D0743681

Finding the Right Texts

SOLVING PROBLEMS IN THE TEACHING OF LITERACY
Cathy Collins Block, Series Editor

Recent Volumes

FINDING THE RIGHT TEXTS

*What Works for Beginning
and Struggling Readers*

Edited by

ELFRIEDA H. HIEBERT
MISTY SAILORS

THE GUILFORD PRESS
New York   London

© 2009 The Guilford Press
A Division of Guilford Publications, Inc.
72 Spring Street, New York, NY 10012
www.guilford.com

All rights reserved

No part of this book may be reproduced, translated, stored in
a retrieval system, or transmitted, in any form or by any means,
electronic, mechanical, photocopying, microfilming, recording,
or otherwise, without written permission from the Publisher.

Printed in the United States of America

This book is printed on acid-free paper.

Last digit is print number: 9   8   7   6   5   4   3   2   1

Library of Congress Cataloging-in-Publication Data

Finding the right texts : what works for beginning and struggling readers / [edited by]
Elfrieda H. Hiebert, Misty Sailors.
    p. cm. — (Solving problems in teaching of literacy)
  Includes bibliographical references and index.
  ISBN 978-1-59385-886-5 (hardcover : alk. paper) — ISBN 978-1-59385-885-8 (pbk. :
alk. paper)
  1. Reading—Remedial teaching.   2. Reading.   I. Hiebert, Elfrieda H.
II. Sailors, Misty.
  LB1050.5.F544   2009
  372.41′4—dc22
                                        2008026744

About the Editors

Elfrieda H. Hiebert, PhD, is Adjunct Professor in the Graduate School of Education at the University of California, Berkeley. She is also a principal investigator at the National Center for Research on the Educational Achievement and Teaching of English Language Learners. Dr. Hiebert has worked in the field of early reading acquisition for 40 years as a classroom teacher, teacher educator, and researcher. Her research addresses methods for supporting students who depend on schools to become literate and for fostering students' reading fluency, vocabulary, and knowledge through appropriate texts. Dr. Hiebert's model of accessible texts for beginning and struggling readers—TExT (Text Elements by Task)—has been used to develop several reading programs that are widely used in schools. Dr. Hiebert was the 2008 recipient of the William S. Gray Citation of Merit, awarded by the International Reading Association, and is a member of the Reading Hall of Fame. Her publications, such as *Becoming a Nation of Readers* (Center for the Study of Reading, 1985) and *Every Child a Reader* (Center for the Improvement of Early Reading Achievement, 1999), have contributed to making research accessible to educators. She is the author or editor of nine books as well as numerous journal articles.

Misty Sailors, PhD, is Associate Professor of Literacy Education in the Department of Interdisciplinary Learning and Teaching at the University of Texas at San Antonio. Her current research includes the instruction that surrounds elementary classroom texts, teacher education, and lan-

guage policies related to reading instruction in international settings. As
the primary investigator of a Teacher Quality Professional Development
Reading Grant, Dr. Sailors is researching comprehension instruction, the
professional development of teachers, and the importance of print-rich
environments for literacy development. In conjunction with the Republic
of South Africa Department of Education and the United States Agency
for International Development, she also oversees the development of two
million supplementary reading and content-integrated learning materials
for elementary learners. Dr. Sailors received the 2007 President's Distinguished Achievement Award for Teaching Excellence from the University
of Texas at San Antonio and the 2007 Recognition Award for Emerging
Scholars from the American Association of University Women. Her writing has been published in journals such as *Reading Research Quarterly*
and the *Journal of Literacy Research*. Collectively, Dr. Sailors's work contributes locally, nationally, and internationally to literacy education.

Preface

A text is central to the act of reading. At first glance, this statement seems too obvious to introduce a book on reading education. However, when a feature of an activity is as ubiquitous or integral to an activity as a text is to reading, its presence can be assumed, glossed over, or even ignored. This is what happened in the National Reading Panel's (National Institute of Child Health and Human Development, 2000) report. Sections on phonological awareness, word recognition, fluency, and vocabulary rarely attended to texts. When references were made to texts, the focus was on the length of texts used in a study or whether students read from a text or a word list.

Although the contributors to this volume differ in the aspects of the text that they emphasize, all assume that the words and structures of text make a difference in the development of proficient word recognition, fluency, vocabulary, and comprehension. The volume is organized around three prominent aspects of text features and content in research literature: linguistic content, conceptual content, and teacher selection and scaffolding of text.

Linguistic content refers to the information about written words that underlies proficient reading. The linguistic content of beginning reading instruction has been the source of the biggest and longest debate in American reading instruction. For example, California (California State Board of Education, 2006) mandates that texts for each of 44 individual phoneme–grapheme relationships are needed in programs adopted for struggling middle school students in 2008, just as these individual phoneme–grapheme relationships have governed textbook selection for grades kindergarten through 2 (California State Board of Education, 1998). Marilyn Jager Adams examines this interpretation of research on linguistic content in the first chapter of Part I. She distinguishes between the need for regularity in linguistic content in beginning reading (which has been validated) and individual phonemes–graphemes as the unit of text design (which have not been validated). This chapter promises to be a landmark paper in early reading education in the next decade.

An equally important topic—and one also ignored by policymakers in the adoption of textbooks for beginning and struggling readers at present—is the degree to which linguistic content needs to be repeated in texts for beginning and struggling readers. In the second chapter of Part I, Elfrieda H. Hiebert and Leigh Ann Martin address this construct, which has a long history in educational psychology but has been virtually ignored in the design and selection of beginning reading texts over the past 25 years. In the final chapter of Part I, Misty Sailors, James V. Hoffman, and Mark W. F. Condon examine the design of texts for multilingual contexts. Sailors and her colleagues raise issues that merit the attention of researchers and textbook publishers in light of the frequent translation of school texts from language to language without consideration of linguistic (or cultural) differences in languages.

The necessity of texts that provide students with compelling content is the focus of Part II. Being able to access the messages and knowledge of text is the raison d'être for literacy. In public debates about what skills and linguistic content should be emphasized in school reading instruction, this goal is often overlooked. As a result, students can spend an inordinate amount of time reading texts that do little to aid them in increasing their background knowledge (Hirsch, 2006). Further, the content of text appears to influence the level of engagement students have in reading (Guthrie, Anderson, Alao, & Rinehart, 1999). Texts that are full of compelling information can be as necessary to the development of proficient reading as having the appropriate linguistic skills. In the first chapter in Part II, Gina N. Cervetti and Jacqueline Barber draw on evidence from a program where texts were effective in supporting students' science knowledge and facility with linguistic content. The subsequent two chapters in Part II show that knowledge acquisition through reading can be part of text experiences from the first—even for young children in the beginning stages of reading and for students who are English language learners (ELLs). Nell K. Duke draws from her decade-long research on increasing opportunities for young children with informational text. She and Alison K. Billman illustrate how, at a time when children are also acquiring linguistic content, publishers can ensure that the content of compelling informational texts is available to young children. Similarly, Young-Suk Kim and Catherine E. Snow draw on a program of research in which ELLs of many different ages have been involved with informational text through skillful modifications and adaptations of texts and interactions with text.

Although the goal of the research summarized in Parts I and II is to support the design and selection of texts with features that support reading development, some texts are difficult for particular students. Part III presents a series of instructional adaptations that researchers have established as effective for supporting teachers in either the selection or the use of texts. Both Heidi Anne E. Mesmer and Staci Cumming (Chapter 8) and Kathleen J. Brown (Chapter 9) focus on the ways in which teachers can be aided in making the right selections for struggling readers on the basis of assessment data. Alison K. Billman, Katherine Hilden, and Juliet L. Halladay take a similar perspective in focusing on the content of professional development for teachers around texts. However, their focus is on teachers' professional development around features in texts that have been selected (or, as is the case in many school systems, mandated). Once teachers recognize features, such as idioms, that make texts difficult for particular students, they can adapt their instructional interactions. In the final chapter of Part III, Mary E. Curtis identifies information for teachers on both kinds of adaptations: the selection of texts and the nature of student–teacher interactions (particularly with a group of students who are still struggling readers). Anne McGill-Franzen completes the volume by drawing on the work of the contributors as well as her studies on the effects of policies and practices on reading development to highlight the next steps in both research and practice on texts and reading.

In the global, digital world of the 21st century, literacy demands can be expected only to escalate as the amount and access to information increases. Creating, selecting, and adapting texts to ensure that students successfully begin on the path to literacy early in their school careers is essential.

ELFRIEDA H. HIEBERT
MISTY SAILORS

REFERENCES

California State Board of Education (1998). *English-language arts content standards for California public schools: Kindergarten through grade twelve.* Sacramento, CA: California Department of Education.

California State Board of Education. (2006, April 17). *Criteria for evaluating instructional materials: Reading/language arts.* Retrieved February 25, 2007, from *www.cde.ca.gov/ci/rl/im/.*

Guthrie, J.T., Anderson, E., Alao, S., & Rinehart, J. (1999). Influences of concept-oriented reading instruction on strategy use and conceptual learning from text. *Elementary School Journal, 99,* 343–366.

Hirsch, E.D., Jr. (2006). *The knowledge deficit: Closing the shocking education gap for American children.* New York: Houghton Mifflin.

National Institute of Child Health and Human Development. (2000). *Report of the National Reading Panel: Teaching children to read: An evidence-based assessment of the scientific research literature on reading and its implications for reading instruction: Reports of the subgroups.* Washington, DC: Author.

Contributors

Marilyn Jager Adams, PhD, Department of Cognitive and Linguistic Sciences, Brown University, Providence, Rhode Island

Jacqueline Barber, BA, Lawrence Hall of Science, University of California, Berkeley, Berkeley, California

Alison K. Billman, MEd, Counseling, Educational Psychology, and Special Education, Michigan State University, East Lansing, Michigan

Kathleen J. Brown, PhD, University of Utah Reading Clinic, University of Utah, Salt Lake City, Utah

Gina N. Cervetti, PhD, Lawrence Hall of Science, University of California, Berkeley, Berkeley, California

Mark W. F. Condon, PhD, Reale Studios, Louisville, Kentucky

Staci Cumming, PhD, Oklahoma State University, Stillwater, Oklahoma

Mary E. Curtis, PhD, Center for Special Education, Lesley University, Cambridge, Massachusetts

Nell K. Duke, EdD, PhD, Literacy Achievement Research Center, Michigan State University, East Lansing, Michigan

Juliet L. Halladay, MA Ed, Teacher Education, Michigan State University, East Lansing, Michigan

Elfrieda H. Hiebert, PhD, Graduate School of Education, University
of California, Berkeley, Berkeley, California

Katherine Hilden, BA, College of Education and Human
Development, Radford University, Radford, Virginia

James V. Hoffman, PhD, Department of Communication and
Instruction, University of Texas at Austin, Austin, Texas

Young-Suk Kim, EdD, School of Teacher Education, Florida State
University, Florida Center for Reading Research,
Tallahassee, Florida

Anne McGill-Franzen, PhD, Reading Education, University of
Tennessee, Knoxville, Tennessee

Leigh Ann Martin, MA, TextProject, Santa Cruz, California

Heidi Anne E. Mesmer, PhD, Department of Teaching and Learning,
Virginia Tech, Blacksburg, Virginia

Misty Sailors, PhD, Department of Interdisciplinary Learning
and Teaching, University of Texas at San Antonio,
San Antonio, Texas

Catherine E. Snow, PhD, Language and Literacy, Harvard Graduate
School of Education, Cambridge, Massachusetts

Contents

1

The (Mis)Match between Texts and Students Who Depend on Schools to Become Literate

ELFRIEDA H. HIEBERT

Texts are central to the act of reading. Children can learn a great deal about the language and content of texts through listening to experienced readers read texts aloud; however, unless children's eyes are making contact with print and translating that print into meaning, they can't be described as reading. The critical role of texts in reading is recognized in the educational marketplace where a substantial amount of money is spent annually on textbooks. The amount of energy devoted to debating appropriate texts for beginning and struggling readers within the educational community is also substantial (Allington & Woodside-Jiron, 1998; Chall, 1967/1983). However, relative to the amount of the expenditure on texts, the amount of research on appropriate texts for beginning and struggling readers has been inconsequential. This sparse research base is surprising in light of claims by policymakers and publishers that the current basal reading programs have been validated empirically. For example, a study on the copyrights of the two basal reading programs mandated for use in California (McGill-Franzen, Zmach, Solic, & Zeig, 2006) appeared in the archival literature just as California issued mandates for its next textbook adoption (California State Board of Education, 2006).

The massive swings in text features for beginning readers over the past 20 years, in particular, have had little research examination (although an extensive amount of rhetoric). Descriptions of the textbook programs adopted in Texas in 1993 (Hoffman et al., 1994) and in 2000 (Hoffman, Sailors, & Patterson, 2002) offer evidence that changes were substantial over this 20-year period. The first-grade texts in the 1993 adoption emphasized literature and deemphasized controlled vocabulary, while those in 2000 had high percentages of decodable words. These rapid changes in policies have produced a scattered approach to the curriculum of basal reading programs with the vestiges of one approach alongside the activities of a second, discrepant approach (Hiebert, Martin, & Menon, 2005). The influence of the literature-based approach is represented in the presence of many multisyllabic words in beginning texts (Foorman, Francis, Davidson, Harm, & Griffin, 2004; Hiebert, 2005a), while the influence of decodable texts is reflected in the presence of many single-appearing words chosen on the basis of individual grapheme–phoneme correspondences (Foorman et al., 2004; Hiebert, 2005a). This seesawing of policies has resulted in texts with features that are contrary to long-standing findings such as Juel and Roper/Schneider's (1985) that beginning readers are challenged by multisyllabic words and Reitsma's (1983) that developing readers require at least a modicum of repetition with some words to develop automatic word recognition.

Shifts in patterns that make texts more difficult (e.g., high percentages of multisyllabic words and many single-appearing words) have occurred during a time of extensive immigration and increased numbers of children who live in poverty (U.S. Census Bureau, 2000). The percentage of students who do not reach the benchmark of basic on the National Assessment of Educational Progress (NAEP) (Perie, Grigg, & Donahue, 2005) has remained fairly robust—approximately 38–40% of a fourth-grade age cohort. Students who are poor and/or speak a first language other than English in their homes have a high probability of being "below-basic." It is these students for whom school instruction makes the biggest difference and who are referred to, throughout this chapter, as students who depend on schools to become literate.

This volume considers responses to the discrepancy between the proficiencies of students who depend on schools to become literate and the typical tasks of texts. Within the volume, ideas are presented for how teachers can adjust, adapt, supplement, and augment instructional texts. To understand the need for this adaptation, the problem needs to be recognized. This chapter lays the foundation by describing the nature and scope of the problem. Specifically, I ask and answer two questions about the nature of the task posed by current beginning reading texts:

1. How does the beginning reading task compare to the proficiencies required to read texts in subsequent grades?
2. How do the task demands of current texts compare with the proficiencies of students in the 10th, 25th, and 40th percentiles?

THE NATURE OF THE TASKS POSED BY TEXTS

Analyses of the features of texts for beginning readers have a fairly long history (see Chall, 1967/1983). Several researchers have described recent changes in texts for beginning readers. As noted earlier, the descriptions of Hoffman and his colleagues (Hoffman et al., 1994; Hoffman et al., 2002) show substantial differences in the features of texts for beginning readers within the Texas textbook adoptions of 1993 and 2000. Whereas texts were chosen for the quality of their literary engagingness in 1993, the texts of 2000 were chosen for the presence of words with particular phoneme–grapheme correspondences. Hypotheses can be offered as to what these differences mean for students learning to read. However, analyses that describe how students at particular stages of development perform with these different types of texts have not been conducted.

In a subsequent study, Hoffman, Roser, Patterson, Salas, and Pennington (2001) examined first graders' ability to read texts similar to those in the 1993 copyrights and ones that continue to dominate the anthologies of basal reading programs. Hoffman and his colleagues examined texts leveled according to the four criteria of Reading Recovery and its classroom application, guided reading (Fountas & Pinnell, 1999): (1) book and print features; (2) content, themes, and ideas; (3) text structure; and (4) language and literary elements. A text is assigned a single level based on a judge's evaluation of all four dimensions. Hoffman et al. gave beginning readers a group of texts that represented different levels. They concluded that students' performances validated the leveling system in that high-performing students read texts at all levels of their distribution, including the highest levels, middle-performing students read texts at the middle levels, and so forth. However, a full 40% of the students were not highly accurate with any of the texts, including those at the earliest levels.

Cunningham et al. (2005) have confirmed that texts, such as those used in Reading Recovery and the basal reading programs, may be difficult for beginning readers who are not proficient at word recognition. Cunningham et al. (2005) analyzed a set of texts based on Reading Recovery levels to determine how supportive such texts are for instruction of word recognition. They concluded that these texts provided only a moderate amount of support for word-recognition instruction and almost none for decoding instruction in the use of onsets and rimes. They also reported that leveled texts do not consistently increase in word-level demands as their levels increase. Johnston's (2000) analyses of student performances with such texts confirm that, even after at least 10 readings of a text, most beginning readers learn a limited number of unfamiliar words. Johnston reported that students who began with low levels of reading learned only a small portion of the words in these texts (approximately 4–5%).

Foorman et al. (2004) analyzed the textbooks that were adopted for use in Texas in 2000 according to phonics patterns, high-frequency word status, and the number of repetitions within and across the six instructional blocks that comprise a school year. They reported that 70% of the words were taught as single units with the percentage reaching 84 in 6-week blocks of several programs. According to Foorman et al., only 229 words were common to all six programs that they analyzed, and 116 of these shared words were on the Dolch list. At the conclusion of their analyses, Foorman et al. questioned how first graders can be expected to acquire and apply letter–sound correspondence knowledge when only 20% of the words in texts are repeated two or three times.

I have used a framework called TExT (Text Elements by Task) to describe the task that a text poses for beginning and struggling readers (Hiebert, 2005a, 2008). Based on reviews of reading acquisition, I have identified two dimensions of texts as most influential on independent word identification: (1) the cognitive load represented by the number of new, unique words per 100 and (2) the linguistic information of the new, unique words. Linguistic content refers to the knowledge about phonology, orthography, and morphology that is required to read words successfully. There are two kinds of linguistic information that are particularly important. The first is the frequency of a word's appearance in written English. I have proposed that the words found in school texts (Zeno, Ivens, Millard, & Duvvuri, 1995) can be classified into seven word zones according to their frequency in written English (Hiebert, 2005b). The word zones differ in size and in the number of times the words in them can be expected to appear in a million-word sample of words. The number of words in the highly frequent zones (zones 0-2), where words can be expected to occur at least 100 or more times per one million words of text, is relatively small (930). Approximately 4,660 words are in zones 3 and 4, where words are predicted to appear with moderate frequency (from 99 to 10 times per one-million words). Zones 6 and 7 are large (approximately 150,000 words). These words appear rarely in texts with likely occurrences from 0.01 to 9 times per million words.

The second kind of linguistic information pertains to common, consistent vowel patterns in words. In order for students to develop automaticity in reading, they must be able to generalize and apply knowledge about the relationships between letters and sounds. The two forms of linguistic information intersect in that all written words in English, no matter how frequent or infrequent, are alphabetic.

I used the TExT framework to analyze the changes in a basal reading program over the 40-year period from 1962 to 2000 (Hiebert, 2005a). I was particularly interested in whether programs showed a developmental pattern with texts becoming increasingly more difficult from grade to grade. The numbers of new, unique words per 100 at the end of first and second grade were as follows: 8 and 11 (1962); 10 and 12 (1983); 20 and 17 (1993); and 19 and 18 (2000). Regardless of the year of the program, the rate at which new words appeared in the programs remained fairly consistent from first grade to second grade. From 1983 to 1993, however, the rate of new, unique words increased substantially in both first- and second-grade texts.

I also analyzed the percentage of words that fall within the 1,000 most-frequent words at the ends of grades 1 and 2, respectively, across these four copyrights: 1962 copyright—60, 40; 1983 copyright—53, 30; 1993 copyright—34, 24; and 2000 copyright—37, 25 (Hiebert, 2005a). While the number of new, unique words remained the same from the ends of grade 1 to 2 for a copyright, the types of words changed. Just as the number of new, unique words changed from 1983 to 1993, so too the percentage of new, unique words accounted for by highly frequent words changed from 1983 to 1993. In the 1962 and 1983 copyrights, highly frequent words consumed a majority of the words through the end of grade 1. Beginning in 1993, highly frequent words did not account for the majority of words even in the latter part of grade 1.

In the same study (Hiebert, 2005a), I examined whether this particular program (one of two that Chall (1967/1983) identified as a prototypical mainstream basal reading program) was representative of five additional basal reading programs. All but one of the six programs was included in the mandated programs in the 2000 Texas textbook adoption. All six programs had a similar rate of introducing new, unique words per 100 at the end of grade 1: a range from 16 to 21. There was somewhat more variation for the exit grade-2 texts: a range from 14 to 22. Percentages of high-frequency words for exit grade 1 were similar (33 to 40), while percentages for the end of grade 2 were lower but within a similar range (20 to 25). The pattern that was apparent in the program used for historical analysis was also evident in the other major programs available in the marketplace in 2000, for both the number of unique words and the percentages of high-frequency words.

In a second study, my colleagues and I (Hiebert, Martin, & Menon, 2005) analyzed the shared words across components of three programs (two of which had been included in Hiebert, 2005a). The three components of the programs were the anthology, decodable texts, and leveled texts. Across the three components of the two programs that are regarded as mainstream basal programs, the percentage of shared words was exactly the same—28%. In the third program (Reading Mastery, a decoding-oriented program), the percentage was higher—40%. In all cases, the majority of shared words fell within the 300 most-frequent words.

AN EXAMINATION OF DIFFICULTY OF WORDS ACROSS A CURRENT PROGRAM

My studies (2005a; Hiebert et al., 2005) and studies by Foorman et al. (2004) indicate that the percentage of unique words in first-grade basal reading programs is high and that the proportion of repeated words consists primarily of high-frequency words. The basal reading programs analyzed in these studies were published from 1995 through 2001. Since features of texts may be specific to a particular program's copyright due to state mandates, one might wonder whether the features of texts reported in the studies (Foorman et al., 2004; Hiebert, 2005a; Hiebert et al., 2005) also apply to recent copyrights of basal programs. Have publishers made changes in programs (and policymakers in mandates) as a result of descriptions of the inaccessibility of basal reading programs, especially for students who depend on schools to become literate? To answer this question, I analyzed a sample of texts from the most recent copyright of a program—the same one used in my historical analyses (2005a). Since I was particularly interested in the developmental changes of the tasks posed by texts, I analyzed a sample of texts from kindergarten through sixth grade.

Database

I chose the Scott Foresman program (Afflerbach et al., 2007) because of its 2007 copyright and because it is the only remaining basal that was included in Chall's (1967/1983) influential analyses. The texts in the program's anthologies were the focus of my analyses since this component is the focus of the teacher's manuals and is the one for which states and districts typically allocate funds.

A corpus of 2,000 words from the middle units of the anthologies for grades 1 through 6 was chosen. The middle unit was used because it captures the typical demands of the grade level. For grades 1 and 2, all of the selections for unit 3 and part of unit 4 were used. Single texts become longer at the upper grades. Initial analyses of 2,000-word corpora, based on a single text at grades 5 and 6, indicated a substantially lower number of unique words per 100 than at grades 1 and 2. Consequently, a consistent sampling procedure of 500-word excerpts from four different texts was used for grades 3 through 6. For kindergarten, where there is no anthology at the present time, the texts from decodables comprised the sample.

The TExT software (Hiebert & Martin, 2003) was used to obtain the following information for each of the seven 2,000-word corpora: (1) number of unique words, (2) number of words within word zones 0–2 (frequent words), 3–4 (moderately frequent words), and 5–6 (rare words), and (3) mean decodability of words within a word zone. The latter was based on the following set of categories: categories 1–3 group words with vowel patterns with a one-to-one phoneme–grapheme correspondence (e.g., *go, at*); categories 4–5 group words with vowel patterns where two graphemes represent a "long" phoneme (e.g., *ate, eat*); categories 6–7 group words with complex vowel patterns (e.g., *oar, owl*); and categories 8–9 group multisyllabic words.

The Nature of the Task from Grades K through 6 in a 2007 Basal Reading Program

Table 1.1 presents a summary of the features of words within each grade-level, 2,000-word sample. Three patterns are evident in the data in Table 1.1. The first has to do with the rate of introduction of new, unique words per 100 running words. There are three different rates of introduction of new, unique words across the seven grade levels: (1) 12 (kindergarten), (2) 22–23 (grades 1 and 2), (3) 30–33 (grades 3 through 6).

The second pattern has to do with the consistency of the distribution of word zones from grades 1 through 6. The percentage of high-frequency words in texts from grades 1 through 6 falls within a fairly narrow range: 82–85. The percentage of rare words (word zones 5–6) is also consistent from grades 1 through 6: 6–7%. Only kindergarten has a different pattern. In the kindergarten texts, a lower percentage of words falls within word zones 0–2 (58%) and a higher percentage falls within word zones 5–6 (19%).

The final pattern addresses the complexity of vowel patterns in monosyllabic words and the presence of multisyllabic words. The pat-

TABLE 1.1. Frequency and Decodability of Words in Grade-Level Text Samples

Word zone	Grade							NAEP
	K	1	2	3	4	5	6	
0–1	37[a] (4.0[b])	63 (5.3)	65 (5.3)	62 (5.4)	62 (5.4)	62 (5.6)	66 (5.0)	58 (5.3)
2	21 (3.7)	19 (5.8)	20 (6.4)	21 (6.5)	19 (6.4)	16 (6.9)	16 (6.2)	22 (5.6)
3–4	23 (2.7)	11 (5.9)	8 (6.3)	10 (5.7)	11 (6.9)	11 (7.0)	12 (7.0)	14 (6.7)
5–6	19 (2.6)	7 (6.9)	7 (6.9)	7 (7.0)	8 (7.4)	11 (7.5)	6 (7.3)	6 (5.9)
New, unique words per 100	12.1	22.9	21.7	29.8	30.8	33.4	32.1	62.6

[a]Percentage of total words in particular word zones.
[b]Average decodability of words in particular word zones.

tern for kindergarten differs from that of the other grades. For all word zones, words in the kindergarten program have a heavy concentration of vowel patterns with a one-to-one correspondence between graphemes and phonemes. The words in the first-grade texts have a higher vowel complexity rating, on average, than the kindergarten texts. Compared to the sixth-grade texts, however, the first-grade texts have less complex patterns. In the first-grade texts, the rarest of words (those in word zone 6) typically have either an *r*-controlled vowel pattern or a consistent but variant vowel pattern (e.g., *old/cold*, *night/right*) in a monosyllabic word. By contrast, the rare words in the sixth-grade texts are primarily multisyllabic or, if monosyllabic, have vowel diphthongs.

What can be concluded about the features of texts that comprise the core of a basal reading program? When a core component is a decodable (as is the case with the kindergarten program), the features differ from those of the anthologies. Differences in the types of words that appear in decodables and anthologies are apparent in the examples of texts that appear in Table 1.2. When writers are responsible for the words in text (as is the case with texts in the anthologies from grades 1 through 6), they are concerned with fulfilling expectations of what constitutes a literary text. They are not concerned about ensuring that students can decode words (as is the case with the example from the kindergarten decodable). Writers of narrative texts select words that communicate the nuances of their characters, settings, and plots, using words such as *chirping* and *balancing* rather than *singing* or *sitting*.

In views of reading acquisition that dominated American instruc-

TABLE 1.2. Examples of Texts

Kindergarten (Afflerbach et al., 2007)	*A Musical Adventure* Sit and play with me, Nat, Lin and Rob. Can you tap and rap and bam? We like to rap on the pot. We like to rap on the lid. We like to bam with the can. Can you tap and rap and bam? Nan can rap the tan pot.
Grade 1 (Afflerbach et al., 2007)	Toad looked at his garden. Little green plants were coming up out of the ground. "At last," shouted Toad, "my seeds have stopped being afraid to grow!" "And now you will have a nice garden too," said Frog. "Yes," said Toad, "but you were right, Frog. It was very hard work."
Grade 3 (Afflerbach et al., 2007)	The tree is old, and she has much to say. Some words are happy ones. They tell of chirping birds and budding leaves and children balancing on her branches. Some words are lonely ones. They tell of birds flying south and leaves blowing away and children staying in their houses,
NAEP (2005 ORF text)	Soon the house was buzzing with excitement. Megan sat on the stool watching while Mom and Aunt Nancy prepared the birthday dinner. Dad wouldn't be back for at least two hours. Jason wandered outside trying to think of something to do, but his thoughts kept returning to the box in the barn.

tion until the past two decades, critical factors in the design or selection of materials for beginning readers were the pace of presenting new information and the repetition of high-frequency words or words with common, consistent vowel patterns (Hiebert & Raphael, 1996). If there is a developmental ramp-up in the pace and repetition of linguistic information in current reading programs, it is in the kindergarten portion of programs. The rate of presenting new words is substantially slower at kindergarten relative to the first- and second-grade programs. While kindergarten programs contain a higher percentage of rare words than subsequent levels, these words are predominantly composed of simple vowel patterns. By the middle of first grade, the profile of moderately frequent and rare words is similar to that of subsequent grades. The profile of linguistic information, at least with regard to high-frequency words, is flat. The decodability of rare words in first grade is somewhat lower than that in the higher grades, indicating that more of the rare words in the grade-six texts are multisyllabic than in the first-grade texts. Even in the first-grade texts, however, the average decodability levels of 6.9 for word zones 5–6 indicate the presence of many monosyllabic words with complex and variant vowels.

A Comparison of the Task of Texts and Proficiency of Students at the 40th Percentile and Below

The level of the texts at kindergarten- and first-grade levels in a current basal reading program would lead to the expectation that students in the United States are reading at earlier points in time. Conclusions about early acquisition of reading by U.S. students are difficult to make because the primary source for understanding the reading performances of U.S. students across states is the NAEP, which is not administered until fourth grade. The results of the NAEP at fourth grade (Perie et al., 2005) do suggest, however, that approximately 38–40% of a grade cohort is not reading texts with the features of current first-grade texts in core reading programs in mid-fourth grade. These fourth graders do not have the skills to read the typical mid-first grade texts accurately and at appropriate rates.

Further substantiation for the mismatch between the typical tasks of core reading programs and students' proficiency comes from a special study of the NAEP (Daane, Campbell, Grigg, Goodman, & Oranje, 2005). The features of the text that was used in this assessment of oral and silent reading appears in the two final columns of Table 1.1. Approximately 80% of the words in the NAEP text and the first-grade texts fall within the 1,000 most-frequent words. The percentage of rare words is almost identical: 7% for the first-grade texts and 6% for the NAEP fourth-grade text. Even the decodability levels are similar. Approximately 35% of U.S. fourth-graders read the NAEP text slowly (Daane, Campbell, Grig, Goodman, & Oranje, 2005). If students in a grade cohort can read the first-grade texts of the basal anthology fluently as first graders, they would be expected to read the text of the fourth-grade NAEP with automaticity, speed, and comprehension 3 years later. That has not proven to be the case.

To examine the match between the task for students in the lowest 40% of the U.S. profile and the task of reading textbooks across grade levels, I compared the task of the texts with students' performances on the sight word efficiency subtest of the Test of Word Reading Efficiency (TOWRE; Torgesen, Wagner, & Rashotte, 1999). The TOWRE is a widely used assessment for both research and instructional purposes. This analysis begins with first grade since the TOWRE does not provide norms for kindergarten students.

Test of Word Reading Efficiency

The sight word efficiency subtest of the TOWRE assesses a student's ability to recognize a particular set of words within a 45-second period. Each of the two forms of the subtest contains 104 words. The analysis of the reading proficiency required for this assessment was based on sets of words in multiples of 20: 20, 40, 60, 80, and 100. Each successive set includes words from each preceding set. Further, the words from both forms of the subtest were included in the analysis. That is, the analysis of Word Set 20 was conducted on 40 words (20 from Form A and 20 from Form B).

With one exception, similar analyses were conducted on these sets of words as had been conducted on the grade-level basal reading texts. The exception was the number of new, unique words per 100. This feature is not relevant for a word list where repetition of words would not be expected. A summary of the frequency and decodability of the words in the four word groups appears in Table 1.3. The data in Table 1.3 are used for two purposes: (1) to describe the proficiency of students in different percentile groups at different grade levels and (2) to compare students' proficiency levels with the tasks of current texts. Before applying the data to these two issues, the proficiencies represented by each benchmark level (e.g., proficiency with Word Set 20) are summarized.

Differences across the Word Sets

As would be expected in an assessment of sight word recognition, the 1,000 most-frequent words figure heavily in the TOWRE sight word efficiency subtest. Only in Word Sets 80 and 100 do less common, multisyllabic words become prominent. The shift from Word Set 60 to 80 is dramatic. Whereas 97% of the words in Word Set 60 are from the 1,000 most-frequent words (and the remaining 3% all have simple

TABLE 1.3. Frequency and Decodability of Words on TOWRE

Word zone	TOWRE20	TOWRE40	TOWRE60	TOWRE80	TOWRE100
0–1	80[a]	67.5	54	42	33
	(3.3[b])	(4.3)	(4.9)	(5.0)	(5.0)
2	20	30	42	42	36
	(3.1)	(4.0)	(5.2)	(5.8)	(6.1)
3–4		3	3	8	13
		(3.0)	(2.7)	(7.2)	(7.8)
5–6				8	18
				(8.2)	(8.6)

[a]Percentage of total words in particular word zones.
[b]Average decodability of words in particular word zones.

vowel correspondences and come from zone 3), 10% of Word Set 80 consists of rare, multisyllabic words.

A benchmark, at least as indicated by the content of this test, is recognition of the 1,000 most-frequent words. Once students have developed automaticity with these words, the test makers needed to draw on words from the entire range of words represented in written English. For students in the bottom 40%, however, automaticity with the 1,000 most-frequent words is a proficiency that takes a long time to attain.

Grade- and Percentile-Group Performances on the TOWRE

TOWRE performances for students from grades 1 through 6 and for six percentile groups (10th, 25th, 40th, 50th, 75th, and 90th) are presented in Figure 1.1. When separate norms were given for the two halves of a grade (as was the case with grades 1 through 3), the norms for the second half of the year were used. In studying the patterns in Figure 1.1, it should be remembered that attainment of a particular level does not mean that students recognized only words within a particular set of words. Especially at the lower grades and lower percentile levels, it is unlikely that students will correctly recognize all of the words consecutively. Likewise, if students are unable to recognize words that occur with high frequency in texts, it is unlikely that they will recognize more infrequent words. Consequently, if 40th-percentile grade 3 students are averaging 50 words on the TOWRE, it is likely that the majority of these words come from Word Set 60.

If recognition of words from the 1,000 most-frequent words (as represented by Word Set 60) is a benchmark, the data in Figure 1.1 provide an indication of when that benchmark is achieved for students in different percentile groups of an age cohort. Students in the 90th percentile attain that benchmark in grade 1, while students in the 10th percentile have yet to attain this level by grade 6. For students at interim points in a grade cohort distribution, this benchmark is attained at different points: 75th: grade 2; 50th: grade 3; 40th: grade 4; and 25th: grade 5.

While students in the 50th percentile and below do not attain this benchmark until grade 3 or later, students in the bottom half of the distribution are able to recognize words. The students in the 10th percentile can recognize a sampling of words from the 1,000 most-frequent words by mid-grade 2.

A Comparison of the Text Demands and Students' Proficiency Levels

The earlier presentation of the tasks posed by the texts of the basal reading anthologies indicated that, already at grade 1, the anthologies have

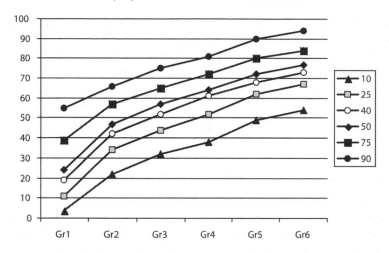

FIGURE 1.1. TOWRE levels for six percentile groups at end of grade.

high percentages of words that fall beyond the 1,000 most-frequent words. The analysis of the TOWRE performances indicated that students in the 90th and 75th percentiles can recognize a sample of words from the 1,000 most-frequent words automatically at grade 1. However, students in the bottom 40th percentile are not automatic with this corpus of words until grade 4 (and those in the 25th percentile, until grade 5). The gap between current texts and the proficiency of students in the bottom 40th percentiles is particularly large in grade 1. This gap decreases over the elementary grades as students gain proficiency with the 1,000 most-frequent words. This proficiency allows students to attend to the approximately one-fifth of new words in texts that, typically, contain complex vowels and/or multiple syllables.

SOLUTIONS TO THE PROBLEM

The task of current reading instructional texts matches the proficiencies of students in the 25% of an age distribution. By mid-grade 1, students in the top 25% of an age cohort are able to recognize words from the 1,000 most-frequent words, leaving sufficient cognitive resources to attend to the one-fifth of words in anthologies that come from the moderate and rare word zones. For students in the bottom 40%, this level of proficiency will be gained much later in the elementary grades. Even so, they are given the same textbooks as their peers who are proficient readers. This volume is about solutions to this mismatch. As an overview for the perspectives developed in this volume, three points are particularly germane: (1) responses to the needs of children who begin kindergarten without extensive book-literacy experiences, (2) responses for older, struggling students, and (3) responses for teachers, including beginning teachers who must rely on teacher's guides as their primary source of learning about reading instruction.

Support for Beginning Readers

The mismatch between existing texts in a basal reading program and the reading proficiency of students in the bottom 40% is greatest at the very beginning levels. For students who have not had the approximately 1,000 hours that Adams (1990) hypothesized some young children receive from birth to age 5 in their homes and communities, the task that confronts them when they enter kindergarten is enormous. In the kindergarten materials of the program reviewed in this chapter, students are introduced to 30 of the 44 grapheme–phoneme correspondences in English over the course of approximately 20 lessons. The underlying assumption is: If a phoneme–grapheme correspondence has been introduced in a lesson in the teacher's guide, students have learned it. Such expectations reflect substantial changes for kindergartners over the past two decades (Hiebert & Papierz, 1990). In the late 1980s, the basal reading programs provided kits, teacher read-alouds, and practice books for kindergartners. The practice books included a handful of foldouts that were intended for students to read. These foldout booklets used 10 to 15 words (e.g., *cat*, *dog*, *a*, *the*) to make stories.

The pace of introduction of new linguistic information has speeded up exponentially for kindergartners and first graders. The repetition of individual words is somewhat higher in kindergarten than in first grade (8 repetitions in kindergarten vs. 4.4 in first grade). Even so, 26% of the words appear a single time in the kindergarten program, and another 25% of the words appear two or three times. Young students who have not had extensive prior experiences with books are likely to see just a blur of illustrations and strange shapes in texts where 12 new words appear in every 100 running words.

Within the paradigm of reading acquisition that underlies the current programs, students who are not successful with this fast pace in kindergarten (approximately 40 to 50% of an age cohort) must be provided similar material (i.e., texts devoted to the 44 grapheme–phoneme relationships in English) in grades 1 and 2 (California State Board of Education, 2006). Further, a similar set of decodable texts must be provided to struggling readers for use in interventions in grades 4 through 8.

An alternative solution would be to involve students with many different texts. As Foorman et al. (2004) have observed, grade-1 basal reading programs have numerous components. However, the teacher's manuals devote most space to the anthologies and provide little guidance on what texts are appropriate for students at various stages of reading development. Decodable texts are available and, as Mesmer (2001) argues, can be accessible for beginning and struggling readers. Programs also have at least one set of leveled texts (Hiebert et al., 2005). These texts, when ordered appropriately, can be another source of exposure to words with consistent, common word patterns (Jenkins, Peyton, Sanders, & Vadasy, 2004; Menon & Hiebert, 2005). The best advice is not to depend on the texts in the anthologies for beginning and struggling readers but to rely on other sources such as decodable, leveled, and high-interest, low-vocabulary texts. The texts in the anthologies may be good for readalouds and follow-up discussions. However, if the teacher and able readers are the only ones who can read these texts, the experience is unlikely to develop independent reading proficiency among beginning and struggling readers (Johnston, 2000).

Support for Older, Struggling Readers

The present analyses show that the mismatch between current texts and students' reading levels decreases once students reach second grade. Students who are able to read approximately 50 words on the TOWRE (as is the case with mid-year third graders at the 25th percentile) will be able to read most of the words in a third-grade text such as the one in Table 1.2. All but five of the words in this excerpt in Table 1.2 fall into the 1,000 most-frequent words: *chirping, budding, balancing, branches,* and *lonely.* The vowel patterns in four of these five words are fairly regular. With several readings of this portion of the text, students from the 20th–40th percentiles should be able to read the text fluently and meaningfully. For these students, it makes sense that they are given the grade-level texts. Opportunities for rereadings of portions of text and guidance with unfamiliar words (especially multisyllabic ones) need to be provided.

Texts are fairly even from grades 1 through 6; thus, teachers have an extensive inventory on which to draw for students who are not automatic, fluent readers. Given the evenness of texts, students can read those texts that are at their grade levels. However, teachers will need to select portions of texts and give students reasons for rereading these portions. One criterion to keep in mind when selecting texts is that the National Reading Panel's (NRP) subgroup on fluency found that the texts used in successful interventions were short—from 50 to 200 words each (NICHD, 2000).

Students in the bottom 10% require more in-depth instruction, including instruction in decoding strategies with morphologically complex words (Nagy, Berninger, & Abbott, 2006). They also require opportunities to read extensively. *Extensive reading* is a term that has been used in instruction and research with college students who are learning English as a foreign language (EFL). As Taguchi, Takayasu-Maass, and Gorsuch (2004) define *extensive reading*, "readers self-select materials from a collection of graded readers (books which have reduced vocabulary range and simplified grammatical structures) with the goal of reaching specified target times of silent sustained reading" (p. 2). Extensive reading has been shown to be as effective as assisted, repeated reading (the technique that was supported by the findings of the subgroup on fluency of the NRP [NICHD, 2000]) in increasing EFL readers' fluency. As has become evident in this chapter, current basal readers do not have the controlled vocabulary that Taguchi et al. (2004) describe as characteristic of the graded readers. I have proposed an underlying curriculum for a concentration of words from particular word zones in the design of texts for struggling readers and have also developed texts that implement that curriculum (Hiebert, 2008). Studies to date have consistently shown that struggling readers improve their fluency when their teachers consistently use the texts that exemplify this curriculum (see, e.g., Wilson, Erickson, & Trainin, 2007).

There is also work demonstrating support for increased reading that can be provided to struggling readers with technology. Shany and Biemiller (1995) showed that participation in an audiotape intervention resulted in more time reading text than in a teacher-guided group. Digital voice recognition increases the quality of a reading experience for struggling readers by providing feedback on specific phrases and words, giving immediate information on accuracy, rate, and comprehension. This also allows students to compare their reading with that of a proficient reader. Adams (2006) reported that, after participating in a voice-recognition repeated reading intervention, students in grades 2 through 5 improved in fluency at levels significantly beyond that of students participating with typical texts. For elementary school students who have not attained the benchmark level of automaticity with the 1,000 most-frequent words, increasing opportunities for reading with voice recognition, especially when the voice recognition uses texts that provide significant exposure to the 1,000 most-frequent words, offers an alternative to the basal texts that, even at grade 1, fail to provide such experiences.

Support for Teachers

For beginning readers who depend on schools to become literate, the prominent nature of existing texts means that teachers will need to do substantial adaptation with texts. Barr (1974) showed that teachers compensated for texts that are too difficult. When texts were too difficult for first-grade readers, effective teachers whom Barr observed in the early 1970s spent considerably more time in instruction and reading. Thirty years later, it is not clear that such compensation is occurring, or even if it can, in the context of Reading First mandates and teacher's manual guidelines.

Teacher scaffolding of text is critical, and chapters in this volume attest to the importance of teacher scaffolding. What is especially critical to consider is how teachers, especially beginning teachers, learn to scaffold. When a minimum of 90 minutes is spent on reading daily (at is the case with Reading First), the teacher's manuals in reading are a primary source of information for teachers. However, the pacing guides within these teacher's manuals offer few suggestions as to how instruction should be adapted to ensure that students in the lowest 40% can be ensured the daily 60–90 minutes of focused reading that has been identified as necessary for struggling readers (Allington, 2001; Fisher & Ivey, 2006).

There are ideas within this volume for how teachers can mediate the difficulty of current texts. Text selection is one of the most basic forms of mediation. If teachers are selecting portions of text for repeated reading from a basal passage, it is useful to have some guidelines as to the length of texts and the features that make a text appropriate for repeated reading. For example, it is useful for teachers to know that the presence of single-appearing, multisyllabic words may require additional attention for developing readers.

Another form of scaffolding is the preteaching of key words prior to the introduction of a text. If students are to become more automatic with highly frequent words and words that have common syllable and grapheme–phoneme correspondences, they cannot spend all of their time on rare words that appear a single time in their texts. They need to have confidence in reading highly frequent words so that they can become more automatic at word recognition. Teachers need to ensure that struggling readers have sufficient encounters in pronouncing and understanding the meaning of these words before they are asked to read along in a text or to read the text independently.

CONCLUSION

If schools are using basal reading programs, students who depend on schools to become literate are being given texts that demand a high level of reading proficiency. While the match is a good one for students who enter kindergarten with hundreds of hours of prior literacy experience, the gap between the task of the texts and the existing proficiencies of students who depend on schools to become literate is significant. Numerous initiatives can be launched to call for greater readiness for school entry. However, no preschool initiative can ensure readiness for a sizable portion of an American age cohort when the task demands of kindergarten and first-grade reading programs escalate as they have in the past 20 years.

Policies are needed that require a developmental trajectory in the task of the basal reading program texts. Until such policies are in place, it is unlikely that any mainstream publishers will provide texts that have a developmental trajectory that moves at an appropriate pace for students in the lowest 40%. Until such policies are in place, students in the lowest 40% will continue to progress poorly unless their teachers have solid understandings of how to select alternative texts and/or how to scaffold existing texts to support learning of critical words and common and consistent patterns within words. The remaining chapters in this volume aim to support teachers in developing an understanding of how to use current reading programs with the many students who depend on schools to become literate.

REFERENCES

Adams, M. J. (1990). *Beginning to read: Thinking and learning about print.* Cambridge, MA: MIT Press.

Adams, M. J. (2006). The promise of automatic speech recognition for fostering literacy growth in children and adults. In M. McKenna, L. Labbo, R. Kieffer, & D. Reinking (Eds.), *Handbook of literacy and technology* (Vol. 2, pp. 109–128). Hillsdale, NJ: Erlbaum.

Afflerbach, P., Blachowicz, C. L. Z., Boyd, C. D., Cheyney, W., Juel, C., Kame'enui, E., et al. (2007). *Reading street.* Glenview, IL: Pearson/Scott Foresman.

Allington, R. (2001). *What really matters for struggling readers.* New York: Addison-Wesley.

Allington R. L., & Woodside-Jiron, H. (1998). Decodable text in beginning reading: Are mandates and policy based on research? *ERS Spectrum: Journal of Research and Information, 16*(3), 3–11.

Barr, R. (1974). The effect of instruction on pupil reading strategies. *Reading Research Quarterly, 10,* 555–582.

California State Board of Education. (2006, April 17). *Criteria for evaluating instructional materials: Reading/language arts.* Retrieved February 25, 2007, *www.cde.ca.gov/ci/rl/im/.*

Chall, J. S. (1967/1983). *Learning to read: The great debate* (3rd ed.). Fort Worth, TX: Harcourt Brace.

Cunningham, J. W., Spadorcia, S. A., Erickson, K. A., Koppenhaver, D. A., Sturm, J. M., & Yoder, D. E. (2005). Investigating the instructional supportiveness of leveled texts. *Reading Research Quarterly, 40,* 410–427.

Daane, M. C., Campbell, J. R., Grigg, W. S., Goodman, M. J., & Oranje, A. (2005). *Fourth-grade students reading aloud: NAEP 2002 special study of oral reading*. Washington, DC: National Center for Education Statistics.

Fisher, D., & Ivey, G. (2006). Evaluating the interventions for struggling adolescent readers. *Journal of Adolescent and Adult Literacy, 50*(3), 180–189.

Foorman, B. R., Francis, D. J., Davidson, K. C., Harm, M. W., & Griffin, J. (2004). Variability in text features in six grade 1 basal reading programs. *Scientific Studies of Reading, 8*, 167–197.

Fountas, I. C., & Pinnell, G. S. (1999). *Matching books to readers: Using leveled books in guided reading*. Portsmouth, NH: Heinemann.

Hiebert, E. H. (2005a). State reform policies and the reading task for first graders. *Elementary School Journal, 105*, 245–266.

Hiebert, E. H. (2005b). In pursuit of an effective, efficient vocabulary curriculum for the elementary grades. In E. H. Hiebert & M. Kamil (Eds.), *The teaching and learning of vocabulary: Bringing scientific research to practice* (pp. 243–263). Mahwah, NJ: Erlbaum.

Hiebert, E. H. (2008). The Word Zone fluency curriculum: An alternative approach. In M. R. Kuhn & P. J. Schwanenflugel (Eds.), *Fluency in the classroom* (pp. 154–170). New York: Guilford Press.

Hiebert, E. H., & Martin, L. A. (2003). *TExT analyzer* (5th ed.). Santa Cruz, CA: TextProject.

Hiebert, E. H., Martin, L. A., & Menon, S. (2005). Are there alternatives in reading textbooks?: An examination of three beginning reading programs. *Reading Writing Quarterly, 21*, 7–32.

Hiebert, E. H., & Papierz, J. M. (1990). The emergent literacy construct and kindergarten and readiness books of basal reading series. *Early Childhood Research Quarterly, 5*, 317–334.

Hiebert, E. H., & Raphael, T. E. (1996). Psychological perspectives on literacy and extensions to educational practice. In D. C. Berliner & R. C. Calfee (Eds.), *Handbook of educational psychology* (pp. 550–602). New York: Macmillan.

Hoffman, J. V., McCarthey, S. J., Abbott, J., Christian, C., Corman, L., Curry, C., et al. (1994). So what's new in the new basals? A focus on first grade. *Journal of Reading Behavior, 26*, 47–73.

Hoffman, J. V., Roser, N., Patterson, E., Salas, R., & Pennington, J. (2001). Text leveling and little books in first-grade reading. *Journal of Literacy Research, 33*, 507–528.

Hoffman, J. V., Sailors, M., & Patterson, E. U. (2002). Decodable texts for beginning reading instruction: The year 2000 basals. *Journal of Literacy Research, 34*, 269–298.

Jenkins, J. R., Peyton, J. A., Sanders, E. A., & Vadasy, P. F. (2004). Effects of reading decodable texts in supplemental first-grade tutoring. *Scientific Studies of Reading, 8*, 53–85.

Johnston, F. R. (2000). Word learning in predictable text. *Journal of Educational Psychology, 92*, 248–255.

Juel, C., & Roper/Schneider, D. (1985). The influence of basal readers on first-grade reading. *Reading Research Quarterly, 20*, 134–152.

McGill-Franzen, A., Zmach, C., Solic, K., & Zeig, J. L. (2006). The confluence of two policy mandates: Core reading programs and third-grade retention in Florida. *Elementary School Journal, 107*, 67–92.

Menon, S., & Hiebert, E. H. (2005). A comparison of first graders' reading with little books or literature-based basal anthologies. *Reading Research Quarterly, 40*(1), 12–38.

Mesmer, H. A. E. (2001). Decodable text: A review of what we know. *Reading Research and Instruction, 40*, 121–142.

Nagy, W., Berninger, V. W., & Abbott, R. B. (2006). Contributions of morphology beyond phonology to literacy outcomes of upper elementary and middle-school students. *Journal of Educational Psychology, 98*(1), 134–147.

NICHD. (2000). *Report of the National Reading Panel: Teaching children to read: An evidence-based assessment of the scientific research literature on reading and its implications for reading instruction: Reports of the subgroups.* Washington, DC: National Institute of Child Health and Human Development.

Perie, M., Grigg, W. S., & Donahue, P. L. (2005). *The nation's report card: Fourth-grade reading 2005.* Washington, DC: U.S. Department of Education, Institute of Education Sciences.

Reitsma, P. (1983). Printed word learning in beginning readers. *Journal of Experimental Child Psychology, 36*, 321–339.

Shany, M. T., & Biemiller, A. (1995). Assisted reading practice: Effects on performance for poor readers in grades 3 and 4. *Reading Research Quarterly, 30*, 382–395.

Taguchi, E., Takayasu-Maass, M., & Gorsuch, G. J. (2004). Developing reading fluency in EFL: How assisted repeated and extensive reading affect fluency development. *Reading in a Foreign Language, 16*, 70–96.

Torgesen, J. K., Wagner, R. K., & Rashotte, C. A. (1999). *Test of word reading efficiency.* Austin, TX: PRO-ED.

U.S. Census Bureau. (2000). *Demographic profile highlights.* Washington, DC: U.S. Government Printing Office.

Wilson, K., Erickson, J., & Trainin, G. (2007, April). *Teaching fluency: Can technology based feedback help?* Paper presented at the annual meeting of the American Educational Research Association, Chicago, IL.

Zeno, S. M., Ivens, S. H., Millard, R. T., & Duvvuri, R. (1995). *The educator's word frequency guide.* New York: Touchstone Applied Science Associates.

Part I

Frameworks for Creating and Selecting Instructional Texts

❧ 2 ❧

Decodable Text

Why, When, and How?

MARILYN JAGER ADAMS

PERSON 2: What is this? This story is about a green eagle? And a
beagle? Does anybody besides me think this is a little weird?

PERSON 1: Well, it needs to be decodable. This is the first story in the
book, so it goes with a long-*e* lesson. The story is designed to
exercise words with spellings for long *e*.

PERSON 3: No, no. This can't possibly be the first story in the book.
Look how difficult it is! And how long! Are you sure this is the
very first story?

PERSON 1: Well, it needs to be long because it needs to tell a good
story. We want to make our commitment to quality literature
clear from the moment people open the very first book.

PERSON 3: Do you honestly think this is quality literature?

PERSON 2: I don't think it's decodable either.

And so it went. This was the conversation held in 1992, near the
outset of developing the 1995 edition of the Open Court basal reading
series *Collections for Young Scholars* (Adams, Bereiter, Hirshberg, Anderson, & Bernier, 1995). In discussion was the first story in the first-

23

grade anthology in the prior edition of the series *Open Court Reading and Writing* (Bereiter et al., 1989). Person 2 and person 3 were two authors, both just being introduced to the to-be-revised first-grade materials.[1] Person 1 was an employee of the publisher who had been involved in developing the materials in review. This chapter is about how the authors went about trying to solve this dilemma for the 1995 edition of Open Court.

Please understand at the outset that, in telling this story, it is not my intention to advocate for the Open Court reading materials. Indeed, not all of our suggestions were faithfully implemented even in the publication of the 1995 edition, and nearly all have been overwritten since the program's acquisition by SRA/McGraw-Hill.[2] I tell this story, instead, to raise issues that seem still to warrant consideration in our collective efforts to create effective, engaging, and manageable materials for first-grade students and their teachers.

Even from so brief a snippet as provided above, the basic dilemma is clear and familiar. There are two key and core goals in designing reading instruction for beginning readers. On one hand, we want to teach first-graders how to read print on their own. To this end, the earliest texts need both to be easy enough to be penetrable by true beginners and to progress by some design that will continually work to strengthen and expand beginning readers' independence with print. On the other hand, we wish to help young students to develop the language, knowledge, literary appreciation, and modes of thought that make reading productive and rewarding.

In support of literacy development, both of these goals are of insuperable importance. Both warrant focused, compelling, effective address at the very start of a child's literacy journey. The dilemma arises because the textual simplicity and control required by the first goal is incompatible with the textual dimensionality and range demanded by the second.

Part of the problem, as so impishly brought to fore in Chall's (1996) discussion of Gray's (1948) perspective on the issue, is that what makes a text interesting or worthwhile is largely in the mind of the beholder.

> Gray views with alarm the swing, since 1900, from one extreme ("an undue emphasis on learning the form and sound of separate words") to

---

[1] I was one of the authors. The other was Valerie Anderson, truly the best curriculum designer with whom I've ever had the pleasure of working.

[2] The Open Court school programs were purchased from Open Court Publishing by SRA/McGraw-Hill in 1995. Three of the authors of the 1995 edition, Valerie Anderson, Ann Brown, and Robbie Case, have since passed away. I resigned my Open Court authorship in 2002.

its opposite ("guessing from context with little attention to the visual form of words"). At the same time, however, he dramatically poses the question: "Shall we, in response to public demand, reinstate the old mechanical phonic drills and content that inevitably result in dull, word-by-word reading?"

You can guess the answer. To Gray, and to other leading researchers in reading, phonics means a return to "drill" and the "dull content" of the phonics readers of the early 1900s. Gray explains his objection as follows:

> In the very nature of things, reading material constructed on this artificial basis [words selected on phonics elements previously taught] was certain to lack continuity of thought. Indeed, pages of such primers and first readers may be read almost as effectively by beginning with the last sentence and reading to the top of the page as by reading in the usual way from top to bottom. (Gray, 1948, p. 19)

He reproduced a page from the Beacon primer, a phonic reader of 1912 to illustrate his points.

I reproduce the same page, together with a page from Gray's own primer, which selects words and content for "meaningfulness" and "continuity of thought," and I invite the reader to try both pages from bottom to top, as well as from top to bottom.

In my opinion, both are improved by being read from bottom to top. They have more punch! At the same time, I imagine we could debate at length which is the duller. (Chall, 1996, p. 96)

The pages referenced are shown in Figure 2.1. In the original, the Beacon primer included a black and white drawing of a horse, and the Dick and Jane text was accompanied by a full color illustration of Dick jumping over blocks, with the entire family looking on.

"Chacun à son goût", as they say. Yet, if you do try to duke it out— as we proceeded to do in the planning of the 1995 Open Court basal— you too will find that many of the very conflicts so untouchably ensconced in "taste" or "literary sensibilities" actually belong to distinct but competing dimensions of literary quality that can be rationally weighed and discussed.

What makes for literary quality? One dimension is plot, or "conflict," as John Le Carré preferred, concretizing the point with his example, " 'The cat sat on the mat' is not a story. 'The cat sat on the dog's mat' is a story" (Barber, 1977). It is the plot of the story that leads the reader's imagination forward, that spawns expectations and, thus, that enables tensions, surprises, happy endings, and tragedies. For stories to have plots is therefore a good thing.

Beyond that, of course, the overarching plot of the first-grade class-

Beacon primer phonic reader	Dick and Jane meaning reader
My name is Dick. I am a big horse. You may pat me. You may ride me. Will you ride on my back, Tom? I will not run fast. I will not kick. I will not jump. I will stand still I like to have Tom ride on my back. I can run like the wind.	**Do What I Do** "See me jump," said Dick. "Oh, my! This is fun. Come and jump. Come and do what I do. Look, look! Who can jump? Who can do what I do?"
Page 50 from J. H. Fassett, *Beacon Primer*, Ginn, Boston, 1912.	Page 41 from W. S. Gray et al., *The New Fun with Dick and Jane (Primer)*. Scott Foresman, 1956.

FIGURE 2.1. Comparison of phonic reader with meaning-based reader. From CHALL. *Learning to Read*, 3E. © 1996 Wadsworth, a part of Cengage Learning, Inc. Reproduced by permission. www.cengage.com/permissions

room is to turn all students into readers. With that in mind, we wish to engage our young students actively in plot, eliciting their reactions and expectations at each juncture. We wish to introduce them to the prototypical garbs that enrobe plots—rags to riches, overcoming adversity, and character testing. We want them to learn about other lands, other times, and other people and their hopes, dreams, and ways of life. We want them to reflect on kindness and cruelty, charity and greed, reason and foolhardiness, honesty and duplicity, pride and arrogance, support and adversity, and hope, perseverance, love, and strength of all kinds. We wish to familiarize them with the best and the best-loved stories that epitomize such plots. We wish to share fairytales, fables, tall tales, and poetry from around the world, exposing them to the cultures of their origins while familiarizing them with their settings, genres, and authors' craft. We want them to learn to love stories, even while using the stories to build in them the linguistic and cultural knowledge and reflective inclinations to get the most from them.

We also wish to introduce them to the world of nonfiction, both in genre and for the treasure trove of information that it opens. We want to engage them with the careful logic of expository text and the special syntax and language through which it is conveyed. We want to introduce them to the physical world, including its geography, climates, continents, people, and their ways of life. We want to pique their curiosity about nature's creatures, their biology, behaviors, and habitats. We want to lead them to appreciate that, whatever they wish to learn, their best bet is to turn to a book. And most of all, we want to instill in them that the key to enjoying informational texts is wondering. Where do frogs go in the winter? How to they breathe down there? And so on.

The wish list went on and on. The more we talked, the more there was that we realized we wanted and truly needed to get done. We also recognized, however, that servicing these goals would be exceedingly difficult with the kinds of short, simple texts suitable for beginning readers.

And then we had an epiphany. No one book need do all! To the contrary, the basic rule of human attention is that it can be focused on only one train of thought at a time. We therefore determined that we would conceive our first-grade materials in separate sets, each designed with a sharp eye toward that which we hoped the children would learn and think about through its use.

Thus, for the beginning of the year, we designed the big books with the specific goal of enabling exploration of informational texts. We did not worry that they were too hard for beginners to read on their own. Instead, we methodically introduced sought topics, concepts, information, puzzles, language, layouts, illustrations, and graphics that would invite the teachers and children to question and wonder, to dwell and revisit. Similarly, in support of literature, we provided an anthology of read-aloud classics and also recommended read-aloud titles to complement and enrich the thematic units throughout the year.

When we turned to the student anthologies, we maintained the same principle. In half the units—we called them "Reflection" units—we focused on universal themes such as courage, persistence, or friendship. In any given unit, we tried to choose each selection so as to bring a dif ferent insight to the theme (e.g., what courage is or isn't and how different people respond to and cope with life challenges that call for courage). The other half of the units, which we called the "Inquiry" units, were each centered on a conceptual space such as fossils, animal habitats, or money, with each selection intended to add new information or perspective on the concept in focus. Again, pursuit of active inquiry was a primary goal. Thus, as students worked through each unit, we asked teachers to help them develop a Question Board, to reinforce wondering, and also a Concept Board through which to display new information, to explore its interrelations and, through that, to recognize still more connections and questions.

The student anthologies, we felt, could be used most powerfully in service of true guided and interactive reading. With that in mind, we set the them aside until the second semester, when students would be better prepared for the intense eyes-on, minds-on reading and interactions they were intended to support.

Across the first semester, we sought to prepare students for this work through two parallel and largely separate sets of activities. The read-alouds and big books were to be the principle vehicles for fostering students' literary stance, as it were. During the first semester, the read-aloud and big-book sessions were also intended to establish appropriate classroom dynamics and discussion, including use of the Concept and Question Boards and comfort with the nature and labels for our six core comprehension strategies (asking questions, clarifying meaning, making connections, making predictions, summarizing, and visualizing). In parallel, to develop students' basic reading skills, we would provide direct instruction and play on phonemic awareness and phonics, complemented with various writing activities and, very importantly, a set of mini-books especially designed for beginners.

THE IMPORTANCE OF DECODABILITY

We had thus separated the challenge of building basic reading skills from those of developing literary language and thought, but we had not yet conquered it. How should texts be designed for beginners so as to be both accessible and instructionally propelling? In fact, techniques abound for making texts "easy": Make the print large; keep the texts short; keep the syntax simple; use familiar vocabulary; ensure repetition of new words. Although there is genuine merit to each of these considerations (for discussion, see Adams, 1990), it is equally obvious that none is sufficient in itself (and remarkably easy to find books where each pretends to be).

Very popular at that time were *predictable* books. Predictable books were expressly designed to support beginners' reading success through pictures and linguistic patterning, such as rhyme and repetition. The drawback to predictable books was that their design tended to be a bit too supportive, allowing children to memorize the words or to figure them out from the pictures or rhymes in place of, rather than in support of, attention to the print. In consequence, and despite their accessibility, predictable books have not been proven good resources for fostering beginners' word recognition growth (Johnston, 2000). Even so, in both spirit and logistics, there was much to be admired about the simple, lively stand-alone book format that had accompanied the predictable text movement.

We imagined producing little books that were similar in spirit and physical format to the predictable books but that were designed to direct the children's attention to the print on the page and, thus, to develop their word recognition skills. To distinguish these books from their predictable cousins, we called them *decodable books*. Hence the term. The challenge was dissolved into two parts: the nature of the texts we wanted the children to read, and the issue of what they would need to know before opening them.

Research indicated a clear advantage of providing beginning readers with books designed to be decodable (e.g., Aukerman, 1984; Bond & Dykstra, 1967; Chall, 1967; Hanson & Farrell, 1995). Yet, the literature offered less guidance on how to design such entry-level books. A provocative exception was a then-recent publication by Juel and Roeper/Schneider (1985).

In the schools in which Juel and Roeper/Schneider (1985) undertook their study, all teachers were required to spend the first 20 to 30 minutes of each reading period instructing the whole class with a synthetic phonics program developed by the district. Because the phonics lessons were scripted, the delivery, as well as the content, of the phonics instruction was effectively controlled across classrooms. Through an observation protocol and teacher interviews, Juel and Roeper/Schneider confirmed that the teachers did indeed use the district's phonics materials as required.

The balance of each reading period, roughly 1 hour each day, was spent in reading activities with selections from the anthologies of one or the other of two different basal programs. The reading selections in one of the basals were anchored on phonics, while those in the other were designed around high-frequency words. The children were drawn from the middle reading group in 11 different classrooms in three different schools. Approximately half of the children were in classrooms that were using the phonics-oriented basal, and a comparable group of children were using the high-frequency basal. In addition to pretesting in September, Juel and Roeper/Schneider evaluated the children's decoding and word recognition growth on completion of the basals' *preprimers* in November, their *primers* in February, and their *first readers* in May.

The November assessment showed that, regardless of their basal program, the children were equally able to read the core vocabulary from their respective preprimers, and that was so whether those words were presented in their original story contexts or in isolated lists. Moreover, a pseudoword test affirmed that, regardless of basal, the children were equally able to decode spelling-to-sound correspondences that they had been taught through the district phonics program. Even so, the children using the phonics-oriented basal significantly outperformed their peers on the pseudoword test. The source of this advantage was that the children using the phonics-oriented preprimers were far more successful with spelling-to-sound patterns that had *not yet* been explicitly taught.

This pattern continued throughout the year. Though the magnitude of the difference dwindled by spring, the children using the phonics-oriented anthology continued to outperform their peers on the pseudo-word assessment. Also, at each testing point, the two groups of children continued to demonstrate comparable accuracy with the core words from their own basal anthologies. In the spring, however, Juel and Roeper/Schneider added an additional, very telling assessment to their evaluation suite. For this last round of assessment, Juel and Roeper/ Schneider asked the children to read not just the core words from their own anthologies, but also the words from the alternate anthology. When the lists were switched, the children who had worked with the phonics-oriented anthology proved far more successful at reading the core vocabulary from the alternate, unfamiliar anthology, than were their peers who had worked with the high-frequency anthology.

Closer analyses of the children's word recognition performance showed that, for both groups, the recognition of core vocabulary was influenced by the number of times the tested word had occurred in their anthologies. Practice makes permanent, but what the children were practicing and learning while reading was evidently significantly different. For children who had worked with the phonic-oriented basal, the best predictor of core vocabulary success—even better than number of repetitions—was the tested words' decodability. For children who had worked with the high-frequency basal, by contrast, the relative decodability of the core words made no measurable difference. Further, for children with the phonics-oriented basal, performance on the word and pseudo-word reading tasks benefited from the number of different words in which their composite letter pairs had been seen in their anthologies. In contrast, for the children who had used the high-frequency basal, just the opposite was true: They were most successful with core vocabulary whose spellings were visually distinctive or unusual.

Use of the phonics-oriented basal qualitatively altered both how and what the children were learning, on their own, through reading. Juel and Roeper/Schneider's data reveal the tendency among the children who used the high-frequency basal to learn words visually, as pictures. In contrast, the children who had used the phonics-oriented basal showed that they had been using their phonics while reading. By dint of so doing, these students had extended their knowledge of spelling-sound relations well beyond what they had been taught and had developed a significantly more agile and productive capacity for reading new words. This finding warrants serious reflection. Is this not the purpose of teaching phonics in the first place?

What exactly was it about the phonics-oriented anthologies that induced this behavior? This, too, seems an aspect of Juel and Roeper/ Scheider's study that is too often overlooked in its frequent citation. The effective difference between the two anthologies lay but entirely within

the preprimers. Though they analyzed the wording of the two anthologies in a host of different ways, Juel and Roeper/Schneider could find
little difference between either the two primers or the two first readers.
In contrast, the difference between the two preprimers was stark. Compared to the high-frequency preprimer, the phonics-oriented preprimers
presented more different words (534 vs. 343), and the words it presented were shorter in letter length (3.7 vs. 4.5), had fewer syllables (1.0
vs. 1.3), were repeated more often (26.3 vs. 15.1), held greater overlap
in spelling patterns as measured by bigram versatility (22.3 vs. 33.6),
and were more decodable (1.2 vs. 1.8 on a scale of 1 to 3).[3]

Taking the issue one step further, we wondered what, cognitively,
might have contributed most to hastening the children's decoding prow-
ess. Was it that words in the phonics-oriented anthologies tended to be
repeated more often (26.3 vs. 15.1 times)? As might be expected, the
number of times a word was repeated was shown to influence its specific
recognition, but that was at least as true for the children who worked
with the high-frequency anthology. Could the greater number of word
repetitions also have contributed to the children's ability to sound-out
never-before-seen words? Indirectly, perhaps. For example, the recur-
rence of secure words might have helped them keep track of the ongoing
context of their readings. It might also have served to free up the energy
and resources needed for sounding out new words. After all, if there are
too many new words in a text, the children get worn out (Hiebert &
Martin, Chapter 3, this volume).

Was it that the words in the phonics-oriented basals were shorter
(3.7 vs. 4.5 letters)? This we thought principally an artifact of the difference in number of syllables (1.0 vs. 1.3). Multisyllabic words bring a
complication to the basic alphabetic principle: They cannot be productively blended letter by letter, start to finish as they must first be broken
into syllables. We therefore decided that we would defer multisyllabic
words until after that strategy had been addressed instructionally.

Some phonics advocates have argued that decodable texts must not
include any irregular words whatsoever (e.g., Hiskes, 2003). Contrary to
this stricture, both programs included many irregularly spelled structure
words, such as *of*, *the*, *do*, and *they*. It follows that the advantage of the
phonics-oriented anthology could not be ascribed to an exclusion of irregular words. On the other hand, where the high-frequency preprimer
was fairly liberal in including content words with irregular or advanced

---

[3]These counts refer to content words only. The two preprimers were relatively comparable
in their usage of structure words (e.g., *the*, *they*, *of*, *to*, *have*, *are*).

spellings, the phonic-oriented preprimer generally avoided them. This, we thought, might well have been a relevant factor.

Recent state adoption specifications require that decodable texts be designed in lockstep pace with students' phonics instruction. According to this position, letters and orthographic conventions that have not yet been explicitly taught must be excluded from decodable texts. Yet, in Juel and Roeper/Scheider's (1985) schools, the phonics lessons were closely aligned with neither of the anthologies as they were written independently of both. Further, as documented by the November assessments, the phonic-oriented preprimer departed from the phonics lessons not merely in specific letters or conventions, but in overall pace. Although the phonics-oriented anthologies required a number of spelling-to-sound relations before they were covered by the phonics lessons, this did not cancel the books' impact.

What was distinctive about the phonics-oriented texts used in Juel and Roeper/Schneider's (1985) study was that content words were introduced categorically, constrained by orthographic conventions and complexity. Thus, for example, the focus was initially on regular single-syllable, short-vowel words which were amply exercised before introduction of long vowel patterns. As far as we could tell, it was this, no more and no less, that principally fueled the advantage of these anthologies.

More specifically, our hypothesis was that there were two major advantages of the phonics-oriented anthologies. The first was that the phonics-oriented books made honest people of the teachers when they dared say, "And if you come to a word that you don't know, sound it out." This sounds silly, but it's potentially very important. As Juel and Roeper/Schneider (1985) mused, "Emphasis on a phonics method seems to make little sense if children are given initial texts to read where the words do not follow regular letter-sound generalizations" (p. 151).

Indeed, one way to summarize the findings of their study is as follows: It barely, if ever, occurred to a number of children who used the high-frequency anthology that what they were taught in their phonics lessons was meant to be applied in the course of their reading. But if what they were taught was not applicable to their reading, then why would they think otherwise? This is pretty basic. Why in the world would anybody teach phonics were it not intended to be useful in learning to read and write?

The second major advantage of the phonics-oriented anthologies, we conjectured, was that they engaged children in attending carefully, left to right, to the spellings and sounds of new words they read. Ensuring that children's earliest books are decodable intrinsically rewards them for applying their phonics while reading, from the outset. Moreover, research and theory urge that the benefits of so doing extend well beyond the learning or generalization of any particular letter–sound correspondence.

Each time the mind attends to information, it creates a trace of that experience, including both the perceived parts and the temporal order in which they were perceived. To sound-out a word, a student must examine the letters left to right, in sequence. This causes the ordered, left-to-right sequence of letters to leave a trace of itself in memory. At the same time, because the student is sounding the word, the trace that results includes the letters' connection to their phonology or speech sounds. That is true for the individual letters and groups of letters, as well as the word as a whole. If the word is in the student's oral vocabulary, connections are also built from its spelling and sounds to its meaning and, one by one, to each of the contexts in which it has occurred. The meaning and usage of the word are like the bow on the parcel, tying its parts and links together into a distinct, integrated, self-supporting whole. Gradually, through repeated encounters, the representation of the word and its parts become so richly and strongly interconnected that the word is recognized virtually at a glance. Its spelling, pronunciation, and meaning seem to come to mind at once. The word has become a *sight word* (see Ehri, 1992, 1998).

In turn, the cumulating trace of the reader's decoding experiences contributes to the more general receptivity of the word recognition system. That is, to the extent that the left-to-right spellings of any two words overlap, they map onto the same internal array of letters. In this way, the orthographic representations of the common parts of words overwrite themselves, gaining strength beyond those of the separate words through which they were learned. Over repeated encounters with words containing the rime, *-at*, for example, the orthographic network will come to respond quickly and strongly to *-at* whether it occurs in *cat*, *bat*, *flat*, or *format*. Similarly, the short-*ă* sound of closed syllables emerges as those words share representation with, for example, *cap*, *bath*, *snack*, and *rabbit*. In the same way, the network will eventually come to respond to the spellings of common syllables and affixes, such as *pre-*, *-tion*, and *-ture* (see Adams, 1990).

As the mind learns the associations between letters, it becomes very fast at recognizing common spelling patterns. Conversely, a handy side effect of this experience-dependent speed is that, relatively speaking, the recognition process stalls on encountering uncommon letter transitions, such as those that typically straddle syllable boundaries: The result of this balk is that, for skilled readers, words are effectively parsed into syllables in the very course of their recognition (see Adams, 1990).

Progressively, as a result of having processed many words letter by letter, left to right, and spelling to sound, a student's mind becomes familiar and responsive to common spelling patterns and their spelling-sound translations, independently of the specific words in which they've been encountered. As this happens, the student gains *decoding automaticity.*

Decoding automaticity is an invaluable asset to the reader. It enables even visually unfamiliar words to be mapped quickly and easily to language, and it allows the reader to progress through new texts and topics with acceptable fluency. At the same time, it provides a support structure by which nearly every new word that is encountered has been partly learned already and, so, is quickly promoted to sight word status (see Adams, 2007). Meanwhile, as written and spoken language become more richly connected to each other, print becomes a full partner rather than a handmaiden to oral language. Through the very structure of the system, what is learned through one medium effectively becomes part of both. This oneness between the language and ideas that we read, write, say, hear, and think is the hallmark of true literacy.

As the knowledge gained through decoding becomes more extensive and responsive, readers appear to recognize nearly all words and, oddly, even pseudowords holistically. But appearances deceive. Again, research shows that the primary dynamic by which skillful readers recognize words as they read is by translating the letters, left to right, into speech (see, e.g., Lukatela & Turvey, 1994; Rayner, 1998; Rayner & Pollatsek, 1989). In effect, skillful readers sound-out the words, much as phonics lessons teach beginners to do. The process differs for beginners principally in that, for them, the recognition, sounding, and mental assembly of the word requires careful attention, active memory, and deliberation. For skillful readers, by contrast, the whole process has become automatized through recognition.

The following meme, which has surely cluttered your own e-mail box in recent years, offers a powerful demonstration of the detail and supportiveness of this orthographic knowledge:

> Aoccdrnig to a rscheearch at Cmabrigde Uinervtisy, it deosn't mttaer in waht oredr the ltteers in a wrod are, the olny iprmoetnt tihng is taht the frist and lsat ltteer be at the rghit pclae. The rset can be a toatl mses and you can sitll raed it wouthit porbelm. Tihs is bcuseae the huamn mnid deos not raed ervey lteter by istlef, but the wrod as a wlohe.

Skilled readers of English are able to read this "mess" not because they recognize the words as wholes, but because the left-to-right order of the letters is an integral part of their orthographic knowledge. Moreover, such automatic correction of perceived letter order is crucial to their ability to read small print with ease and accuracy (see Adams, 1990, Chapter 6)—something that children will very soon need be able to do themselves.

In short, because of the cumulative and self-organizing nature of the knowledge underlying decoding, orthographic knowledge is expected to beget orthographic learning. The richer one's orthographic knowledge, the easier the reading act and the more rapid the acquisition of sight words.

Importantly, however, acquiring new sight words is the direct outcome of neither careful instruction in phonics, phonemic awareness, or letters, nor even of prior decoding sophistication. All of those factors are but enablers. Rather, the prepotent determinant of sight word acquisition is whether, on encountering a new word in print, the student actually does try and does succeed in decoding it (Cunningham, 2006; Cunningham, Perry, Stamovich, & Share, 2002; Share, 1999). Whether or not students do so depends not just on whether they have learned to decode but, equally pivotal, on whether they have developed the inclination to do so when encountering new words as they read (Byrne, Freebody, & Gates, 1992; Connelly, Johnston, & Thompson, 1999; Frith, 1980). As demonstrated by the Juel and Roeper/Schneider (1985) study, the latter may be significantly influenced by whether decoding is useful in students' very earliest efforts to read by themselves.

DESIGNING THE DECODABLES

In designing the entry-level texts for the 1995 Open Court program, our overarching goal was bald and simple: to reward the children, in success and learning, for using their decoding skills while reading. At a cognitive level, what we envisioned was essentially a receptive equivalent of inventive spelling. As with inventive spelling, the message we wished to secure was: "If you are unsure of a word, try sounding it out." Also, as with inventive spelling, the tacit entailment was: "Each time you do, you will make it easier the next."

To achieve this goal, the challenge was necessarily divided into two parts: The nature and progression of the texts we would give the children to read, and the issue of what they would need to know before opening them.

Preparatory Knowledge

Phonics

Given that the goal is leading children to decode as they read, phonics instruction is an obvious prerequisite. Yet, phonics has its own prerequisites, including knowledge of letters and their sounds, phonological and phonemic awareness, and an appreciation of the basic alphabetic principle.

Of these, the most fundamental and difficult is that of ensuring children can confidently recognize the letters of the alphabet. Indeed, of all of the literacy challenges that students will ultimately confront, learning the letters of the alphabet is the only one that depends exactly and only on sheer rote memorization, and it requires meticulous, secure memorization—at that. There is no gain in teaching letter–sounds or decoding unless and until children can confidently discern one letter from another.

With this in mind, we began letter work at the beginning of the kindergarten year and continued it daily. In course, the children were led to sing, recite, name, recognize, copy, and write the letters over and over through a host of different activities, including wake-me-up and transitional activities that allowed for quick and frequent repetitions.

Research shows that learning letter–sounds is greatly facilitated by knowing the names of letters (Adams, Treiman, & Pressley, 1997; Treiman, Weatherston, & Berch, 1994). Nevertheless, productive decoding requires that the letters' sounds be firmly distinguished, one from another, and learned well. Letter–sound instruction began about a quarter of the way into the kindergarten year and moved from isolated sounds and initial-letter alliteration games to the use of letters in phonemic awareness, word building, and writing activities.

Among letters, the vowels are trickiest in both their sounds and spellings. If this is true for all children, then it is only more so for English language learners (ELLs). That English vowels have two primary sounds, long and short, warrants explicit attention. Since this is true of few other languages, such attention is only more important for ELLs. In addition, the names and sounds of English letters differ from the Latinate languages in befuddling ways; for example, the name and long sound of the English letter *Aa* rhymes with the name and sound of the letter *Ee* in Spanish, while the long sound of the English letter *Ee* rhymes with the name and sound of the Spanish letter *Ii*.

In our classroom display of the alphabet, vowels were printed in red to emphasize their "special" status. They were called *vowels* and treated with special attention from the start, including, for example, rhymes and songs that were targeted at making sure the children knew which letters were vowels and could confidently recall and produce the two major sounds of each.

In prior editions of the Open Court reading program, phonics instruction focused first on long vowels. The rationale for this approach was that the sounds of long vowels are easier to hear and distinguish from one another than are those of short vowels. We honored this observation in the phonemic awareness activities, which were initially focused on listening for and discriminating between the long sounds of vowels. At the next step, however, we turned to discriminating between the long and short sounds of each particular vowel, tying these activities to tall-and-squat graphics of each vowel. The goals were to establish firmly not just that each vowel has two major sounds but, further, to seat those sounds well and to attach them to labels (e.g., long *a* vs. short *a*) for downstream use.

The phonemic awareness strand began with listening and ordering games, partly to develop children's auditory attention and partly for purposes of anchoring terminology (e.g., *first, last, middle, one by one, without*) and attendant analysis on which later phonemic and phonics activities would depend. The listening games were followed by activities focused on rhyming, word awareness, and syllable awareness before turning to phonemic awareness proper. After introducing phonemic awareness through oral activities, we frequently used the letters themselves to mediate phonemic awareness activities. Using letters, instead of, for example, bingo markers, in this way allowed us to shift seamlessly in phonics instruction proper (see Adams, Treiman, & Pressley, 1998, for research on this option).

In the initial phonics lessons, the modes of thought were the same as those developed through the phonemic awareness activities. The principle difference was that attention was now shifted from simply hearing the separate speech sounds to tying them to letters. The tasks were alternately structured around determining the letters for representing phonemes, as in word building and spelling activities, or identifying the speech sounds represented by the letters, as in decoding. In contrast to earlier editions of the Open Court curriculum, entry level phonics was focused on short vowel words for reason that a primary concern was in instilling the basic alphabetic principle: left to right, letter to sound.

Structure Words

Over the years, considerable controversy has been directed to the dilemma of when and how to introduce those words that Juel and Roeper/Schneider termed "structure words," such as *the, of, to, is, are, you, they,* and *there.* On one hand, these are the matrix words of the English language; it is extremely difficult to write coherent, natural, well-formed sentences without them. On the other hand, the spellings of these words are not simple. Even the most frequent among them entail spelling-sound correspondences that are beyond the first few phonics lessons. Worse still, the spelling of many of these words is just plain irregular.

Because of the orthography of these words, some have argued that such words should categorically be avoided in decodable texts (e.g.,

Hiskes, 2003). Yet, avoiding such words in the earliest texts does not solve the problem. For how long should these words be deferred? Waiting until all regular spelling-sound correspondences have been duly taught and exercised is untenable. Yet, at any point in between, the issue is the same.

The second, and perhaps most common, strategy for dealing with the structure words is to introduce each in preview of the reading selection where it is first needed. We did not think this approach sensible either. In effect, it amounts to saying, "If you come to a word you don't know, try sounding it out—unless it is irregular in which case you will fail." What kind of guidance is that?

By process of elimination, the only option left was to teach core structure words *before* introducing the decodables. Happily, unlike its competitors, this option had many positives. We selected the 25 most indispensable of these words and exercised them throughout the kindergarten year so that we would then be able to use them in the decodables without worrying about mixed messages. After all, nobody, neither child nor adult, pauses to deliberate on a sight word while reading. Structure words were introduced by having the kindergartners find them, chime them, and count them in their big books (e.g., "Hey Diddle Diddle" was used to introduce *the*.) Their spellings and usages were exercised frequently through sentence building and grammatical play. In addition, a set of rebus books was developed for the kindergartners toward the joint goals of securing the structure words and easing the students into reading books on their own (see Biemiller and Siegel, 1997; MacKinnon, 1959).

First Grade Redux

In the best of all possible curricular worlds, all children in a first-grade program would have completed the preparatory kindergarten program, and none of them would have forgotten a thing. Regrettably, neither of these is a good bet in the real word. During the first few weeks of grade 1, the reading skills strand was therefore devoted to reseating (or seating) the alphabetic basics and the core structure words. The activities were more systematic and focused and were punctuated with assessment tips to help teachers discern which children and which activities were in need of additional attention.

The Decodables

The plan for the phonics scope and sequence and the decodables was guided by three precepts: (1) fostering conceptual clarity, (2) respecting individual differences, and (3) moving children into real books as soon as they are ready.

Conceptual Clarity

With respect to conceptual clarity, our goal was to convey the message that phonics is worth learning and worth using. Toward this end, we organized the phonics scope and sequence categorically by orthographic conventions.

For English, the most basic convention, of course, is the fundamental alphabetic principle. Its application consists of sounding all letters in a word, left to right, in sequence. To give the alphabetic principle due priority, we began with short-a consonant–vowel–consonant (CVC) patterns. The scope and sequence then marched through the short vowels, adding consonants and consonant blends along the way, before moving to long vowels, which began with the consonant–vowel–consonant–final *e* (CVCe) families.

We also argued (albeit unsuccessfully) that the basic consonants (simple, primary sounds and spellings only) should be permitted in the decodables from the start. We argued that free use of the consonants would reinforce the "figure it out" message. It would allow us to exercise word families more richly and flexibly, thus discouraging children from trying to rote memorize their way to literacy, while hastening decoding habit and, through that, the growth of the underlying orthographic representations. Besides which, we argued, nobody had ever seen a child whose inventive spelling extended only through the letter *Mm* on *Mm* day. To the contrary, provided that children know their ABCs and have had the phonemic insight, research shows that learning how to sound one or two letters transfers readily and independently to sounding others (Byrne, 1992).

Bear in mind, too, that prior to opening the decodables, the children had already been engaged in a great deal of letter–sound, segmenting, and blending practice with the same sorts of single syllable, short-vowel words. Thus, the challenge at this point, as we saw it, was less teaching individual letter–sound correspondences than leading children to make use of these correspondences in the course of connected reading and, through that, to build larger orthographic structures into their reading repertoire.

Accordingly, the decodables were centered on word families. Among word families we included enduringly popular onset–rime patterns (e.g., *sit, pit, fit; past, last, blast*). However, because orthographic growth depends on attending to the middles and ends of words as well as their beginnings, we also included word families built on vowels (e.g., *stick,*

stack, stuck) and consonant codas (e.g., *fan, fat, fast*). The risk in designing beginning texts around multiple types of word families is that it potentially admits a degree of orthographic dispersion that can be over-
whelming for the young reader (see Hiebert, 1999). This was to be
avoided; the very reason for building the texts around word families was
to ensure that each new word the children conquered would make it easier for them to read the next. Thus, although the decodable writing rules
allowed more than one new word per sentence, they did not permit more
than one new word family per sentence (e.g., "It was a *fat, cat*"; "He
had a *hat*"; "He put the *big, bug* in the *bag*").

In similar spirit, there were other rules, too. For example, any spelling pattern used in a story was to be used at least five times. Repeated
use of any given word was encouraged, albeit with the caveat that doing
so was not sufficient. It was decoding facility, as distinct from word
memorization, that we were after. A complementary set of rules was directed toward ensuring that the children received feedback as to whether
they had decoded the new words correctly. As in the predictable books,
we encouraged use of patterned text and common sentence frames to
ease and support decoding (e.g., letting new words fall in predictable
spots: "There was a *bump*. There was a *thump*. . . . "), while cautioning
that the wording must not be so predictable as to permit the children to
avoid decoding by glossing or guessing.

In both the phonics lessons and the decodables, we endeavored to
use contrasts methodically so as to make focal points salient. For example, _____*nk* and _____*ng* words (e.g., *bang–bank, sing–sink*) were taught
together so as to encourage children to attend closely to the relatively
subtle difference in their final sounds. In turn, using such words together
in the decodables served to reinforce this phonological distinction by tying it to differences in the words' meanings. Similarly, when the time
came, we designed both the activities in the phonics lessons and the
decodables to contrast vowel spelling conventions (e.g., *cap–cape, slim–
slime* and, later, *men–mean, peck–peek, stop–stoop*), final consonant
conventions (e.g., *face–fake, hug–huge, lick–like, jug–judge*), inflectional
conventions (e.g., *pack–packed–packing; sit–sitting; name–naming; hopping–
hoping*), and derivational affixes (e.g., *big–bigger–biggest; zip–unzip;
do–redo*).

In all, our goal was to convey to children that, irregularities notwithstanding, there is a system and logic to the spellings of English
words. Our goal was to reduce the phonics challenge from a myriad of
microrules to a few big ones and to persuade children that they could
understand, learn, and thoughtfully apply these rules on their own.
Again, it is only through its application that phonics instruction can productively promote acquisition of sight words and decoding automaticity.

Respect for Individual Differences

In every first-grade classroom, some children arrive knowing how to read, while others are lacking the minimal basics. For some children, reading comes with remarkable ease, while for others it is a daunting challenge. This gave us three more goals in designing the decodable books and their usage. We wished, at once, to (1) ensure adequate practice for every child, (2) provide adequate challenge for children who advance more quickly, and (3) provide teachers with the information they would need in order to guide each student toward reading and rereading books as would serve her or him best.

For the true beginner, reading is lots of work. Getting through a 100-word story just once may well require 5 minutes of disciplined effort and can be wholly exhausting. Yet, where children struggle with a story, there is value in reading it again, and more than once. Immediate rereading of a text helps to complete and refine the trace its new words leave in memory. Once the words have been established in memory, reading the text again after a day or so provides the kind of spaced practice that makes learning permanent. For these children, we hoped to provide lots of gently graduated books and ample time to read and reread each.

In contrast, readers who are more advanced may need only a minute or so to complete a 100-word story. Research shows further that, beyond the very beginning levels, a single encounter with a new and meaningful word is very often sufficient to anchor it as a sight word (see Adams, 2007). Forcing these children to read and reread books beneath their level did not strike us as educationally responsible.

We knew, too, that in the classroom, one of the more difficult aspects of independent activities is that children who finish quickly make it awkward for those who require more time to concentrate and complete their work. We wanted to be sure that, during each such session, *all* children would spend the full duration reading productively. For management purposes, we therefore made a rule that all children were always to begin each session reading the book of the day. Otherwise, whenever they had finished reading any book twice, they were to go on to their next incomplete book, even where that meant moving to ahead of the nominal schedule. The children were to keep track of first and subsequent readings of each title on their personal progress charts.

To manage this dynamic, we developed two sets of decodable books. The books in the first practice set were organized into subseries, corresponding to units in the phonics scope and sequence. Each of these books was designed to emphasize the specific foci of a specific phonics lesson. The children were to read these books with partners, one reading the odd-number pages and one reading the even-numbered pages, and then swapping.

The second, complementary set of books was designed to capitulate each subseries in the first set of books. More specifically, the second set was comprised of two books for each of the subseries of the practice set, such that the combined sequence can be schematized:

$$a_{1,1}, a_{1,2}, a_{1,3}, a_{1,4}, b_{1,1}, b_{1,2}, a_{2,1}, a_{2,2}, a_{2,3}, a_{2,4}, b_{2,1}, b_{2,2}, a_{3,1}, a_{3,2},$$
$$a_{3,3}, a_{3,4}, b_{3,1}, b_{3,2}, \ldots$$

While $a_{i,j}$ represents the jth book in the ith subseries of the practice bookset, $b_{i,1}$ and $b_{i,2}$ represent the two books in the complementary bookset designed to go with that subseries.

The purpose of the second, cumulative bookset was to help teachers manage and guide their students' progress. That is, each book in this set contained all of the orthographic patterns and conventions that were exercised across the subseries that it followed. Thus, by listening to a child read from either book in this set, teachers could discern whether the child was ready to move on or whether he or she was in need of additional practice or review. In an effort to make re-assessment easier where needed, we included two different titles at each level in this set.

Meanwhile, the second set of books also gave teachers a way to let speedier students advance at an individually appropriate pace. That is, because the design of the phonics instruction was progressive while that of the decodables was cumulative, a comfortable cold reading of any book in the second set could be taken as a check-off for all earlier titles in both booksets. Consider, for example, a child who had quickly surged through the whole subseries ahead of schedule. If a reading of either of the final summative books affirmed that the child was indeed in command at that level, then the teacher could safely permit her or him to continue moving forward without a need for evaluating the child's mastery of earlier books.

The books in the first practice set were black and white and fully reproducible so that teachers could encourage children to take them home without concern for damage or loss. The books in the second, summative set were softbound and full-color in hopes of making them more rewarding for children and less likely that they would leave the classroom.

Reading Real Books

Any decent children's library has shelves and shelves of books, especially for beginning readers, that are written by truly talented authors with the express intention of writing good books, and that have been filtered for quality and appeal by the marketplace. The problem with these books is that, by and large, they are leveled for children at the end of first grade or the beginning of second grade. Although we tried to make the decodables as good as they could be, we did not suffer the illusion that they would rival these books in interest or delight. Our purpose, instead, was to provide children with the sort of entry-level material that would fill the gap.

As soon as children completed the decodable series, as affirmed by their teacher, they were to turn their efforts to tradebooks during daily independent reading sessions. To be sure, some children would be ready to move into the tradebooks before mid-year while others would need work with decodables for a bit longer; the accordion-like pacing of the decodable series allowed for such differences. Nevertheless, the modal expectation was that the decodable series would be done by the end of the first semester.

We proposed a similarly structured set of books for the first 4 weeks of grade 2, but that never came to be. Instead, states soon began to require the inclusion of decodable books in basal reading packages and, as they did so, they also took over specification of the design and scheduling.

AFTERMATH

In 1997, Texas required that reading textbooks to be adopted for the 2000–2001 school year include decodable texts as part of the first-grade program, defining "decodable texts" as "engaging and coherent texts in which most of the words are comprised of an accumulating sequence of letter–sound correspondences being taught" (Texas Education Agency, 1998, Chapter 110.3b, 1.7G). Some protested that this requirement was inadequately supported by research (e.g., Allington & Woodside-Jiron, 1998). Others felt strongly that Texas's request was neither well-defined nor stringent enough.

The latter group won and, in November, 1999, the Texas State Board of Education (2000) revised its textbook specifications, requiring that "decodable text for practice of letter–sound correspondences across the first-grade program meet a minimum average of 80% decodability using the methodology approved by the board." In December, 1999, California (California Department of Education, 1999, lines 144–158) followed suit, requiring that programs submitted for its 2002 reading adoption include decodables in which "at least 75% of the words are comprised solely of previously taught sound–spelling correspondences." California further required that the decodables be introduced in the end of kindergarten and be continued throughout grade 1 and, "for students who still need this instruction," extended into grade 2.

The methodology for gauging decodability that was adopted by Texas and California, and by others in their wake, consists of counting a word as decodable if, and only if, it contains no grapheme–phoneme correspondences that have not been previously taught. The percent decodability of a text is given as the ratio of the number of fully decodable words to the total number of words in the text. In producing their first-grade decodables, some publishers found the most expedient way to meet the criterion was to excise nonconforming words, offering texts with as few as two or three words per page. Others conformed by tallying letter–sound correspondences, seemingly without heed of number of syllables per word, sentence complexity, or vocabulary and much less considerate of repetition of words or orthographic patterns. In California, whatever may have been intended by "students who still need this instruction," decodables became a core component of the second-grade programs. If there exist data, theory, or cogent argument for extending decodables beyond the very beginning levels of reading, then I am unable to find it.

To offer texts with which the children can succeed and, through that, will learn seems the minimal responsibility of any vendor that accepts money from our schools for instructional reading materials. At the entry level, the argument for offering books designed to seat and reinforce the decoding habit is theoretically, empirically, and clinically persuasive (e.g., Aukerman, 1984; Bond & Dykstra, 1967; Chall, 1967; Hanson & Farrell, 1995; Juel & Roeper/Schneider, 1985). A case can also be made for such materials at the very outset of grade 2, whether to reboot the children or to find out which are in need of special help. In addition, decodable texts have been shown valuable in helping delayed students to catch on and catch up (Torgesen et al., 2001). Regardless of level, however, the difficulty of a text depends on many other considerations besides its letter–sound correspondences (see Hiebert & Mesmer, 2005) and so, too, does its instructional, informational, and literary value.

REFERENCES

Adams, M. J. (1990). *Beginning to read: Thinking and learning about print.* Cambridge, MA: MIT Press.

Adams, M. J. (2007). The Limits of the Self-Teaching Hypotheses. In S. Neuman (Ed.), *Literacy achievement for young children from poverty.* Baltimore: Brookes.

Adams, M. J., Bereiter, C., Hirshberg, J., Anderson, V., & Bernier, S. A. (1995). *Collections for Young Scholars: Framework for effective teaching.* Chicago and Peru, IL: Open Court.

Adams, M. J., Treiman, R., & Pressley, M. (1998). Reading acquisition. In I. Sigel & A. Renninger (Eds.), *Handbook of child psychology: Vol. 4. Child psychology in practice* (pp. 275–356). New York: Wiley.

Allington, R. L., & Woodside-Jiron, H. (1998). Decodable text in beginning reading: Are mandates and policy based on research? *ERS Spectrum, 16*(2), 3–11.

Aukerman, R. C. (1984). *Approaches to beginning reading* (2nd ed.). New York: Wiley.

Barber, M. (1977, September 25). John le Carré: An interrogation. *New York Times Books in Review,* pp. 9, 44.

Bereiter, C., Scardamalia, M., Brown, A. L., Anderson, V., Campione, J. C., & Kintsch, W. (1989). *Open Court reading and writing.* LaSalle, IL: Open Court.

Biemiller, A., & Siegel, L. S. (1997). A longitudinal study of the effects of the "Bridge" reading program for children at risk for reading failure. *Learning Disability Quarterly, 20*(2), 83–92.

Bond, G. L., & Dykstra, R. (1967). The cooperative research program in first-grade reading instruction. *Reading Research Quarterly, 2,* 5–142.

Byrne, B. (1992). Studies in the acquisition procedure for reading: Rationale, hypotheses, and data. In P. B. Gough, L. C. Ehri, & R. Treiman (Eds.), *Reading acquisition* (pp. 1–34). Hillsdale, NJ: Erlbaum.

Byrne, B., Freebody, P., & Gates, A. (1992). Longitudinal data on the relations of word-reading strategies to comprehension, reading time, and phonemic awareness. *Reading Research Quarterly, 27,* 140–151.

California Department of Education. (1999). *2002 K–8 reading/language arts/ English language development adoption criteria.* Sacramento, CA: California Department of Education.

Chall, J. S. (1996). *Learning to read: The great debate.* San Francisco, CA: Cengage Learning.

Connelly, B., Johnston, R. S., & Thompson, G. B. (1999). The influence of instructional approaches on reading procedures. In G. B. Thompson & T. Nicholson (Eds.), *Learning to read: Beyond phonics and whole language* (pp. 103–123). New York: Teachers College Press.

Cunningham, A. E. (2006). Accounting for children's orthographic learning while reading text: Do children self-teach? *Journal of Experimental Child Psychology, 95,* 56–77.

Cunningham, A. E., Perry, K. E., Stanovich, K. E., & Share, D. L. (2002). Orthographic learning during reading: Examining the role of self-teaching. *Journal of Experimental Child Psychology, 82,* 733–740.

Ehri, L. (1992). Reconceptualizing the development of sight word reading and its relationship to recoding. In P. B. Gough, L. C. Ehri, & R. Trieman (Eds.), *Reading acquisition* (pp. 107–143). Mahwah, NJ: Erlbaum.

Ehri, L. (1998). Grapheme-phoneme knowledge is essential for learning to read words in English. In J. L. Metsala & L. C. Ehri (Eds.), *Word recognition in beginning reading* (pp. 3–40). Mahwah, NJ: Erlbaum.

Fasset, J. H. (1912). *Beacon primer.* Boston: Ginn and Company.

Frith, U. (1980). Unexpected spelling problems. In U. Frith (Ed.), *Cognitive processes in spelling* (pp. 495–516). New York: Academic Press.

Gray, W. S. (1948). *On their own in reading.* Chicago: University of Chicago Press.

Gray, W. S., Artley, A. S., & Arbuthnot, M. H. (1956). *The new fun with Dick and Jane.* Chicago: Scott, Foresman.

Hanson, R. A., & Farrell, D. (1995). The long-term effects on high school seniors of learning to read in kindergarten. *Reading Research Quarterly, 30*(4), 908–933.

Hiebert, E. H. (1999). Text matters in learning to read. *The Reading Teacher, 52,* 552–568.

Hiebert, E. H., & Mesmer, H. (2005). Perspectives on the difficulty of beginning reading texts. In S. Neuman & D. Dickinson (Eds.), *Handbook of research on early literacy: Vol. 2* (pp. 935–967). New York: Guilford Press.

Hiskes, D. G. (2003). Decodable readers. *Phonics Talk, 6.* Retrieved September 2007 from *www.nrrf.org.*

Johnston, F. R. (2000). Word learning in predictable text. *Journal of Educational Psychology, 92*(2), 248–255.

Juel, C., & Roeper/Schneider, D. (1985). The influence of basal readers of first-grade reading. *Reading Research Quarterly, 20*(2), 134–152.

Lukatela, G., & Turvey, M. T. (1994). Visual lexical access is initially phonological: Evidence from associative priming by words, homophones, and pseudo-homophones. *Journal of Experimental Psychology: General, 123*(2), 107–128.

MacKinnon, A. R. (1959). *How do children learn to read: An experimental investigation of children's early growth in awareness of the meaning of printed text.* Toronto: Copp-Clark.

Rayner, K. (1998). Eye movements in reading and information processing: 20 years of research. *Psychological Bulletin, 124*(3), 372–422.

Rayner, K., & Pollatsek, A. (1989). *The psychology of reading.* New York: Prentice-Hall.

Share, D. L. (1999). Phonological recoding and orthographic learning: A direct test of the self-teaching hypothesis. *Journal of Experimental Child Psychology, 72,* 95–129.

Texas Education Agency. (1998). *Chapter 110. Texas essential knowledge and skills for English language arts and reading.* Austin, TX: Author.

Texas State Board of Education. (2000). Report on percentage of decodable text in conforming first grade language arts-reading instructional materials. Austin, TX: Author.

Torgesen, J., Alexander, A., Wagner, R., Rashotte, C., Voeller, K., Conway, T., et al. (2001). Intensive remedial instruction for children with severe reading disabilities: Immediate and long-term outcomes from two instructional approaches. *Journal of Learning Disabilities, 34,* 33–58.

Treiman, R., Weatherston, S., & Berch, D. (1994). The role of letter names in children's learning of phoneme-grapheme relations. *Applied Psycholinguistics, 15,* 97–122.

❧ 3 ❧

Repetition of Words

The Forgotten Variable in Texts for Beginning and Struggling Readers

ELFRIEDA H. HIEBERT
LEIGH ANN MARTIN

At the present time, repetition of specific words does not appear to be a factor in the design or selection of individual texts or sets of texts in instructional programs for beginning readers in the United States. As illustrated in Chapter 1 of this volume, approximately 22.9 new unique words appear per every 100 words in the 2007 copyright of a U.S. mid-first-grade textbook. In 1962, the rate in this same program was 7.4. These rates reflect historical events, changes in theory and perspectives, and critiques of education that have occurred over the past 45 years. The interest in this chapter is to review research to determine whether this dramatic shift represents a practice that emanates from work that qualifies as scientifically based reading research (Slavin, 2002).

We preface this review with a comment about its comprehensiveness. In 1995, while working with students in a graduate course at the University of Michigan on an analysis of then-current basal reading programs, the first author was confronted with the paradigm shift in the nature of reading textbooks that resulted from changes in guidelines and policies (California English/Language Arts Committee, 1987; Texas Education Agency, 1990). Reading textbooks had shifted from controlled vocabulary texts to anthologies of authentic children's literature. The effects of this shift on the features of words in first- and second-grade reading programs were reported in several publications (Hiebert, 2005; Hiebert, Martin, & Menon, 2005). These analyses showed high percentages of single-appearing words and patterns of word repetition that can be described as serendipitous (i.e., reflecting the typical use of high-frequency words in written language). These results were the impetus for a search of literature on the role of repetition and the pace of new information in learning to read.

Our aim in this chapter is to summarize critical literature that we have identified in this decade-long search. We do not claim that the literature summarized in this chapter represents all that is known about the role of repetition and pacing in learning to read. We are aware that individual studies, and even particular literature that represents particular paradigms, have not been addressed. For example, substantial literature exists on massed and distributed practice of word learning (Bloom & Shuell, 1981). There is also a research literature (although not large) on repetitions in vocabulary learning (McKeown, Beck, Omanson, & Pople, 1985; Wysocki & Jenkins, 1987) and on learning vocabulary in a foreign language (Kyongho & Nation, 1989). We have chosen to focus on particular literatures and, within those literatures, particular studies to provide an overview of the current research on the repetition of words and linguistic units in learning to read.

Our focus in this chapter is on those students who depend on schools to become literate, not those who come to first grade reading or become proficient readers within the few first months of school (Lesgold, Resnick, & Hammond, 1985). As was demonstrated by Hiebert (Chapter 1, this volume), automaticity with the 1,000 most-frequent words is not reached until the fourth grade by the 40th percentile and fifth grade by the 25th percentile. It is the role of word repetition in the reading development of this portion of an age cohort that provides the focus of this chapter.

A HISTORICAL PERSPECTIVE ON REPETITION
IN TEXTS FOR BEGINNING READERS

In a historical review of the texts used for beginning reading instruction in American schools from 1640 to 1940, Monaghan and Barry (1999) showed that, at least prior to the 1930s, the text genres thought appropriate for young students meant that particular words were often repeated in the texts given to beginning readers. The excerpt of a text (Norton, 1902) that appears in Table 3.1 illustrates one of the text genres that was often used in beginning reading programs—poems or stories with repeated elements. The repetitive nature of *The House that Jack Built* meant that words such as *this, is, the,* and *that* appeared numerous times, as did words such as *rat, malt, house, Jack,* and *built.*

It was during the period that Venezky (1984) has described as the scientific period in American reading instruction—1914 to 1940—when repetition of words was formalized. The first generation of American educational psychologists such as Thorndike (1903, 1921) drew heavily on explanations from Gestalt psychology to explain and define *learning.* As interpreted by these early educational psychologists, what needed to be learned (i.e., the stimulus) was the whole word. Words that held high interest for students (e.g., *truck, car, bus*) or those that represent frequently occurring patterns in English (e.g., *cat, rat, hat*) could have become the focus. Instead, Thorndike (1921) in *The Teacher's Word Book* identified the words that occurred most frequently in samples of written language—words such as *the, a, and, at, as,* and *be.* Rather than using texts that had been used up to this point such as *The House That Jack Built,* publishers, with the advice of educational psychologists, devised little stories that used these high-frequency words in a formulaic way. An example of a text that appeared in the 1940 Scott Foresman series (Gray, Baruch, & Montgomery, 1940) is included in Table 3.1.

The formula for the repetition of words in such texts came from the work of Gates (1930). Gates described observations in classrooms that showed that students spent 50% of the reading period practicing words that they would read in their texts as the incentive for his experiments on word repetition. This word study was necessary, Gates claimed, because his analyses of the textbooks of the era showed that 1 out of every 16 running words was a new, unique word. Gates believed that this rate of introduction (approximately 6.25 new words per 100 running words of text) exceeded the number of new words that most students could recognize with accuracy. If new words were repeated more frequently in texts, more of students' time could be spent reading and less on word study.

Gates (1930) conducted research on a set of texts that he designed where 1 of every 150 words was a new, unique word (150 Materials). The same teacher taught two groups which were equated on mental age, intelligence quotient (IQ), and scores on a series of reading tests, with one group reading the typical materials (i.e., 1 new, unique word out of 16 words) and the other the 150 Materials. The students in the 150 group spent the entire reading period with these materials, while the comparison students also engaged in word study to ensure that they could read the words in their texts. Accuracy levels of the majority of

TABLE 3.1. Illustrations of Texts from First-Grade Reading Books

The Heart of Oak Books (1st book) (Norton, 1902)	*The House That Jack Built* This is the house that Jack built. This is the malt That lay in the house That Jack built. This is the rat That ate the malt That lay in the house that Jack built. This is the cat, That killed the rat, That ate the malt That lay in the house that Jack built.
Elson Readers (Book 1) (Elson & Runkel, 1928)	*Little Gustava* Once there was a little girl. Her name was Gustava. One day she heard a little bird. It sang and sang and sang. "Oh, spring has come," said Gustava. "Mother, do you hear the bird? I am so happy! I love the spring!" Her mother gave her some bread and milk. She sat in the warm sun to eat it.
Basic Readers: Curriculum Foundation Series (1st preprimer) (Gray, Baruch, & Montgomery, 1940)	*Tim and Spot* Go up, Tim. Go up. Go up, up, up. Go down, Tim. Go down. Go down, down, down. Oh, Jane. See Spot and Tim. See Spot run. Funny, funny Spot. Funny, funny Tim.

students led Gates (1930) to conclude that the 150 Materials were superior only for the very lowest students and that most students in the 150 group could have acquired more words. At the same time, Gates concluded that the students in the 16 Materials group were asked to progress too rapidly, as evident in erroneous recognition of words.

For the next study, Gates (1930) created the 60 Materials where one out of every 60 running words of text was a new word. At posttest, students who received the 60 Materials recognized more words on the Gates Reading Vocabulary test than the students who received the 150 Materials (12 for the former; 9 for the latter). Students in the 60 group also performed better on phrase, sentence, and paragraph reading. In a subsequent study with the 60 Materials and existing materials where one in every 14 words was a new, unique word, Gates reported that the students with the 60 Materials had superior performances by 30 to 40%.

Gates (1930) used this research to generate what he called "guesses" as to the number of repetitions per word that must be provided during the first year for students to become successful readers. He associated the numbers of repetitions with IQ bands, with 20 repetitions recommended for the highest band of 120–129 and 55 for the lowest band of 60–69. As this set of hypotheses was translated into textbook programs, it was the number of repetitions for the average band of 90–109—35 repetitions—that came to govern textbook design.

Educational psychologists subsequently combined Gates's (1930) hypotheses regarding number of repetitions with Thorndike's (1903) laws of learning (readiness, exercise, and effect) to guide publishers in the design of beginning reading texts (Smith, 1934/1965). The laws of learning translated into attention to the pace at which new words were presented (effect) and the number of repetitions (exercise). With respect to the law of readiness, the words for which young children were regarded to be ready were high-frequency words that the children were already using in their speech.

The application of the laws of learning to texts for beginning readers is evident in the features of text in Excerpts 2 and 3 in Table 3.1. Excerpt 2 is from the text published by Scott Foresman (Elson & Runkel, 1928) prior to the application of Gates's (1930) hypotheses regarding word repetition to the creation of beginning reading texts. In Excerpt 2, words such as *bread* and *milk* appeared a single time in the text (and for the first time in the program). The one-third of the unique words that were repeated were either high-frequency words (e.g., *it*, *I*, *a*) or words relevant to the storyline (e.g., *Gustava*, *spring*, *sang*). Once the laws of learning were applied by Gray et al. (1940) in the Scott Foresman reading program (Excerpt 3), new words were distributed in particular sequences and with a specific number of repetitions. In the text represented in Excerpt 3, all words but *go* and *down* had appeared in previous texts in the first preprimer. The two new words in this text, *go* and *down*, were repeated six and five times, respectively. The two words that appeared for the first time in the previous text—*Tim* and *up*—each appeared five times. By the end of the first preprimer, 17 words each had appeared a minimum of seven times and an average of 10 times.

This pattern suggests an algorithm. However, while specific formulas based on behaviorist principles are evident in readability formulas (Klare, 1984), we have been unable to find any articles in the archival literature that either describe the algorithm or research that supports its use. By the 1960s, the pattern was applied so rigidly that, as Chall's (1967/1983) analyses showed, students saw few new words. Despite Chall's (1967/1983) critique, highly constrained texts continued to characterize beginning reading programs through the late 1980s. The instructions in the teacher's guides changed as a result of Chall's critique to emphasize greater phonics instruction. However, the texts became even more formulaic. For example, the 1983 Scott Foresman first-grade program had even fewer unique words than had been in the case in the 1940 program represented in Table 3.1 or the 1962 program that Chall reviewed (Hiebert, 2005). The number of total words within the program had increased substantially, but the average number of repetitions per word went from 10 in the 1962 program to 20 in the 1983 program (Hiebert, 2005). There was a strong backlash to this tight control in beginning texts in the late 1980s. While policies on the kinds of words that should be prominent in beginning texts has vacillated from highly meaningful words in authentic literature to highly decodable words over the past two decades, the decrease in word repetition that occurred with the textbook adoptions of the late 1980s and early 1990s has not been addressed by policymakers or researchers.

CURRENT PATTERNS OF REPETITION
IN BEGINNING READING TEXTS

A sea change in text features of reading programs occurred in the late 1980s and early 1990s when the model of beginning texts shifted from the controlled vocabulary recommended by Gates (1930) to the authentic text of children's literature. According to the perspective that was evident in the California and Texas guidelines for publishers (California English/Language Arts Committee, 1987; Texas Education Agency, 1990), authentic text had features that would engage students and support comprehension. The support for comprehension was claimed on the basis of cohesiveness and coherence—features that the controlled texts often lacked. In that studies on the effects of controlled texts on comprehension were conducted almost exclusively with students who had at least a modicum of reading proficiency (e.g., Beck, McKeown, Omanson, & Pople, 1984), the generalizability of results to students at the very earliest stages of reading had not been established when policies calling for no controlled vocabulary for all levels went into effect. One aspect of this shift was an increase in the number of unique words at the earliest stages. From the 1983 copyright of Scott Foresman, where the average number of repetitions per word was 20, the average number of repetitions in the 1993 plummeted to 3.4.

When the first state-by-state comparison on the National Assessment of Educational Progress (NAEP) (Miller, Nelson, & Naifeh, 1995) showed Californian fourth graders to be performing poorly, policies that favored whole language, including authentic texts, were viewed to be the culprit. Subsequently, policymakers in Texas and California mandated decodable texts as the basis of the next textbook adoption cycles (California English/Language Arts Committee, 1999; Texas Education Agency,

1997). Decodable texts in these policies were defined on the coverage of phonemes in instruction, not on the number of repetitions of linguistic units or words in texts. The repetition of words within the 2000 copyright of Scott Foresman (and other publishers) remained fairly consistent to that of the beginning reading programs that had used authentic literature: 4.8 (Hiebert, 2005). Analyses of the 2007 copyright that were described in Chapter 1 of this volume indicate that the pattern is holding steady. In the 2007 program, the average repetition of words was 4.5.

Hiebert et al. (2005) have shown that the distribution of word repetitions is skewed. Most of the repetitions occur with a small group of words, while a large number of words appear a single time. In their examination of the core vocabulary across three components of three beginning reading programs, Hiebert et al. found that two of the three programs (both mainstream basal programs but differing in their emphasis on decoding) had the same percentage of words that occurred four times or more (30%), and the same percentage of single-appearing words (50%). In the third program—a program that emphasizes decoding, 45% of the words appeared four times or more, while 38% appeared a single time. In the two mainstream programs, the 100 most-frequent words accounted for only 4% of the unique words in the corpora but 20% of the words that were repeated four times or more (Hiebert et al., 2005). Foorman, Francis, Davidson, Harm, and Griffin (2004) similarly reported that 229 words were common to the six first-grade programs they analyzed, and 116 of these words were on the Dolch list.

In summary, recent policies by major textbook adoption states that have focused on different features of texts for beginning readers have failed to attend to the repetition of words. As a result, the words that occur most in texts (by virtue of being high-frequency words) occur a lot. However, they are interspersed with many different words—words with diverse meanings and patterns. As will become evident in the following review of literature, many beginning readers fail to learn high-frequency words either quickly or automatically when they are presented with numerous other unknown words.

CURRENT THEORY AND EMPIRICAL EVIDENCE ON THE REPETITION OF LINGUISTIC UNITS AND WORDS

We have classified research that gives insight into the number of repetitions that support beginning readers' word recognition into four groups: (1) studies of the repetition of letter–sound units, especially the rime (i.e., the vowel and consonant(s) in a syllable), (2) studies of the self-teaching hypothesis that address learning of orthographic patterns, (3) studies of

the repetition of words in experimental tasks where texts are constrained to either a handful of sentences and/or lists, and (4) studies of the repetition of words in instructional texts used as part of classroom instruction. While the first two categories both deal with orthographic units within words, they represent different approaches and traditions in the research literature and consequently will be reviewed separately.

Repetition of Rimes

We begin with a brief overview of research that has compared beginning readers' attention to the grapheme–phoneme correspondences within words relative to rimes. While this review is far from comprehensive, it is an important literature since the policies of large states with textbook adoptions, specifically California (California English/Language Arts Committee, 1999) and Texas (Texas Education Agency, 1997), mandate that texts be designed around phoneme–grapheme correspondences. In that the mandates of these two states call for texts to be designed around this feature through the end of second grade (and, for struggling readers in California, through the end of middle school [California State Board of Education, 2006]), evidence that individual grapheme–phoneme correspondences continue to be salient for developing readers is sparse.

The literature on students' ongoing use of grapheme–phoneme correspondences (especially beyond early stages of reading acquisition) has not been extensive. One pattern evident in the research is that the frequency of the letter–sound correspondence in written language differentially influences the recognition of children at the very earliest stages of reading. Thompson, Cottrell, and Fletcher-Flinn (1996) established that *b* and *th* in the final position of words occurred significantly less often than *t* and *m*. Based on this information, they assessed 24 children on consonant–vowel (CV) and vowel–consonant (VC) pseudowords incorporating the target consonants. Words with *b* and *th* in the final position were read with significantly lower accuracy than words with *m* and *t* in the final position. In a second experiment, Thompson et al. (1996) manipulated the amount of exposure beginning readers had to words containing the consonant *b* in the final position by having children read sentences with a target word that ended in *b*, or sentences where the target words were omitted in the text but supplied orally by the investigator. The former group significantly improved in the accuracy with which pseudowords with *b* in the final position were read, while the latter group made no improvement.

Once beginning readers attend to grapheme–phoneme correspondences or are in the partial alphabetic stage as Ehri (1998) has described it, their attention moves to units of written language that are larger than individual grapheme–phoneme correspondences, especially rimes (i.e., the vowel and the following consonants). When rimes are regular (Stuart, Masterson, Dixon, & Quinlan, 1999), and when rimes appear in frequently occurring words (Treiman, Goswami, & Bruck, 1990), beginning readers tend to use them more than individual grapheme–phoneme correspondences in recognizing and remembering words.

The rime is a particularly salient unit in word recognition once students have grasped the alphabetic principle. The effects of rime family size (e.g., a large rime family such as *cat, hat, bat, sat, mat, pat* relative to a small rime family such as *rough, tough*) and frequency of words within rime families (e.g., *cat* vs. *gnat*) on students' word recognition have been examined in a number of studies. An example of a research program in which these factors have been a focus is that of Leslie and Calhoon (1995; Calhoon & Leslie, 2002).

Leslie and Calhoon (1995) compared reading of words and nonwords based on large-, medium-, or small-rime neighborhood size and the frequency (high, low) of words in lists or stories. The frequency of words, as well as the size of their rime neighborhoods, influenced less skilled readers' recognition of words on lists, with high-frequency words and words with rimes from large neighborhoods being read more accurately. Reading words in context helped more for low-frequency words in large and medium rime neighborhoods than those in small neighborhoods and for high-frequency words. Since word frequency significantly predicted less skilled readers' ability to read words, Leslie and Calhoon concluded that rime neighborhood size has no influence when students are in the partial-alphabetic stage, but the frequency of the word does.

Subsequently, Calhoon and Leslie (2002) examined the word learning of students from first through third grades receiving whole language instruction. Within these classrooms, letter–sound correspondences were not taught explicitly except through the strategy of cross-checking where readers confirm a word's pronunciation with illustrations or sentence context (Clay, 1985). Calhoon and Leslie asked whether the size of the rime neighborhood was a factor with low-frequency words that had a high-frequency counterpart (e.g., low-frequency: *zip*; high-frequency: *ship*). During first grade, words from large neighborhoods were read more accurately in texts than words from medium neighborhoods which, in turn, were read more accurately than those from small neighborhoods. Unlike first grade where the accuracy of high-frequency words on the list did not differ by rime neighborhood, second graders read high-frequency words on the list more accurately than words from medium and small neighborhoods. With low-frequency words, the effects of rime family size were the same. By third grade, rime neighborhood size had little effect on accuracy in reading words on a list. In stories, however, words from large rime neighborhoods were read significantly better than words from medium neighborhoods (which did not differ from words from small neighborhoods). Students read low-frequency words with similar levels of accuracy in stories and word lists. Calhoon and Leslie took these results to confirm their model that rime neighborhood size-effects occur once students have reached the partial-alphabetic phase. They concluded that word learning occurs as a result of frequent exposure to words that share rimes.

Similar effects for rime family size and word frequency results have been reported in other studies. Laxon, Smith, and Masterson (1995) reported that there were significantly more errors on words from small rime neighborhoods, while Laxon, Gallagher, and Masterson (2002) reported that more errors were made on nonwords than words, and more errors were made on nonwords with small rime neighborhoods (although the last difference was not significant). Weekes, Castles, and Davies (2006) compared reading of high- and low-frequency words with consistent and inconsistent rime pronunciations, controlling for the age at which children acquire the words orally. Significantly more words with consistent rimes were read correctly, regardless of the age of oral acquisition of the word. When rimes were inconsistent, significantly fewer errors were made on high-frequency than low-frequency words.

There is sufficient evidence to conclude that the frequency with which letter–sound correspondences, rimes, and words appear in texts influences the accuracy and speed of recognition of words by beginning readers. The evidence does not provide specific numbers of repetitions that support this accuracy and speed of recognition. The evidence does, however, point to general directions: words with more frequent letter–sound correspondences and rimes are recognized better than words with less-frequent patterns. Even when these units appear in nonwords, the frequency of appearance in written language influences students' accuracy and speed (with more-frequent patterns recognized more readily than less-frequent ones). Further, the frequency with which words appear in texts also predicts accuracy and speed in beginning readers' recognition of words.

Self-Teaching Hypothesis

Similar to the analyses conducted by Foorman et al. (2004) and Hiebert (2005), Jorm and Share (1983) reported that many words in texts of beginning reading instruction appeared a single time. While many students struggle in becoming proficient readers with such texts (Hiebert, Chapter 1, this volume; Lesgold et al., 1985), Share (1995) focused on the students who had learned to read with these texts. He proposed the self-teaching hypothesis as an explanation for beginning readers' ability to form the orthographic representations needed for fast sight word recognition through phonological recoding (decoding) of unknown words. According to the self-teaching hypothesis, words that are successfully decoded are added to a lexicon of sight vocabulary by items, not stages. As more and more words are added to readers' lexicons of sight vocabulary, decoding moves beyond the decoding of one-to-one letter–sound correspondences to include larger units such as rimes and morphemes. Both phonological and orthographic components are involved in the self-teaching mechanism. The phonological component is primary as unknown words must be successfully decoded before correct orthographic representations can be formed.

Share (1999) initiated an experimental paradigm that has been used in subsequent tests of the self-teaching hypothesis. Students orally read texts in which one unfamiliar word (the target) has been inserted and, typically, is repeated more than once. Usually, the target word is a pseudoword for the name of something like an animal, city, or fruit. In a session at least a day later, students are given between one and three assessments of orthographic learning. The orthographic-choice task requires students to select the target word from four choices: the target (e.g., *Yait*—the name of a hypothetical city in a study conducted by Cunningham, Perry, Stanovich, & Share [2002]), a homophonic version of the target word (e.g., *Yate*), and up to two similar words containing transposed or visually similar substituted letters (e.g., *Yoit, Yiat*). In a second task, the time it takes students to read target words and homophones that are displayed one at a time on a computer (onset latency) is assessed. The third task involves spelling target words and homophones.

Several studies testing the self-teaching hypothesis have considered the effects of repeated exposures in the formation of orthographic representations of target words. Two studies involving second- and third-grade readers reading in English (Bowey & Muller, 2005; Nation, Angell, & Castles, 2007) found that increasing the target repetitions within a text resulted in significantly more targets being identified on the orthographic-choice task. However, Share and his colleagues (de Jong & Share, 2007; Share, 1999, 2004; Share & Shalev, 2004) reported that increasing the number of repetitions of targets for students reading in Hebrew did not result in significantly higher accuracy rates on the orthographic-choice measure. The differing results from these studies may be due to the orthographic depth of the languages involved. In languages with deeper orthographies, such as English, the correspondence between letters and sounds is more complex, often depending upon larger units such as rimes and morphemes. More exposure to target words may be needed with deeper orthographies to form detailed orthographic repre-

sentations within memory. This may also explain why self-teaching studies in English have reported that targets were named significantly faster
than homophones (Bowey & Miller 2005, 2007; Cunningham et al.,
2002), while studies in Dutch and Hebrew—languages that have more
transparent orthographies—(de Jong & Share, 2007; Share, 2004) reported no significant differences.

One interpretation of the findings within the self-teaching paradigm
is that some amount of orthographic knowledge is necessary for more
orthographic learning to occur. Cunningham and her colleagues found
that neither general cognitive ability nor rapid automatized naming
(RAN) ability predicted significant amounts of variance in the orthographic learning of target words by first and second graders (Cunningham, 2006; Cunningham et al., 2002). However, in both of these studies, one or more measures of *existing* orthographic knowledge were
administered prior to reading the experimental texts. These measures of
existing orthographic knowledge predicted a significant amount of additional variance in orthographic learning beyond that due to decoding
ability: 11% for first-grade students and 20% for second-grade students.
These measures of existing orthographic knowledge mainly tested the
ability of the students to identify common vocabulary words from homophones that differed mostly in their vowel spellings. The results of
these studies suggest that repetitions of orthographic patterns, such as
common vowel spellings or rimes, as well as words, are important for
developing readers.

Share (2004) has theorized that the first encounter with a new word
may result in the most orthographic learning, particularly with students
possessing some orthographic knowledge. For example, Share noted that
when third-grade students initially encountered a target, they typically
decoded the word letter by letter. When these students encountered the
same target a second or third time, their pronunciations became much
more fluent. While most learning may occur during the first exposure,
additional exposures may be needed to refine this knowledge, particularly for beginning readers. Share (1995) recognized that, while too
many unfamiliar words will influence comprehension, the occasional unfamiliar word is the impetus whereby beginning readers develop into fluent readers.

Share's (1995) hypotheses are consistent with several theories of
sight word acquisition. In connectionist theory, the first encounter with a
novel word results in the largest changes to the weight of the connections, while subsequent encounters refine the system by making smaller
or even minimal changes (Seidenberg & McClelland, 1989). Logan
(1997) theorizes that the first encounter with a new word establishes an
initial trace within memory, and that subsequent encounters increase the

number of memory traces that can be accessed, resulting in faster and less effortful recognition of specific words. Ehri (1998) and Perfetti (1992) have also theorized that the initial encounter with a novel word results in a representation being formed within memory that maps the word's orthography to its pronunciation and meaning. This initial representation may be partial, since a beginning reader may only partially decode a word, but each successful encounter with a word refines the representation. Regardless of whether a single exposure to a new word is enough to result in orthographic learning, repeated exposure to these words is important to firmly establish them within memory as sight words.

An important issue that these studies do not address is the ratio between the numbers of unfamiliar words to known words during text reading. Share (1995) suggests that too many unfamiliar words will disrupt comprehension during reading. The texts used within examinations of the self-teaching hypothesis were designed so that only the target word would be unfamiliar (with the exception of de Jong and Share, 2007). While such control is necessary in experimental studies, it is not reflective of the types of reading texts that beginning readers encounter (Hiebert et al., 2005). More experimental study is needed on this issue, although Menon and Hiebert (2005) did find that first-grade students who read texts that contained more repetitions of both words and rimes learned more words overall than students who read from literature basals containing more single-appearing words and words that were more difficult to decode, such as multisyllabic words.

Repetition of Words in Experimental Texts

To guard against the vagaries of word repetition in already existing texts and to control for variables such as words already known by readers, some studies have used carefully constructed texts and/or word lists that are studied under laboratory conditions. For example, Reitsma (1983) investigated how frequency of exposure to individual words affects the speed with which mid-year first graders and older, struggling readers recognized words. Children read sentences with a target word two, four, or six times, followed by post-tests which assessed the speed of recognizing individual words. The assessments included homophonic versions of the target words, where spellings differed by only one letter such as *read* and *red* and *to* and *too*. First graders' speed of responding to target words decreased systematically with exposure, with a leveling off between four and six exposures. Apparently, first graders were recognizing words automatically at around four exposures. Further, since first graders recognized the homophonic variants more slowly, Reitsma concluded they were internalizing the spellings of the target words. Based on these find-ings, it has been suggested that beginning readers need four to six expo-sures with unfamiliar words before achieving automaticity (Share, 1999). However, it is important to note that many of the first graders in this study (conducted at mid year) had some reading proficiency. Further, the students were reading in Dutch, a language with a more consistent or-thography than English (i.e., a shallow orthography). As demonstrated in the review of self-teaching studies, the number of repetitions required by students to recognize words (and orthographic patterns) may be fewer in languages with shallow orthographies.

Another study sometimes cited to suggest that additional practice beyond six repetitions is redundant is that of Ehri and Wilce (1983). In this study, skilled (second graders only) and less-skilled readers (first graders and two second graders) practiced reading high-frequency words and consonant–vowel–consonant (CVC) pseudowords. There was no significant difference between pretest and posttest times for the target high-frequency words, whether practiced 6 or 18 times. However, the high-frequency words were common to beginning reading texts, and the study did not control for prior exposure. Consequently, the lack of im-provement in word naming latencies may be due to prior exposures to these words. This interpretation is supported by the fact that the skilled readers were able to recognize these words as quickly as they could name digits, an indication that the words were being recognized auto-matically. In contrast, the naming latencies for the pseudowords prac-ticed 18 times decreased significantly between pretest and posttest for both skilled and unskilled readers.

Findings from a study by Lemoine, Levy, and Hutchinson (1993) provide stronger evidence that additional practice with words is neces-sary in order to achieve long-term automaticity. In their experiment, 40 third graders who were reading at a second-grade level were trained to read either 50 regular or 50 irregular words. Each word was encoun-tered 5, 10, 15, 20, or 25 times. During training, speed and accuracy gains leveled off after five to seven repetitions, but during the retention test 1 week later, the words that had been practiced 15 to 25 times were read significantly faster and more accurately than those words only practiced 5 to 10 times. These results suggest that "overlearning" is im-portant in establishing sight vocabulary. Further studies by Levy and her colleagues examining the acquisition, retention, and transfer of new words in both text reading and in isolation by second through fourth graders have also found main effects due to exposure (up to 12) on accu-racy and speed (Martin-Chang & Levy, 2005, 2006; Martin-Chang, Levy, & O'Neil, 2007).

The laboratory research on word repetition indicates that beginning readers typically require at least a modicum of repetition to read a word. To date, however, the studies have failed to carefully delineate how these repetitions differ as a function of word features, students' prior word-recognition knowledge, and number of new words within a text. Particular features of words have yet to be systematically examined in laboratory studies. For example, there is evidence that the imageability of a word influences the ease with which beginning readers learn to read words (Hargis, Terhaar-Yonkers, Williams, & Reed, 1988; Sadoski & Paivio, 2001) and the speed with which particular rimes are recognized and retained in memory (Laing & Hulme, 1999).

Repetition of Words in Instructional Texts

There are a handful of studies that have considered the relationship among words in instruction, the amount of repetition in texts, and students' word recognition. During the 1990s, researchers were particularly interested in determining how beginning readers fared with predictable or authentic literature texts where the level of repetition was not controlled. Predictable texts typically contain a pattern (a phrase or sentence(s) that is repeated) with small variations (e.g., "I see a dog"; "I see a cat") and often incorporate rhyme and concrete illustrations as further support. These texts can provide a successful entrée for beginning readers, allowing them to focus on comprehension (Leu, DeGroff, & Simons, 1986). However, the overuse of predictable texts may encourage overreliance on recitation and rhyme rather than actual reading (Johnston, 2000; Landi, Perfetti, Bolger, Dunlap, & Foorman, 2006; Leu et al., 1986).

Stuart, Masterson, and Dixon (2000) examined the words encountered by 20 five-year-old students during their first term of reading instruction. These students were nonreaders at the beginning of the term and were taught using a whole-language approach that involved the repeated reading of books with an adult, focusing on meaning. During the term, students encountered an average of 126 different words across books. Of the approximately 4 words that were repeated more than 20 times, beginning readers were able to recognize 1.3. Furthermore, when Stuart et al. exposed these students to 16 target words within the context of shared-book reading, they found that students recognized an average of 4.95 words soon after exposure, and 3.6 words a month later. Similarly, Johnston (2000) found that first graders who were exposed to 41–66 new words per week in predictable texts learned only an average of 5.7 words.

By contrast, first graders who read from texts where words were repeated—whether high-frequency words in a mainstream program or highly decodable words in a phonics program—learned substantially more words. Evidence for this finding comes from Juel and Roper/Schneider (1985) who examined the effects of textbooks with different emphases on first-grade children's word learning and strategies. Half of the students read from a basal series that employed decodable words that were repeated an average of 26.3 times, accounting for 69% of the total text. The other students read from a basal preprimer that emphasized high-frequency words that were longer, less decodable, and repeated on average 15.1 times, accounting for 44% of the total text. Once students had finished the preprimers, subsequent texts in the two programs (i.e., primers and first readers) were very similar in the kinds of words they used. All students also received the same districtwide phonics instruction.

Word repetition was a significant factor for all students; however, the students who read from the high-frequency preprimers were more dependent upon the amount of word repetition for successful word recognition in their basals. Furthermore, the students who had read from the decodable preprimers were able to read more new words at the end of the year than the students who had initially read from the high-frequency preprimers, suggesting that their early reading experience affected their subsequent ability to read new words.

The studies on predictable text where repetition is serendipitous indicate that, without explicit guidance, beginning readers fail to learn many words. In Juel and Roper/Schneider's (1985) study, repetition of words was a factor for both the decodable and mainstream programs, although more so for the mainstream program that emphasized high-frequency words in the preprimer. One aspect of the Juel and Roper/Schneider study that should be kept in mind when extending the findings to current texts is that the repetition of the decodable words in their study was substantially higher than is the case in current decodable texts. Studies that include data on students who have gone through current programs of decodable texts, where the concern is with the match between individual grapheme–phoneme correspondences and the instructional sequence in the teacher's manual (Stein, Johnson, & Gutlohn, 1999) rather than repetition of words or words with particular patterns, show that many students who depend on schools to become literate fail to learn many words in either classroom instruction (Hiebert & Fisher, 2006) or in intensive interventions (Vaughn et al., 2006).

DISCUSSION

The first observation from this review of research is how sparse the literature is on repetition of words in beginning reading. However, patterns from the various literatures that we have reviewed are evident. First, the familiarity of orthographic and phonological patterns of words influences beginning readers' recognition of words. Students generalize knowledge of frequent and familiar patterns and use this knowledge with new words. Second, high-frequency words are learned more rapidly than low-frequency words.

But, within the literature, the specificity is simply not there. In particular, there is a paucity of information on the pace at which unfamiliar words should be introduced and the ratio of unknown to known words within texts. We are far from having the research base that is needed, particularly when large states, such as California, Texas, and Florida, mandate substantial changes in their textbooks. What can we expect from a research base in the future? Before we explore that question, we examine what we cannot expect.

One response that we cannot expect from the research base is to have algorithms at the level specified in current textbook adoptions. For example, specifications of percentages of decodable words that are now mandated by the states of California (California English/Language Arts Committee, 1999) and Texas (Texas Education Agency, 1997), as well as numbers of books mandated per phoneme, are simply not justified. The process of learning to read is simply too complex. The variables that enter into the reader–text interaction are simply too many and too complex to isolate. As Gray and Leary (1935) showed, the variables that can be distinguished across texts are numerous—topics, sentence types and complexity, and frequency and commonality of words. Experiments where "ideal" texts are compared to typical texts are difficult to conduct. One reason is that the variables that need to be controlled are many. It is unlikely that all permutations that will need to be considered can be established, even in ambitious programs of research. Further, the production of texts, including illustrations that are comparable to those of existing texts, are expensive and prohibitive without ambitious research funding. At the present time, none of the calls for research from the U.S. Department of Education has made such research a priority.

Within the existing literature, however, several models can be identified that illustrate directions for research programs. One model is a careful documentation of student learning as a result of particular conditions of instruction and text, as illustrated by several studies (Juel & Roper/Schneider, 1985; Lesgold et al., 1985; McGill-Franzen, Zmach, Solic, & Zeig, 2006). Juel and Roper/Schneider (1985) and McGill-Franzen et al. (2006) contrasted student learning as a result of different features of textbook programs that had been implemented in classrooms. Such contrasts can be useful, and there are numerous opportunities for them in current policy contexts. For example, over the past textbook adoption, school districts in California have been limited to the purchase of two basal reading programs with state funds. A group of policymakers have compared student progress as a function of the two programs (Williams, Kirst, Haertel et al., 2005). However, documentation of how the two programs were different was not provided. In the case of McGill-Franzen et al., the manner in which two programs differed in comprehension instruction as well as fluency experiences was provided. This project was conducted with third graders and did not address the issue of repetition. But we provide it as a model for how students' learning can be documented within the current context of textbook programs being designed to fulfill particular mandates of state policymakers.

Another model comes from two interventions where texts were organized in particular configurations, and the effects on beginning readers' performances were documented over a period of time (Jenkins, Peyton, Sanders, & Vadasy, 2004; Menon & Hiebert, 2005). While the amount of repetition of individual words was not analyzed relative to student performances in these studies, such analyses could be included in future interventions of this type. In that there are numerous interventions going on right now in the United States (see, e.g., Vaughn et al., 2006), there is no reason why the nature of word repetition—and the features of this repetition—could not be considered at different points in students' development and for students with different learning trajectories and performances.

Hiebert and Fisher (2006), in their design of a set of texts, provide a third model. They based their text design on specific information about the most critical features of written language such as Wylie and Durrell's (1970) identification of the most frequent and prolific rimes and the most frequent words in written language (Carroll, Davies, & Richman, 1971). They were especially interested in identifying words that intersected in prolificacy of rimes, frequency of appearance of at least one or more members of the rime family, and imageability. While the experimental comparisons of these texts with existing texts have been limited in duration, initial analyses show the following: Texts that include words that have been carefully chosen for these features produce significantly higher levels of speed and accuracy among young English language learners (ELLs) than decodable texts that use the phoneme as the unit of learning and where word repetition is not of concern.

Research on the self-teaching hypothesis illustrates a fourth model. While the work on self-teaching to date has been limited in scope, attention to the ratio of known to unknown words within this model could be the focus of experiments. One would hope that, in this work, information on students' existing knowledge would be documented thoroughly. Cunningham (2006) has demonstrated how such documentation can be done and how this information illuminates what students are learning.

We reiterate our belief that algorithms should not be the aim of this work. Students' experiences with texts spill over into their home lives. They see words in the environment, in the media, and in a variety of contexts within the school and the input can be, at best, described with broad strokes. However, guidelines can be provided, especially for students who have particular skill profiles. Such guidelines can respond to current policy mandates and contexts. For example, patterns that have been reported in this review call into question the use of texts with, on average, four repetitions of words. Such texts, as an example, are mandated in California where a significant portion of a grade cohort is learning to speak English at the same time that they are learning to read. If nothing else, the achievement outcomes in that state (and others) suggest that there are problems with current texts (Perie, Grigg, & Donahue, 2005). The amount of input that the children are expected to process is massive, particularly those children who are not reading when they come to school.

We are hopeful that others will join us in identifying areas of already existing research that sheds light on the role of the repetition of words and linguistic units in reading acquisition, especially that of students who depend on schools to become literate. We are also hopeful that this review will spark the interest of researchers in considering the role of a variable—the repetition and pacing of unknown words—that has long been recognized as a critical contributor to the ease and automaticity of reading development.

REFERENCES

Beck, I. L., McKeown, M., Omanson, R., & Pople, M. (1984). Improving the comprehensibility of stories: The effects of revisions that improve coherence. *Reading Research Quarterly, 19,* 263–277.

Bloom, K. C., & Shuell, T. J. (1981). Effects of massed and distributed practice on the learning and retention of second-language vocabulary. *Journal of Educational Research, 74,* 245–248.

Bowey, J. A., & Miller, R. (2007). Correlates of orthographic learning in third-grade children's silent reading. *Journal of Research in Reading, 30*(2), 115–128.

Bowey, J. A., & Muller, D. (2005). Phonological recoding and rapid orthographic learning in third-graders' silent reading: A critical test of the self-teaching hypothesis. *Journal of Experimental Child Psychology, 92,* 203–219

Calhoon, J., & Leslie, L. (2002). A longitudinal study of the effects of word frequency and rime-neighborhood on beginning readers' rime reading accuracy in words and nonwords. *Journal of Literacy Research, 34,* 39–58.

California English/Language Arts Committee. (1987). *English-Language Arts Framework for California Public Schools (Kindergarten Through Grade Twelve).* Sacramento: California Department of Education.

California English/Language Arts Committee. (1999). *English-Language Arts Content Standards for California Public Schools (Kindergarten Through Grade Twelve)*. Sacramento: California Department of Education.

California State Board of Education (April 17, 2006). *Criteria for evaluating instructional materials (Reading/Language Arts)*. Retrieved January 12, 2007 from *www.cde.ca.gov/ci/rl/im*.

Carroll, J. B., Davies, P., & Richman, B. (1971). *Word frequency book*. Boston: Houghton Mifflin.

Chall, J. S. (1967/1983). *Learning to read: The great debate*. New York: McGraw-Hill.

Clay, M. M. (1985). *The early detection of reading difficulties* (3rd ed.). Portsmouth, NH: Heinemann.

Cunningham, A. E. (2006). Accounting for children's orthographic learning while reading text: Do children self-teach? *Journal of Experimental Child Psychology, 95*, 56–77.

Cunningham, A. E., Perry, K. E., Stanovich, K. E., & Share, D. L. (2002). Orthographic learning during reading: Examining the role of self-teaching. *Journal of Experimental Child Psychology, 82*, 185–199.

de Jong, P. F., & Share, D. L. (2007). Orthographic learning during oral and silent reading. *Scientific Studies of Reading, 11*(1), 55–71.

Ehri, L. C. (1998). Grapheme–phoneme knowledge is essential for learning to read words in English. In J. L. Metsala & L. C. Ehri (Eds.), *Word recognition in beginning literacy* (pp. 3–40). Mahwah, NJ: Erlbaum.

Ehri, L. C., & Wilce, L. S. (1983). Development of word identification speed in skilled and less skilled beginning readers. *Journal of Educational Psychology, 75*(1), 3–18.

Elson, W. H., & Runkel, L. E. (1928). *The Elson readers: Book 1*. Chicago: Scott Foresman.

Foorman, B. R., Francis, D. J., Davidson, K. C., Harm, M. W., & Griffin, J. (2004). Variability in text features in six grade 1 basal reading programs. *Scientific Studies of Reading, 8*, 167–197.

Gates, A. I. (1930). *Interest and ability in reading*. New York: Macmillan.

Gray, W. S., Baruch, D., & Montgomery, E. (1940). *Basic readers: Curriculum foundation series* (PP1). Chicago: Scott Foresman.

Gray, W. S., & Leary, B. W. (1935). *What makes a book readable?* Chicago: University of Chicago Press.

Hargis, C. H., Terhaar-Yonkers, M., Williams, P. C., & Reed, M. T. (1988). Repetition requirements for word recognition. *Journal of Reading, 31*, 320–327.

Hiebert, E. H. (2005). State reform policies and the task textbooks pose for first-grade readers. *Elementary School Journal, 105*, 245–266.

Hiebert, E. H., & Fisher, C. W. (2006). Fluency from the first: What works with first graders. In T. Rasinski, C. L. Z. Blachowicz, & K. Lems (Eds.), *Teaching reading fluency: Meeting the needs of all readers* (pp. 279–294). New York: Guilford Press.

Hiebert, E. H., Martin, L. A., & Menon, S. (2005). Are there alternatives in reading textbooks? An examination of three beginning reading programs. *Reading and Writing Quarterly, 21*, 7–32.

Jenkins, J. R., Peyton, J. A., Sanders, E. A., & Vadasy, P. F. (2004). Effects of reading decodable texts in supplemental first-grade tutoring. *Scientific Studies of Reading, 8,* 53–85.

Johnston, F. R. (2000). Word learning in predictable text. *Journal of Educational Psychology, 92*(2), 248–255.

Jorm, A. J., & Share, D. L. (1983). Phonological recoding and reading acquisition. *Applied Psycholinguistics, 4*(2) 103–147.

Juel, C., & Roper/Schneider, D. (1985). The influence of basal readers on first grade reading. *Reading Research Quarterly, 20*(2), 134–152.

Klare, G. R. (1984). Readability. In P. D. Pearson, R. Barr, M. L. Kamil, & P. Mosenthal (Eds.), *Handbook of reading research* (Vol. 1, pp. 681–744). New York: Longman.

Kyongho, H., & Nation, P. (1989). Reducing the vocabulary load and encouraging vocabulary learning through reading newspapers. *Reading in a Foreign Language, 6,* 323–335.

Laing, E., & Hulme, C. (1999). Phonological and semantic processes influence beginning readers' ability to learn to read words. *Journal of Experimental Child Psychology, 73*(183–207).

Landi, N., Perfetti, C. A., Bolger, D. J., Dunlap, S., & Foorman, B. R. (2006). The role of discourse context in developing word form representations: A paradoxical relation between reading and learning. *Journal of Experimental Child Psychology, 94,* 114–133.

Laxon, V., Gallagher, A., & Masterson, J. (2002). The effects of familiarity, orthographic neighbourhood density, letter-length and graphemic complexity on children's reading accuracy. *British Journal of Psychology, 93,* 269–287.

Laxon, V., Smith, B., & Masterson, J. (1995). Children's nonword reading: Pseudohomophones, neighborhood size, and priming effects. *Reading Research Quarterly, 30*(1), 126–144.

Lemoine, H. E., Levy, B. A., & Hutchinson, A. (1993). Increasing the naming speed of poor readers: Representations formed across repetitions. *Journal of Experimental Child Psychology, 55,* 297–328.

Lesgold, A., Resnick, L. B., & Hammond, K. (1985). Learning to read: A longitudinal study of word skill development in two curricula. In G. E. Mackinnon & T. G. Waller (Eds.), *Reading research: Advances in theory and practice* (Vol. 4, pp. 107–138). New York: Academic Press.

Leslie, L., & Calhoon, A. (1995). Factors affecting children's reading of rimes: Reading ability, word frequency, and rime-neighborhood size. *Journal of Educational Psychology, 87*(4), 576–586.

Leu, D. J. Jr., DeGroff, L. J. C., & Simons, H. D. (1986). Predictable texts and interactive-compensatory hypotheses: Evaluating individual differences in reading ability, context use, and comprehension. *Journal of Educational Psychology, 78*(5), 347–352.

Logan, G. D. (1997). Automaticity and reading: Perspectives from the instance theory of automatization. *Reading and Writing Quarterly, 13,* 123–146.

Martin-Chang, S. L., & Levy, B. A. (2005). Fluency transfer: Differential gains in reading speed and accuracy following isolated word and context training. *Reading and Writing, 18,* 343–376.

Martin-Chang, S. L., & Levy, B. A. (2006). Word reading fluency: A transfer appropriate processing account of fluency transfer. *Reading and Writing, 19,* 517–542.

Martin-Chang, S. L., Levy, B. A., & O'Neil, S. (2007). Word acquisition, retention, and transfer: Findings from contextual and isolated word training. *Journal of Experimental Child Psychology, 96,* 37–56.

McGill-Franzen, A., Zmach, C., Solic, K., & Zeig, J. L. (2006). The confluence of two policy mandates: Core reading programs and third-grade retention in Florida. *Elementary School Journal, 107,* 67–92.

McKeown, M. G., Beck, I. L., Omanson, R. C., & Pople, M. T. (1985). Some effects of the nature and frequency of vocabulary instruction on the knowledge and use of words. *Reading Research Quarterly, 20,* 522–535.

Menon, S., & Hiebert, E. H. (2005). A comparison of first graders' reading with little books or literature-based basal anthologies. *Reading Research Quarterly, 40*(1), 12–38.

Miller, K. E., Nelson, J. E., & Naifeh, M. (1995). *Cross-state data compendium for the NAEP 1994 grade 4 reading.* Washington, DC: U.S. Government Printing Office.

Monaghan, E. J., & Barry, A. L. (1999). *Writing the past: Teaching reading in colonial America and the United States, 1640–1940.* Newark, DE: International Reading Association.

Nation, K., Angell, P., & Castles, A. (2007). Orthographic learning via self-teaching in children learning to read English: Effects of exposure, durability, and context. *Journal of Experimental Child Psychology, 96,* 71–84.

Norton, C. E. (Ed.). (1902). *The heart of oak books* (1st book). Boston: D.C. Heath.

Perfetti, C. A. (1992). The representation problem in reading acquisition. In P. B. Gough, L. C. Ehri, & R. Treiman (Eds.), *Reading acquisition* (pp. 145–174). Hillsdale, NJ: Erlbaum.

Perie, M., Grigg, W., & Donahue, P. (2005). *The nation's report card: Reading 2005* (U.S. Department of Education, National Center for Education Statistics). Washington, DC: U.S. Government Printing Office.

Reitsma, P. (1983). Printed word learning in beginning readers. *Journal of Experimental Child Psychology, 36,* 321–339.

Sadoski, M., & Paivio, A. (2001). *Imagery and text: A dual coding theory of reading and writing.* Hillsdale, NJ: Erlbaum.

Seidenberg, M. S., & McClelland, J. L. (1989). A distributed, developmental model of word recognition and naming. *Psychological Review, 96*(4), 523–568.

Share, D. L. (1995). Phonological recoding and self-teaching: Sine qua non of reading acquisition. *Cognition, 55,* 151–218.

Share, D. L. (1999). Phonological recoding and orthographic learning: A direct test of the self-teaching hypothesis. *Journal of Experimental Child Psychology, 72,* 95–129.

Share, D. L. (2004). Orthographic learning at a glance: On the time course and developmental onset of self-teaching. *Journal of Experimental Child Psychology, 87,* 267–298.

Share, D. L., & Shalev, C. (2004). Self-teaching in normal and disabled readers. *Reading and Writing: An Interdisciplinary Journal, 17,* 769–800.

Slavin, R. E. (2002). Evidence-based education policies: Transforming educational practice and research. *Educational Researcher, 31,* 15–21.

Smith, N. B. (1934/1965). *American reading instruction.* Newark, DE: International Reading Association.

Stein, M. L., Johnson, B. J., & Gutlohn, L. (1999). Analyzing beginning reading programs: The relationship between decoding instruction and text. *Remedial and Special Education, 20*(5), 275–287.

Stuart, M., Masterson, J., & Dixon, M. (2000). Spongelike acquisition of vocabulary in beginning readers? *Journal of Research in Reading, 23*(1), 12–27.

Stuart, M., Masterson, J., Dixon, M., & Quinlan, P. (1999). Inferring Sublexical correspondences from sight vocabulary: Evidence from 6– and 7–year-olds. *The Quarterly Journal of Experimental Psychology, 52A*(2), 353–366.

Texas Education Agency. (1990). *Proclamation of the State Board of Education advertising for bids on textbooks.* Austin, TX: Author.

Texas Education Agency. (1997). *Proclamation of the State Board of Education advertising for bids on textbooks.* Austin, TX: Author.

Thompson, G. B., Cottrell, D. S., & Fletcher-Flinn, C. M. (1996). Sublexical orthographic-phonological relations early in the acquisition of reading: The knowledge sources account. *Journal of Experimental Child Psychology, 62,* 190–222.

Thorndike, E. L. (1903). *Educational psychology.* New York: Lemcke & Buechner.

Thorndike, E. L. (1921). *The teacher's word book.* New York: Columbia University Press.

Treiman, R., Goswami, U., & Bruck, M. (1990). Not all nonwords are alike: Implications for reading development and theory. *Memory and Cognition, 18,* 559–657.

Vaughn, S., Cirino, P. T., Linan-Thompson, S., Mathes, P. G., Carlson, C. D., & Cardenas-Hagan, E. (2006). Effectiveness of a Spanish intervention and an English intervention for English-language learners at risk for reading problems. *American Educational Research Journal, 43*(3), 449–487.

Venezky, R. L. (1984). The history of reading research. In P. D. Pearson, R. Barr, M. L. Kamil, & P. Mosenthal (Eds.), *Handbook of reading research* (Vol. 1, pp. 2–38). New York: Longman.

Weekes, B. S., Castles, A. E., & Davies, R. A. (2006). Effects of consistency and age of acquisition on reading and spelling among developing readers. *Reading and Writing, 19,* 133–169.

Williams, T., Kirst, M., Haertel, E., et al. (2005) *Similar students, different results: Why do some schools do better? A large-scale survey of California elementary schools serving low-income students.* Mountain View, CA: EdSource.

Wylie, R. E., & Durrell, D. D. (1970). Teaching vowels through phonograms. *Elementary English, 47,* 787–791.

Wysocki, K., & Jenkins, J. R. (1987). Deriving word meanings through morphological generalization. *Reading Research Quarterly, 22,* 66–81.

4

The Challenges of Developing Leveled Texts in and for Developing Countries

The Ithuba Writing Project in South Africa

MISTY SAILORS
JAMES V. HOFFMAN
MARK W. F. CONDON

J essica arrives early to school. She decides she would like to spend some time reading before class begins, so she ventures to the bookshelf in the far corner of the classroom and selects a book from a dusty corner entitled *On We Go*. Jessica does not know that this book was published as part of a basal reading program 50 years earlier and could well have been read by her grandparents when they were in first grade. Eight thousand miles away, Prudence has finished her assignments early and has some free minutes before school dismissal. She decides she would like to spend this time reading, and so she ventures to the bookshelf in the far corner of the classroom and selects a book from a dusty corner entitled *On We Go*. Prudence does not know that this book was written for children in the United States, nor does she know that this book was donated to her school by an international charitable organization.

Children, classrooms, schools, books, and reading—so much is the same around the world. But there are differences. There are 21 students in Jessica's class. She selected her book from a classroom collection of over 600 books (tradebooks mostly but a few out-of-adoption basals, and there is a library down the hall offering thousands of books to choose from). There are 61 learners in Prudence's classroom. She selected her book from a shelf of 30 books—all U.S.-produced out-of-adoption basal readers with a couple of teacher guides thrown into the mix. There is no library in her school. Prudence speaks mostly isiXhosa at home, but because her father's family speaks Sepedi, she is comfortable in this language as well. English is her third language, and she uses it only at school. Jessica speaks only English.

As authors of this chapter, we have over 100 years of combined experience working in classrooms with students like Jessica and over 20 years of combined experience working in classrooms with students like Prudence. We are committed to the principle that children have certain basic rights and among these are the rights to be taught to read and write in languages they know (UNESCO, 2003) with texts that reflect their lived experiences. We are also committed to the principle that there are qualities of the texts used to support learning in schools that are generally valid across languages, nationalities, and cultures. In this chapter, we will describe our current work in the development of texts for children in the developing world. Specifically, we will describe our work in three provinces of South Africa. Before describing this project, we will offer some background on the research perspective we use to guide our development effort.

BACKGROUND ON LEVELED TEXTS

The *On We Go* text read by both Jessica and Prudence was first published as a leveled reader for a basal reading program in 1951. The book was designed to be read by students in the second grade. Basal reading programs are rooted historically in the "progressive" readers of the mid to late 19th century (Smith, 1964). The McGuffy readers are recognized as the prototype of modern basals with some attention to control over repetition of new vocabulary and a separate book designed for each elementary grade. The evolution of basal readers through the first half of the 19th century can be characterized primarily through the increased attention to word selection and word repetition (Hoffman, 2002). Basal readers were designed to support the reader toward automatic word recognition through repeated encounters with the same words, growing out of the research of Gates (1961). The words in the most popular basal series were selected on the "meaning frequency" principle (Chall, 1967). In other words, the words were selected for introduction starting with the most frequent words appearing in oral (and written) texts. Because these high-frequency words tended to be the most "irregular" words in terms of grapheme–phoneme correspondences, there tended to be little attention at the early levels to the teaching of decoding skills (e.g., phonics) and extreme attention to memorization through repetition. Chall used the term *look-say* to characterize the pedagogy imbedded in popular basal programs like the Sally, Dick and Jane readers published by Scott Foresman, the Jack and Janet readers published by Hougton-Mifflin, or the Alice and Jerry readers published by Harper, Row & Peterson.

The consensus surrounding leveled readers that focused around the repetition of high-frequency words and sight word teaching crumbled in the late 1960s and early 1970s. Different theories emerged regarding the processes of learning to read and the texts that would best support readers in schools. Politics played a significant role in the rapidly changing materials and approaches, with radical swings back and forth from a focus on isolated skills instruction, to literature-based, to whole language. Regrettably, most of these shifts in materials were based on competing ideologies and market forces—not on research. There were few evaluation studies conducted that examined the effects of different approaches to the leveling of texts on learning to read, and there were few theories to guide the development of leveled readers.

A FRAMEWORK FOR LEVELED TEXTS

There is growing evidence that beginning and struggling readers must be provided with appropriately leveled texts (Hiebert, 1999; Hoffman, Roser, Patterson, Salas, & Pennington, 2001) as part of a well-designed instructional plan. There are several considerations when leveling books for instructional purposes—some of these considerations are focused at the word level and others at larger linguistic units and broader design features. We offer a conception for leveled texts in beginning reading materials that addresses specifically these important considerations. The framework draws on current research and is considerate of the historical trends in the United States. The framework (nowhere near a theory at this point) has evolved over the past decade of research in texts for beginning reading. This framework draws attention to a set of key factors that relate text features to the acquisition of decoding skills and fluency. The framework rests on three major factors: instructional design, engaging qualities, and accessibility.

Instructional Design

The instructional design factor addresses the question of how words in the various selections included in leveled texts reflect an underlying instructional design for building decoding skills. Certainly, Beck's (1981, 1997) writings reflect a concern for the matching of skills taught to word features as critical to instructional design. This valuing of instructional consistency and alignment of skills taught and words read is not the only perspective one might adopt in considering instructional design. A sight word or memorization perspective, for example, might emphasize repetition and frequency over alignment of skills.

Or, as Hiebert (1999) has argued, the text might provide practice with words and within-word patterns referenced to a developmental perspective. Instantiations of patterns in a variety of contexts lead to automaticity in word recognition. The instantiations may take the form of high-frequency words. Or, the instantiations may take the form of common rimes (e.g., -og, -ip). Text that has strong instructional design features for beginning readers provides for repeated exposure to these patterns, starting with the simple, most common, and most regular patterns and then building toward the less common, less regular, and more complex. Another view on instructional design is seen in the Reading Recovery program, where skill and strategy instruction rely on a diagnostic or opportunistic approach to skills teaching that arises out of a learner's interactions with text. This differs from skill and strategy instruction that relies on an explicit, prescriptive sequence. The texts used in Reading Recovery offer highly supportive contexts for word identification to encourage the development of varied and flexible word identification strategies.

There are other likely perspectives one could take in asserting the instructional design of text in promoting decoding and word recognition. The key to evaluating the instructional design of a series of leveled texts rests on an examination of the underlying principles for the development of the program as they interface with the words students are expected to read in texts.

Engaging Qualities

No attempt to value leveled text for the development of decoding abilities can ignore issues of content, comprehension, and motivation. The construct of engaging qualities draws on a conception of reading that emphasizes its psychological and social aspects (Guthrie & Alvermann, 1999). Three qualities of engaging texts have guided our work: *content*, *language*, and *design*.

Content

Content refers to what the author has to say. Are the ideas important? Are the ideas personally, socially, or culturally relevant? Is there development of an idea, character, or theme? Does the text stimulate thinking and feeling? High-quality texts for children are characterized by the expression of important and worthwhile ideas and are socially relevant and complex. Narrative texts may introduce complex ideas, themes, and characters. Characters may change throughout the text, providing children with opportunities to consider the behaviors of the characters and their own lives. Expository texts of the highest quality for children present concepts in the abstract rather than the concrete. Furthermore, high-quality texts (fictional and expository) stimulate the reader to think about issues and may evoke strong emotions.

Language

Language refers to way in which the author presents the content in a linguistic and literary form. Is the language rich in literary quality? Is the vocabulary appropriate but challenging? Is the writing clear? Is the text easy and fun to read aloud? Does the text lend itself to oral interpretation? A high-quality text for children that is considerate of language calls attention to itself in positive ways through the stylized use of words that are expressive, unusual, idiomatic, and/or metaphorical. Compound or complex sentences may be present. Further, the complex ideas in the text are supported by causal, sequential, and associative connections among propositions and may suggest multiple interpretations, allowing children to make high-level inferences and evaluations of the characters and ideas in the texts. Where uncommon vocabulary is presented, it is done so in ways representative of the discourse pattern; the language in the text is playful and invites oral interpretation by the reader.

Design

Design refers to the visual presentation of the text. Do the illustrations or photographs enrich and extend the text? Is the use of design creative and attractive? Is there innovative use of print? Higher levels of engaging qualities are associated with greater effectiveness in supporting the development of motivation and comprehension. Simply stated—the design of the text is aesthetically pleasing. Included in the considerations of the design is the layout and format of the book, the use of media, line, color, shape, and texture. The images in the text call attention to themselves for their creativity and stand-alone beauty; they are children's first encounter, perhaps, with works of art. When revisited by the reader, they may invoke new interpretations or noticings. The design extends the text, and both recursively support the reader in comprehending the story and/or information presented in the book.

Accessibility

In contrast to utility that considers the overall program design and interface between instruction and text features, accessibility is judged specific to a text selection that is to be read. The accessibility factor addresses such important questions as: How demanding is the text in relation to the decoding demands it places on the reader? How supportive is the text for the reader in the identification of challenging words? How does the physical display of the text make reading easy or difficult? The construct of accessibility is tied to three principle factors: *decodabilty, predictability*, and *format*.

Decodability

Decodability is focused at the word level and reflects the degree to which the words in texts reflect a combination of high-frequency words as well as words that are phonically regular. What decoding demands does the text language (at the isolated word level) place on the reader? The evidence for the critical role of decodability in making texts accessible for developing readers seems irrefutable. In former studies we have conducted that looked at the nature and effects of changes to texts for beginning readers, we used a computer-based text analysis program (Martin, 1999) to estimate the degree of decodability of words presented to beginning readers (Hoffman et al., 1994; Hoffman et al., 1998; Hoffman, Sailors, & Patterson, 2003). This program offered us the opportunity to investigate the number of rimes and instantiations for each rime, the repetition rate of high-frequency words, and the average number of words a reader would encounter before meeting a unique (i.e., new) word. Texts that support the development of decoding must attend to all of these factors. Texts that consist mainly of sight words with lots of redundancy and few digraphs or vowel combinations are considered highly decodable. Texts that consist of one- or two-syllable words, are still very repetitive, and contain multisyllabic words that are strongly cued by the sentences or images are considered moderately decodable. Finally, texts that have no apparent attention to vocabulary control and contain many multisyllabic words are more difficult for children to decode. All of these factors must be considered when designing texts for children.

Predictability

Predictability refers to the surrounding linguistic and design support for the identification of challenging words (e.g., rhyme, picture clues, repeated phrases, linguistic structures). Decodability and predictability work together, creating an internal balance within a text. Together they determine the accessibility of the text for a reader. The qualities of decodability and predictability are challenging constructs to measure. Here again, though, we have found that holistic scales, rubrics, and anchor texts can be used effectively (e.g., Peterson, 1987). Such scales for accessibility have validity in relation to student performance in texts and provide more reliable estimates of pupil success at beginning levels than traditional readability formulas (Hoffman et al., 2001).

Finally, the construct of accessibility includes consideration of the text format itself—an area where research has been lacking. Current mandates for the use of text—for example, with a particular size of font and a set number of words per page—have limited research support. These kinds of prescriptions restrict creative design considerations and would leave the Bill Martin, Jrs. and the Shel Silversteins out of leveled texts altogether. Before we go too far in this direction, we need more research.

It is critical to note that texts rated high in instructional design and accessibility can also be highly engaging. Trends over the past two decades would suggest falsely that these are antithetical constructs. Decodability declined in basals when engaging qualities increased in 1993 and engaging qualities declined when decodability increased in 2000 (Hoffman et al., 2003). This is simply a case of the commercial publishers responding to shortsighted, simplistic mandates. There are highly engaging texts that are high in accessibility and high in instructional design. This framework is intended for use at the conceptual and design levels. Any consideration of leveled text for use in instruction must take into account the reader and the match of text to the reader's needs and strengths. This framework for evaluating the quality of leveled texts is complex and still incomplete. It is based as much on speculation as it is on synthesis, but it does offer a framework for further inquiry.

DEVELOPING READERS IN AND FOR DEVELOPING COUNTRIES

Although a chapter about texts created in the South Africa might appear to be misplaced in a book structured and organized for the creation and use of leveled texts in classrooms in the United States, it is, in fact, well placed. Our work in the United States and in South Africa has led us to a federally funded development project in which we are facilitating the design and creation of supplementary reading materials for South African children in grades 4, 5, and 6. In this section, we discuss learning materials in developing countries and the role of (or lack of) appropriately leveled texts in the development process of texts in those countries. We then offer our insight on leveled texts for readers based on the work we have conducted in the United States. Finally, we offer concluding thoughts for the way in which our work in South Africa might inform the process of text development.

READING MATERIALS IN SUB-SAHARAN AFRICA

Texts that support learning in developing countries are important. Several studies have demonstrated the importance of textbooks for children's academic achievement. For example, Farrell and Heyneman (1989) and Lockheed and Vespoor (1991) demonstrated that children with access to textbooks performed higher on measures of achievement than did students without access. Interestingly, textbooks were reported to be important in the achievement of children when the teachers of those children were using teacher's guides (Craig, Kraft, & du Plessis, 1998, p. 16). Further, effective teachers in developing countries use the state-issued textbooks, but they also produce local teaching and learning materials (Craft et al., 1998).

In recent years, and in economically developed countries, the focus on texts has moved beyond subject-area textbooks to the literacy environment broadly considered—to include trade books as part of the total literate environment in classrooms. Further evidence points to the importance of giving children in developing countries this same access to trade books when considering the resourcing of classrooms. For example, Elley (2000) pointed to evidence in his summarization of the findings of Book Flood studies in Niue, Fiji, Singapore, Sri Lanka, South Africa, and the Solomon Islands that it is possible to double the rate of reading achievement of primary-age students in developing countries by flooding classrooms with approximately 100 high-interest books (per class) and by providing teachers with instruction on how to use the books. Book flooding appeared to improve children's writing, listening comprehension, and related language skills, which are traditionally slow to develop under traditional styles of teaching (Elley, 2000, p. 250).

However, knowing what is helpful to learning does not necessarily mean that students have access. Various reports describe the state of affairs of learning materials in sub-Saharan African countries. For example, researchers in the early 1990s indicated that there was wide variance in the amount of books offered to children in these countries. In the best case, Namibia offered free books to both urban and rural school children on a one book per child basis. Kenya, on the other hand, could only sell books to their students; consequently, in rural areas, the ratio of books to students was 1:30 (Montagnes, 2000). In addition to the quantity issue, there are issues around the quality of the materials. Often the materials available to teachers and students are poorly designed, contain factual inaccuracies, do not support higher-level thinking, do not represent the lived experiences of the children using them, and reinforce gender stereotypes (Baine & Mwamwenda, 1994; Craig, Kraft & du Plessis, 1998; Montagnes, 2000). In some cases, such as that in South Africa, the materials available to support instruction were simply not available in the home languages of the children (Makalela, 2005).

Many international organizations have recognized the need to supply learning materials to sub-Saharan Africa, including the United Nations Educational, Scientific, and Cultural Organization (UNESCO) (*www.unesco.org*), the World Bank (*www.worldbank.org*), the United States Agency for International Development (*www.usaid.gov*), and the African Union (*www.africa-union.org*). These organizations recognize the need to raise literacy levels, and thus the educational, health, and economic equity of and within these countries. In addition to the financial aid to support the access to books, these organizations have called for the development of new materials to support learning and teaching and have identified a set of recommendations for the development of materials. Synthesizing across these calls, there seem to be a set of considerations for materials developers espoused by these organizations, including the support for gender sensitivity, science and technology (linked to culture and environment), the language of the learners, life-long learning, and leadership skills (Africa Union, 2006; Montagnes, 2000; UNESCO, 2005; World Bank, 2002).

While these are valuable considerations and should be heeded by development organizations and workers, there is scant attention to the importance of the leveling of texts for learners, even though researchers have documented the need for it (Craig et al., 1988, p. 9). We draw from our work in the United States in the leveling of texts and our previous research in South Africa (Hoffman, Pearson, Beretvas, Matthee, & Hugo, 2004; Sailors, 2004; Sailors, Hoffman, Pearson, Beretvas, & Matthee, 2008; Sailors, Hoffman, & Matthee, 2007) and extend these into our current project—developing leveled stories for children in rural South Africa.

THE *ITHUBA* WRITING PROJECT

In the opening scenario for this chapter we described Prudence, a South African student, reading from an old, American, basal reading book. Although the intentions surrounding used, donated books are rooted in a caring philosophy, there are many problems that come with the importation of reading materials for children in developing countries. Included in these are the mismatch between the lived experiences of the recipient children and a void of culturally relevant and/or inappropriate language presented in the texts. Our recent work in South Africa has focused on the development of supplementary readers to support the teaching of literacy skills and content. The *Ithuba* Writing Project is funded under a cooperative agreement between the University of Texas at San Antonio and the United States Agency for International Development under the Textbooks and Learning Materials Program of the African Education Initiative. The goal of the program is to develop and produce educational materials for primary school students in select sub-Saharan African countries; the *Ithuba* Writing Project is one of six projects currently in operation. Loosely translated in isiZulu (one of the indigenous languages of South Africa in which we are working), *Ithuba* means "opportunity."

The target for the *Ithuba* Writing Project is to create a minimum of 2 million supplementary readers and teacher's guides through collaborative interactions with U.S.-based literacy experts, South African universities, and nongovernmental organizations. To that end, our team is facilitating the authoring of a targeted 140 titles, written for students in grades 4, 5, and 6, in all 11 official South African languages. Nine of these languages are mother-tongue languages. The books are designed to serve multipurposes. They are, first and foremost, reading materials that engage children with high-quality stories representative of the various home languages as well as the South African experience. These books are also tied to the National Curriculum Standards of South Africa. Thus, they will become, when implemented in rural South African classrooms, the impetus for mathematics, natural science, or social studies lessons that follows the reading of the books. Third, they are the beginning of a potential leveling process for materials written in home languages for learners in grades 4, 5, and 6.

The books are written by South African classroom educators who are engaged as authors through a series of workshops. All of our participating teachers are home-languages speakers and represent all nine official indigenous languages in South Africa. Through these workshops, the teachers are engaged as authors where they learn to document and describe experiential events and expert self-knowledge that will be of interest to children. The teachers are learning the craft of authoring as their stories undergo several revisions throughout the workshops. The authoring teachers are encouraged to keep their audience in mind as they revise their stories based on knowledge gained through craft mini-lessons within the workshops. Mini-lessons include discussion of content, word choice, and imaging decisions. The teachers write in their home language and then create a version of the story in English for further development. Once the stories are developed in English, the teachers revise their home-language versions accordingly.

As an intermediary step in the process, members of the development and editing team (which consists of U.S. and South African writing and content experts) further develop English versions for quality purposes, to both tie the books to the national curriculum and to, as much as possible in working with the English versions of the stories, level them. As we have not discovered a leveling system in South Africa when writing for intermediate-aged children, we have borrowed from our work in the United States. In the next section, we address each of these qualities.

Because these stories are not part of a basal series (and are, rather, supplementary readers), the instructional design is not a pervasive part of our work. Although we do not have set of words that make up any core set of words for intermediate-aged learners, we watch very carefully the words that our development team uses in the stories, keeping close to the more regular patterns and then building toward the less common, less regular, and more complex. When our teachers revise their home-language versions based on the developed English versions, we ask that they keep issues such as this in mind.

We are cognizant of the construct of the engaging qualities when developing the stories, as we are interested in creating stories with rich content and opportunities for comprehension instruction that motivate and inspire these students to read. We closely follow the qualities of engaging texts that have guided our work over the years. The books that are being developed in the *Ithuba* Writing Project must contain personally, socially, and/or culturally relevant ideas without being didactic and boring to children. Many of our stories are centered on strong grandmothers who are raising children because of the HIV/AIDS epidemic. We strive to incorporate as much diversity as we can, while keeping the stories interesting to children. Complex characters guide our work, especially strong female role models.

We are also very cognizant of the linguistic and literary form of the books in which we are facilitating the development. For example, teachers in these workshops learn to "stretch the truth" and "show, not tell" as a way of introducing literary form into these experiential-based stories. Additionally, we encourage them to use words that stretch the vocabulary of children, but to maintain a readability that children can access. Since these books are for intermediate-phase learners, we invite the teachers to use compound or complex sentences and allow for children to make high-level inferences and evaluations of the characters and ideas in the texts.

Finally, we are cognizant of the design features of the books. The South African illustrations and art enrich the text and are creative and attractive. In a society where there is scant attention paid to the creation of texts in home languages for young children, our artist, Vusi Malindi, is consciously incorporating a variety of medium into his work for our books. Simply stated—the design of the texts is aesthetically pleasing.

The accessibility factor offers much more of a challenge to our work that the engaging qualities, as these stories are being authored in one of the nine indigenous languages—most of these languages are not represented in original books for children. There has been an attempt throughout South Africa to provide translated materials for children; currently, there are very few books authored in these home languages. We have accounted for a lack of attention to this feature through the final stage of the books—field testing with learners in the appropriate grade levels. For example, we have the teachers read their books with four learners, two of the assigned grade level (assigned by the authoring teacher) and two more children—one above and one below that grade level. In addition, another teacher in the group is field-testing that same book with four other learners. Each book, therefore, is field tested with eight learners. From this field testing, we can account for the comprehension of the story, the engagingness of the story (and illustrations), and the word choice within the text with regard to the accessibility factor. We ask the teachers to consider the support of the reader when he or she encounters a challenging word and whether that word might be too challenging. As in our work in the United States, we have found that decidability and predictability (especially at an intermediate level) are difficult constructs to measure, especially in light of a lack of anchor texts in these languages.

CHALLENGES AHEAD

The *Ithuba* Writing Project seeks to address concerns of relevance and effectiveness of design for leveled texts by facilitating the creation of texts for South African children by their teachers. We are, at the writing of the chapter, in the second year of the project. We have made progress, but we have also faced challenges. In this section, we will describe these challenges in the context of our experiences in South Africa.

Issues of Instructional Design

With regard to instructional design, although South Africa does have a set of curriculum standards that are innovative in nature, there is no underlying instructional design in regard to material development in the nine indigenous and official African languages. In the United States, and more specifically in Texas, instructional design is more a result of the shifting winds of policy than an attempt to be inclusive in the way in which texts are designed for children. South Africa, on the other hand, is moving away from the former educational system (that limited the educational experiences of children of black South African heritage) to a system that is much more inclusive of a quality and empowering education for all children. Because of this, South Africa may be able to construct an instructional design feature that is inclusive of the developmental perspective of learning to read. Our project, because of its supplemental nature, may offer an opportunity to examine the texts for patterns of isolated word use that might be helpful in creating texts from an instructional design perspective in the future.

Issues of Engaging Qualities

With regard to issues of engaging qualities, we have discovered that there are, in fact, trade books that are being published in South Africa in the indigenous languages. Many of these books are translated from one of the two colonizing languages in the country—English and Afrikaans. The publishing industry simply has not grown to fill the need of books written in home languages. Therefore, we have discovered that using a set of anchor texts from which we can judge the quality and merit of the books created in the *Ithuba* Writing Project is not possible. Using translated texts, which do not necessarily represent the vast cultural and linguistic diversity that exists in South Africa, to judge the merit of the uniquely South African experiences portrayed by the authors of the stories is unfair to the author and, more importantly, unfair to the children who will use the books for literacy and subject-area learning.

The *Ithuba* books, because of the nature of the authorship, surely offer uniquely South African content (the teacher-authors represent all of the cultural groups in South Africa, with a priority to the most marginalized groups) in that the ideas are personally, culturally, and socially relevant. The teachers are writing with their audience in mind, and they maintain the idea that their books must be interesting to children but also must be driven by important ideas that stimulate discussions of relevant topics to children and society. Additionally, the books are being authored in the home language of the authors; teachers are discouraged from translating texts from English, as the African languages have their own rich vocabulary and literary quality to them. To translate from English is to lose much of that richness, and vice versa.

The challenge that we have encountered in our work on the *Ithuba* project centers on not just the protection of the mother tongue, but also on the development of languages through the design of these books. Several groups, including the Pan South African Language Board (*www.pansalb.*

org.za), have been charged with the maintenance of the home languages in South Africa (both official and unofficial), along with the development of these languages. As in all languages that are in the process of developing, technical words that did not exist before must be developed in order for language to survive.

Many of the teachers with whom we are working are proficient in multiple languages but still need support in revising their stories. Our favorite quote comes from one of our participants who decided two things. First, she was writing a story in a language for which she had never read a book before (a result of the Apartheid government), and second, she found the need to, "Call my mom, because I have no idea how to say what I want to say in isiNdebele." While we have laughed with our teachers at the use of cell phones to "find words," the reality is that for some of the authors, words simply did not exist (or they did not know them) in their home language. Substituting an English word may have worked, but in the spirit of protection and development, they struggled to find words in their home language to convey the ideas and meanings in ways that were true to the culture of their story. This is a matter that is seriously being considered in South Africa; the *Ithuba* Writing Project may be able to set a standard for the development of words in texts for children that are tied directly to the national curriculum and subject-area learning.

Issues of Accessibility

Issues of accessibility are connected to the lack of materials available to children in their home languages (Makalela, 2005). And, thus, issues of decodability are inextricably linked to the lack of a core set of high-utility words in these home languages, also because of the lack of materials. To our knowledge, a core set of words that are developmentally aligned do not exist in the home languages in South Africa. Issues of accessibility in the *Ithuba* project are currently addressed through the field testing of the books with home-language speakers. The author-teachers record the usefulness of the design of the books with learners, based on how well the images support the learners in picture-walking their way through the books prior to reading. Feedback on the images furthers the development process of the books, allowing the authors and the development team to make them as supportive of readers as possible.

The authors also collected data on the readability of the texts through running records; they revised their story based on words that were problematic for learners during these field tests. This will work for now, until a core set of words might be developed that will guide the appropriateness of the words used in materials; a set that takes into account much more than the number of syllables per word and words per sentence, and includes the cultural and contextual relevance of the texts with the readers for which it was intended.

CONCLUDING REMARKS

Our work with children and teachers in rural South African classrooms leads us to believe that there are issues surrounding the creation of high-quality, leveled texts that transcend geographical locations. The teachers with whom we are working on the *Ithuba* project are excited to be part of something that offers "opportunities" to them and their children. We, too, are excited about these opportunities. We have observed, in the field testing of the first set of *Ithuba* books, children like Prudence engage successfully with and respond enthusiastically to the stories they read. We are convinced that our work with the authoring teachers will lead to the development of authors of high-quality reading materials for children in South Africa, as well as a deeper understanding that the role of leveling plays in that process. Finally, as our work progresses, we envision a larger contribution to the research and policy communities of both of our countries and to development work in other countries around the world that struggle with education and literacy.

REFERENCES

Africa Union. (2006). *Second decade of education for Africa (2006–2015): Draft plan of action.* Addis Ababa, Ethiopia: Author. Available at *www.africa-union.org/root/AU/Conferences/Past/2006/August/HRST/Draft%20Plan%20of%20Action-%20B.doc.*

Baine, D., & Mwamwenda, T. (1994). Education in Southern Africa: Current conditions and future directions. *International Review of Education, 40,* 113–134.

Beck, I. L. (1981). Reading problems and instructional practices. In G. E. MacKinnon & T. G. Waller (Eds.), *Reading research: Advances in theory and practice* (Vol. 2, pp. 53–95). New York: Academic Press.

Beck, I. L. (1997; October/November). Response to "overselling phonics" [Letter to the Editor]. *Reading Today, 17.*

Chall, J. (1967). *Learning to read: The great debate.* New York: McGraw-Hill.

Craig, H. J., Kraft, R. J., & du Plessis, J. (1998). *Teacher development: Making an impact.* Washington, DC: Academy for Educational Development.

Elley, W. (2000). The Potential for book floods to raise literacy levels. *International Review of Education, 46,* 233–255.

Farrell, J. P., & Heyneman, S. P. (1989). Textbooks in the developing world: Economic and educational choices. Washington, DC: The World Bank.

Gates, A. I. (1961). Vocabulary control in Basal reading materials. *The Reading Teacher, 15*(2), 81–85,

Guthrie, J. T., & Alvermann, D. E. (Eds.). (1999). *Engaged reading: Process, practices, and policy implications*. New York: Teachers College.

Hiebert, E. (1999). Text matters in learning to read. *The Reading Teacher, 52,* 552–566.

Hoffman, J. V. (2002). *Words on words: The texts for beginning reading instruction.* 51st Yearbook of the National Reading Conference. Oak Creek, WI: National Reading Conference.

Hoffman, J. V., McCarthey, S. J., Abbott, J., Christian, C., Corman, L.,& Dressman, M. (1994). So what's new in the new basals?: A focus in first grade. *Journal of Reading Behavior, 26,* 47–73.

Hoffman, J. V., McCarthey, S. J., Elliott, B., Bayles, D. L., Price, D. P., & Ferree, A. (1998). The literature-based basals in first grade classrooms: Savior, satan, or same-old, same-old? *Reading Research Quarterly, 33,* 168–197.

Hoffman, J. V., Roser, N., Patterson, E., Salas, R., & Pennington, J. (2001). Text leveling and "little books" in first-grade reading. *Journal of Literacy Research, 33, 507–528.*

Hoffman, J. V., Sailors, M., & Patterson, E. U. (2003). Decodable texts for beginning reading instruction: The year 2000 basals. *Journal of Literacy Research, 34,* 269–298.

Lockheed, M. E., & Verspoor, A. (1991). *Improving Primary Education in Developing Countries.* New York: Oxford University Press.

Makalela, L (2005). We speak eleven tongues: Reconstructing multilingualism in South Africa. In B. Brock-Utne & R. Hopson (Eds.), *Language of instruction for African emancipation: Focus on postcolonial contexts and considerations.* (pp. 147–174). Cape Town: CASAS.

Martin, L. A. (1999). *CIERA TExT (Text Elements by Task) Program.* Unpublished manuscript. Ann Arbor, MI: CIERA.

Montagnes, I. (2000). Textbooks and learning materials 1990–1999: A global survey. Paris: UNESCO.

Sailors, M. (2004). READ Educational Trust of South Africa. *Thinking Classrooms, 5,* 34–36.

Sailors, M., Hoffman, J. V., & Matthe, B. (2007). South African schools that promote literacy learning with students from low-income communities. *Reading Research Quarterly, 42,* 364–387.

Sailors, M., Hoffman, J. V., Pearson, P. D., Beretvas, N. S., & Matthe, B. (2008). "Learning to read with READ: Testing the effectiveness the "Learning for Living" project." In C. S. Sunal & K. Mutua (Eds.), *Research on Education in Africa, the Caribbean, and the Middle East.* Greenwich, CT: Information Age Press.

Smith, N. (1964). *American reading instruction.* Newark, DE: International Reading Association.

United Nations Educational, Scientific and Cultural Organization. (2003). *Education in a multilingual world.* Paris: Author.

World Bank. (2002). *Opening doors: Education and the World Bank.* Washington, DC: Author.

Part II

Addressing the Content of Texts for Beginning and Struggling Readers

The Role of Informational Texts

5

Text in Hands-On Science

GINA N. CERVETTI
JACQUELINE BARBER

Over the past several years, we have been engaged in a curriculum development and research project focused on the integration of science and literacy. Our approach to integration ties reading, writing, and speaking to science inquiry in order to build students' scientific skills and understandings and to give context and purpose to students' experiences with nonfiction reading and writing. This paper describes one aspect of our work—the development of science texts and their use in inquiry-based science curriculum. While we position science skills and understandings as essential ends of our work, we also set out to explicitly target literacy learning goals. Toward those dual objectives, we have been searching for the "sweet spot" between text and experience, where the use of text supports students in conducting scientific investigations and making sense of scientific ideas, and science investigations and ideas support students' development of academic vocabularies and world knowledge, their facility with content-rich text, and their comprehension of nonfiction materials.

SCIENCE TEXT IN THE ELEMENTARY CLASSROOM

Over the last decade, researchers have documented a genre imbalance in early-reading instruction (e.g., Duke, 2000). This work has resulted in a heightened awareness that students' early-literacy instruction is dominated by fictional texts, while, as Palmer and Stewart (2005) point out, "simply put, we live in an expository world" (p. 426). That is, most of the reading students do in schools is of nonfiction materials, and adults, likewise, do most of their out-of-school reading with nonfiction materials (McKee & Ogle, 2005). However, when it comes to school instruction, students have few experiences with informational text (Duke, 2000).

Arguments for the importance of including nonfiction and informational text in literacy instruction at the primary level have been presented elsewhere (e.g., Duke & Bennett-Armistead, 2003). One compelling rationale concerns students' preparedness for content-area learning, which inevitably involves students in learning from nonfiction texts. The assumption that text is text—that students will easily transfer generic reading skills from fictional literature to other genres of text—has been called into question as research has documented that students across grade levels struggle with reading and understanding nonfiction text (McGee, 1982; Meyer, Brandt, & Bluth, 1980). This research suggests that, if we want students to use nonfiction text effectively, they must be taught how. According to the 2002 Rand report, *Reading for Understanding*, teachers need to directly instruct students on how to navigate and extract information from text (RAND, 2002). In addition, the failure to include more content-rich texts in elementary reading instruction is seen by some as a missed opportunity to develop powerful world knowledge that can support students' later reading comprehension (Walsh, 2003).

At the same time that literacy educators have come to recognize the importance of nonfiction text genres, science educators have started to revisit the relationship of text to science learning. There is no dispute that inquiry-based science, or science that involves students in hands-on experiences and investigations, is the accepted standard for elementary science instruction (American Association for the Advancement of Science [AAAS, 1993]; National Research Council [NRC], 1996, 2000). However, controversy does continue to surround what inquiry-based instruction involves operationally and what role text can play. This controversy centers on questions about the authenticity, efficacy, and efficiency of hands-on science experiences in helping students master the broad array of science content standards that are laid out by current state and national standards, and conversely, on the efficacy of text in helping students to learn science with understanding and to develop the skills of inquiry (Bransford, Brown, & Cocking, 2000).

Over the past few decades, this controversy has played out between the extremes of text-only versus experience-only science instruction. Textbook science programs once included little or no firsthand experience for students, and a generation of hands-on science programs supported by the National Science Foundation (NSF) included no texts for students. Emblematic of the controversy is the tussle that occurred in 2003–2004 over California's criteria for K–8 science instructional materials. The proposed wording of the 2003 California Curriculum Commission's (CCC) *Criteria for Evaluating K–8 Science Instructional Materials in Preparation for the 2006 Adoption* specified that materials include *no more than* 20 to 25% hands-on instruction (Strauss, 2004). In the end, and after much struggle, the final wording now specifies that *at least* 20 to 25% of science instructional materials must be hands-on (California Department of Education, 2004).

Recently, science educators in the inquiry-based tradition have started to acknowledge that reading and writing are important tools in scientific inquiry and argumentation—that scientists are reliant on literacy skills particularly as they access ideas from text and communicate the results of their investigations. Yore et al. (2004) note that "scientists rely on printed text for ideas that inform their work before, during, and after the experimental inquiries" (p. 348). Nevertheless, the integration of text-into-inquiry science programs has been particularly tentative. Yore (2000), like many other inquiry-based science educators, suggest a limited role for text, where students *"do first and read and write later"* (p. 105). In addition, the past 5 to 10 years have witnessed a cautious approach to integrating text into inquiry-based science curricula and vice versa, where text-based programs have added materials kits to their programs, and inquiry-based programs have added student readers, each without changing the basic structure of the curriculum.

As we have created student texts and a related program of instruction, we have been confronted with the questions of how we can create a more meaningful form of integration and how text can support students' involvement in hands-on science, rather than supplanting their investigations. Our answer has been to offer students opportunities to use reading and writing in the service of conducting investigations, making sense of their investigations and sharing their learning—much as scientists do. In this chapter, we present (1) a model of text in inquiry science that prioritizes students' firsthand experiences, (2) guidelines for selecting texts that supports this kind of involvement in science, and (3) considerations that have guided our development of student text for inquiry science.

WHY FOCUS ON THE USE OF TEXT
IN INQUIRY-BASED SCIENCE?

Much has been written lately about nonfiction and informational text genres and the use of these texts in subject-matter learning. While teachers are being encouraged to provide opportunities for students to read in content areas such as science, the question of what kinds of text students should be reading and when and how these texts should be used remains open. This question is particularly sensitive in science, where inquiry-based science educators have been tentative in their embrace of text, concerned that it might constitute a slide backward toward textbook science.

In designing an approach to using text in science, we have been aware of strong concerns from inquiry-oriented science educators about the ways that text has sometimes been used to misrepresent science and exclude students from involvement in inquiry. Inquiry-oriented science educators have expressed concerns about the use of text that represents science as a set of facts. Yager (2004) suggests that the typical content of science textbooks or supplemental materials is not *science*, but rather, statements of *fact* based on explanations of how the natural world has come to be accepted by most scientists. Trade books and textbooks about science often fail to represent "the heart and soul of the scientific enterprise"—the nature and processes of science—but instead emphasize the facts and generalizations that are the products of science (Yager, 2004, p. 95; Armbruster, 1992/1993).

Perhaps the most significant concern about text for educators in the inquiry tradition of science education is that texts often take the place of students' involvement in firsthand investigation and experimentation. Short and Armstrong (1993) emphasize that texts should support the doing of science, rather than replace it. Palincsar and Magnusson (1997) interviewed teachers about the role that secondhand (text-based) investigations can play in scientific investigations. They found that there was a shared view among teachers that emphasizing text too much in science can be risky. The risk lies in students' deference to the authority of the text even though they are capable of investigating and generating their own answers. In part as a result of these concerns, inquiry-oriented science educators have often shied away from the use of text, or they have positioned text experiences after firsthand experiences in inquiry-based science programs that include reading. Often, firsthand inquiry experiences set the context for the introduction of new science concepts or inspire further investigation in text. For example, in the in-depth expanded application of science (IDEAS) program (Romance & Vitale, 1992) and the concept-oriented reading instruction (CORI) program (e.g., Guthrie

& Cox, 1998), experience generally precedes reading. While the CORI creators do not make any explicit claims about order, hands-on exploration is the first phase of the program. The teachers that Palincsar and Magnusson (2001) interviewed supported this approach: "The teachers cautioned against introducing text early in the investigation and urged that text be used following a significant amount of firsthand inquiry" (p. 160). The teachers recommended that text be used to *extend* hands-on experiences. In the Explorers program aimed at upper-elementary students, Bruning and Schweiger (1997) used hands-on experiences to "energize" literacy learning. They suggest that "observation and active involvement provide immediate, compelling, memorable sensory experiences" for subsequent experiences with text (p. 149).

Despite widespread apprehension about the use of text in inquiry science, some inquiry-oriented science educators have become interested in the role of reading and writing in science education (Glynn & Muth, 1994; Lemke, 1990; Yore, 2000; Yore et al., 2004), recognizing that reading and writing are authentic ways that scientists and non-scientists learn about and do science outside of school. In addition, the goals that reading and science inquiry share are being recognized. That is, students read to find out about the natural world much like they inquire. Pratt and Pratt (2004) suggest that "the commonality between the science and reading comprehension goals should be obvious; both place the understanding of subject matter content as the ultimate outcome" (p. 396).

Several programs of research have demonstrated how inquiry-based science experiences combined with science text can support students in building scientific understanding. Most notably, Guided Inquiry Supporting Multiple Literacies (GISML; Palincsar & Magnusson, 2001) and IDEAS (Romance & Vitale, 1992, 2001) use domain-appropriate experiences and text to build knowledge about the world that students then bring to bear on their understanding of related text. The GISML project demonstrates how hands-on experiences in combination with reading can be used to deepen students' conceptual understanding by helping them to extend, sharpen, and clarify their knowledge. By foregrounding conceptual understandings in science, and by using reading, writing, and concept mapping in combination with hands-on experiences in support of the understandings, the IDEAS program has produced positive learning outcomes and attitudes in reading and science compared with traditional instruction involving the use of a district-adopted basal reading series and science textbook with a few supplemental hands-on activities. Our own research has demonstrated that students in combined science-literacy curricula involving text and hands-on experiences exhibit greater growth in science knowledge and science vocabulary than students who participate in curriculum focused exclusively on hands-on inquiry experiences or reading science text (Cervetti et al., 2006).

It may be that students can't learn all they need to know about science from firsthand experiences alone. Palincsar and Magnusson (2001) problematize the notion that inquiry is exclusively activity based, noting "the impossibility that children will come to meaningful understandings of the nature of scientific thinking simply through the process of interacting with materials and phenomena" (p. 152).

In addition, researchers working at the interface of science and literacy have documented positive effects of a combined science-literacy approach involving the use of both text and hands-on experiences on student learning in both science and literacy (Guthrie & Ozgungor, 2002; Klentschy, Garrison, & Amaral, 2001; Romance & Vitale, 1992; Varelas & Pappas 2006). The CORI project provides especially powerful evidence that connecting reading and writing to expertise in content areas can engage students and support strategic reading, as well as improved science understanding. For example, Guthrie et al. (2006) have shown that stimulating firsthand experiences result in more motivated reading and improved reading comprehension when compared with instruction that includes a similar focus on reading comprehension and science understanding but uses fewer firsthand experiences related to the reading. Reading and hands-on investigations can be mutually reinforcing in the service of a knowledge goal such as understanding how animals survive in their habitats.

A FRAMEWORK FOR THE ROLES
OF TEXT FOR HANDS-ON SCIENCE

In our work, we have focused on using text in the context of inquiry-based science instruction in support of students' hands-on experiences. We have been committed to creating texts that represent the processes and products of science and to using these texts in ways to support students' inquiry experiences. This approach involves students in using text before, during, and after their firsthand investigations.

We have developed a framework of the roles that texts can serve in supporting inquiry science. These roles appear in Table 5.1: providing context, modeling, supporting firsthand inquiry, supporting secondhand inquiry, and delivering content. To provide a context for the description of the text roles that follow, we describe a short sequence from a curriculum unit about the shoreline ecosystem as an example of the relationship between text and experience.

In this sequence, students learn about the physical characteristics,

TABLE 5.1. Functions and Illustrations of Five Roles of Text in
Inquiry-Based Investigations

Function	Examples of texts

Role 1. Provide context for inquiry-based investigations

• Inviting students to think about their everyday experiences in a new way (e.g., about all of the organisms that live in the soil beneath their feet) • Sharing an aspect of the natural world that is unfamiliar to students (e.g., how everyday objects are made or organisms that live in caves) • Introducing the natural contexts in which scientific phenomena operate (e.g., the habitats in which organisms under study live) • Connecting students' everyday experiences to classroom investigations (e.g., where chemical reactions happen in everyday life) • Connecting students' investigations to big ideas in science (e.g., the use of models or systems in science) • Connecting students' investigations to a specific domain (e.g., field of chemistry or forensic science) • Connecting students' investigations to the work of professional scientists (e.g., scientists who research new medicines)	• *Where Butterflies Grow* by Joanne Ryder • *Beach Postcards* by Catherine Halversen and Nicole Parizeau • *What the Moon Is Like* by Franklyn Branley and True Kelley

Role 2. Model scientific processes

• Modeling inquiry processes, such as observing, recording, comparing, planning and conducting investigations, and making sense of data • Modeling scientific dispositions, such as posing questions, exploring, and testing • Depicting scientists and their work (e.g., biographies and portrayals of the dispositions of curiosity, passion, persistence, and open-mindedness that characterize good scientists)	• *Wild Mouse* by Irene Brady • *Protecting Primates* by Kate Boehm Nyquist • *Jess Makes Hair Gel* by Jacqueline Barber

Role 3. Support for firsthand investigations

• Providing science information to supplement the evidence students are collecting in a firsthand way (e.g., a handbook with information to help students make sense of their observations) • Providing information to help students create a firsthand investigation (e.g., a book about how to build a habitat for an organism under study)	• *Tracks, Scats, & Signs* by Leslie Dendy • *Snails and Slugs* by Chris Henwood • *Gary's Sand Journal* by Gary Griggs, Catherine Halversen, and Craig Strang

(continued)

TABLE 5.1. (*continued*)

Function	Examples of texts
Role 4. Provide opportunities for secondhand investigations	
• Providing data for the reader to interpret. These data can be pictorial (e.g., a collection of pictures or graphics that represents a set of data), qualitative (in tables or organized in other ways), or quantitative (numbers in tables or on graphs). • Communicating visual information based on data (e.g., pie charts, bar graphs)	• *What Do You Do with a Tail like This?* by Steve Jenkins and Robin Page • *Introducing Frogs and Toads* by Graham Meadows and Claire Vial • *Snail Investigations* by Gina Cervetti
Role 5. Deliver content	
• Providing information about or illustrating phenomena that would otherwise be unobservable in a classroom context (e.g., internal structures of organisms or solar system objects) • Addressing misconceptions that might arise in the conduct of firsthand investigations • Supplementing, extending, and providing opportunities to apply what students are learning (e.g., detailed information about an organism or planet provided in a reference book)	• *Zipping, Zapping, Zooming Bats* by Anne Earle • *What Color Is Camouflage?* by Carolyn Otto • *Handbook of Interesting Ingredients* by Jacqueline Barber

composition, and formation of sand through firsthand investigations and reading specific texts that have been designed to accomplish particular goals.

1. *Read to set context.* Students read *Beach Postcards*, a text about beaches and shorelines (Halversen & Parizeau, 2006). By reading and comparing a set of postcards that feature different beaches around the world, students learn that a shoreline is a place where water meets land, that there are shorelines all around the world, and that a sandy beach is one kind of shoreline. For the many students who have never been to a shoreline, the text also communicates information about the experience of being at a shoreline and provides wide and close views of river, lake, and ocean shorelines.

2. *Investigate things that can be found on a sandy beach through hands-on activities.* Students explore a model beach (a bucket with sand and other materials found on sandy beaches). Students observe the materials they find and sort them into categories that suggest something about their origins (e.g., evidence of animals, plants, humans, or rocks).

In using the beach bucket, students examine real beach objects firsthand, experience the power of models to investigate questions about the world, and look for evidence to support explanations. Students' hands-on investigations suggest that many different kinds of objects from living and nonliving sources can be found on sandy beaches.

3. *Investigate the formation of sand.* Students investigate to learn more about how sand is made by using hard candy to model the process. Different colored candy represents different objects the students found in their model beaches, including rocks, shells, seaweed, and trash. Students shake the jar of candy to model wave action at the beach and watch how the candy breaks into smaller and smaller pieces and mixes together to form candy sand.

4. *Investigate the composition of sand.* Students investigate to learn more about what sand is made of. Students use magnifiers, magnets, and mineral kits to make inferences about the composition of sand: What are the observable properties of the sand grains? Are any of the sand grains metallic? Do some sand grains resemble particular minerals? Students record their observations in their own sand journals. Their investigations suggest that sand is composed of the different materials found at the beach.

5. *Read for modeling and for information to inform investigations.* Students read *Gary's Sand Journal*, a text about a real shoreline scientist that presents a model of the nature of science (how scientists view the world and how they investigate) and information about the composition of sand that can inform students' investigations (Griggs, Halversen, & Strang, 2006). The text shows how Gary uses the properties of sand as evidence to determine the sand's origin and composition and how he records his observational notes. The text also provides information that would be difficult to gather in a firsthand way in classrooms—for example, how different kinds of waves influence the size and shape of sand grains found on the beach.

6. *Continue to investigate.* Students continue their hands-on investigations, using the information from the text to inform their inferences about what the observable properties of individual sand grains tell them about the age, origin, and formation of the sand. They are given mystery sand and asked to identify its age.

Using Texts to Connect Students' Hands-On Experiences in Science with the World Outside of School: Providing Context

In the sequence just described, students begin their investigation of the shoreline ecosystem with a text that describes various shorelines around the world. The unit of study focuses on only one kind of shoreline, the sandy beach, but *Beach Postcards* situates students' investigations in the context of a world etched with thousands of miles of shoreline. Texts can be used to set a context for students' hands-on experiences in science. When students engage in classroom-based investigations, context-setting texts can situate their firsthand experiences in the contexts of the natural world, the scientific discipline, and society.

Contexts provide a natural link to the knowledge and experience that students bring to science investigations and can prepare students for inquiry-based investigations by provoking them to look at the natural world in new ways and by inspiring them to wonder about science. In a study by Anderson, West, Beck, Macdonell, and Frisbie (1997), students read texts to stimulate their wondering about a scientific topic. They asked questions about the topic and engaged in investigations to answer their questions. Students selected texts by asking, "Is this interesting? Does it make us wonder about science things? Do we want to talk about these wonderments with our friends?" (Anderson et al., 1997, p. 714). Collectively, the students found many texts that prompted wonderments that led them to conduct substantive explorations.

Text can also help students connect their firsthand investigations to the natural world and to the work of scientists. For example, many teachers offer students the opportunity to observe the development of a butterfly, from egg to butterfly. While students can observe this metamorphosis firsthand in the classroom, many students know very little about the natural habitat of butterflies. Ryder's (1996) *Where Butterflies Grow* shows how caterpillars are camouflaged in the surroundings they choose, how they move through the foliage of their habitat, and how and where caterpillars attach to vertical surfaces as they metamorphose into chrysalises. Reading this text can provide students with a rich understanding of the natural context in which butterflies live even as they observe an important event in the life cycle of butterflies.

In our own work, we have developed texts that connect students' hands-on investigations with desktop terrariums to the forest floor that the terrariums model. We connect model oil spills to a real oil-spill disaster in the ocean. We connect students' firsthand experiences designing new soda recipes with the work of professional food scientists.

Using Text to Demonstrate Science Skills and Dispositions: Modeling

Texts can model important science processes. In the sequence from the shoreline ecosystem unit described earlier, students' involvement in investigations of the composition and origins of sand is supported by

Gary's Sand Journal, a text that models how a scientist uses observations of sand to make inferences about its formation. Text is used not only to model the scientific process of observing and making explanations from evidence, but also to offer models of the written products of science (i.e., what observational notes look like).

Texts can model the entire inquiry process from question to conclusion, and they can provide rich models of specific inquiry skills, including what careful observation involves, how to compare and classify things, and how to make inferences and explanations based on collected evidence. Brady's (1976) *Wild Mouse* is a true account of a writer who discovers that a mouse has nested in the drawer of her desk. The writer goes on to make systematic observations and drawings every day for a month of what turns out to be a pregnant mouse. The text models careful observation and description and the use of drawings to amplify particular parts of the text. It also models fundamentals of observation over time, including dating each observation.

Text can provide insights into the scientific enterprise and scientific dispositions, as well as science processes. Text can model the wondering and exploration that are the heart of science (Yager, 2004). Texts can model missteps and dead ends, as well as successes of science. They can demonstrate how science is applied to everyday dilemmas. They can share the life and/or work of particular scientists in which they describe their interest in science, demonstrate scientific habits of mind, such as persistence and curiosity, and share aspects of their work.

Texts can provide models that support students in developing literacy skills associated with scientific inquiry. Just as stories can provide models for students' own narratives, science texts can provide models of how particular text genres are constructed, as well as scientific modes of communication, including argumentation and creating evidence-based explanations. Texts can even model the writing process, providing examples of the steps a writer might go through in recording observations or creating a journal or report.

In our work, we have developed texts that model the inquiry processes that students use in their own hands-on investigations. We provide biographical sketches of scientists (novice and professional) that provide a window into the processes and products of these scientists' work and share their excitement, commitment, and passion for science. For example, *Jess Makes Hair Gel* (Barber, 2006), a text for a unit about design and invention, describes one boy's attempt to design a mixture that will work as hair gel. The text models a design process, and students can use this process to develop other useful mixtures. The text also models the process of taking notes and analyzing data, as well as the need to sometimes rethink a design in the face of failure.

Using Texts to Provide In-the-Moment Support
for Hands-On Investigations: Supporting Firsthand Inquiry

Texts can directly support students' involvement in firsthand investigations. Just as scientists rely on the work of other scientists to provide information they need in their investigations, texts provide this kind information for students. In the sequence from the unit on shoreline ecosystems, described earlier, *Gary's Sand Journal* is used to infuse new information that compels students to investigate their sand samples further and to make even more sophisticated explanations about their sand observations.

Informational texts, including field guides, handbooks, and other reference texts, can provide information that informs in-progress investigations. Just-in-time information can help students make sense of their observations (and other data they collect) and can inform their emerging conclusions. Dendy's (1998) *Tracks, Scats, and Signs* is an example of a field guide that can be used to identify evidence of animals the reader might see on a nature walk. Students might not encounter animals on a walk, but the opportunity that this text affords to identify evidence of animals' presence can inform and motivate careful observation.

In our own work, one of us (Barber) has written a reference text, *Handbook of Interesting Ingredients*, which provides information on the properties of a collection of substances that students can use to design their own products, such as glue and soda (Barber, 2006). Students use the text to look up properties of potential ingredients for their mixtures. The information they find in the text supplements the information they gather through hands-on experience and provides a richer collection of evidence than students can gather alone firsthand. For example, the text provides information about where the ingredients come from and other things that can be created with the ingredients.

Using Texts to Provide Opportunities to Interact
with Data: Supporting Secondhand Inquiry

Students need opportunities to collect data, but they often have an even stronger need for repeated opportunities to practice the challenging skill of interpreting data. Secondhand investigations can also allow students to investigate phenomena in ways that are not easily accomplished in classrooms by providing students with information and data that would be difficult or impossible to gather through hands-on classroom inquiry. In secondhand investigations, readers interpret data presented in text and draw conclusions based on those data.

Secondhand data can also provide a common data set for a class of students, which might be presented in a variety of forms (numeric, tabular, and pictorial, for example), and which might be more easily interpreted than data students collect themselves.

The data students collect in classrooms can be imprecise, making interpretation challenging. Data provided in text can have greater accuracy and consistency, making it more likely that students will draw meaningful conclusions. Providing data in text increases the likelihood that students will be able to make sense of a set of data and draw reliable conclusions about the scientific phenomena under study.

Palinscar and Magnusson (2000) investigated the power of second-hand investigations—opportunities for students to make sense of someone else's data provided in text. Students were provided with science notebook entries of a fictional scientist, including data related to students' own firsthand investigations. The researchers observed that students were better able to coconstruct information about the topic under study (light) when they used science-notebook style texts that provided interpretable data in combination with their own inquiry experiences than when they used traditional, considerate expository text on the same topic.

Trade texts that provide interpretable data are harder to come by than texts that serve the other four roles in our framework. However, especially for younger students, there are a handful of trade selections that provide pictorial data that can support secondhand investigations. In Jenkins and Page's (2003) *What Do You Do with a Tail like This?* students draw conclusions about the function of specific animal structures based on illustrations of those animal structures. One spread of the text shows images of animal "feet" and asks, "What can you do with feet like these?"

In our own work, we have developed texts that provide students with opportunities to interpret data that augment their firsthand experiences and support their growing conceptual understandings. Our texts also provide students with practice interpreting data similar to the data they are collecting. In one unit, students read *Snail Investigations*, a text that models the inquiry process with an emphasis on the recording of data (Cervetti, 2006). Students are challenged to interpret some of the data tables in the text in preparation for their own firsthand investigations.

Using Text to Supplement Investigations with Information That Is Difficult to Access in Classrooms: Delivering Content

Text can present scientific concepts and facts. The presentation of information is the most traditional role for text in science, and it is the role that most concerns inquiry-oriented science educators. In the sequence from the shoreline ecosystem unit, described earlier, students are presented with scientific information in both texts. For example, they are told that water covers most of the earth, the difference between a beach and a shoreline, and that black sand is often composed of lava rock. All of these are facts that would be difficult to learn in a firsthand way in classrooms.

At its best, the delivery of information through text connects, supplements, and extends, rather than supplanting students' firsthand investigations. In combination with inquiry experiences, texts can lend cohesion to series of hands-on investigations. Texts can also expand and build upon the ideas that students explore in their firsthand investigations. And, texts can provide information about and even illustrate phenomena that would otherwise be unobservable in a classroom context. There are limits to the amount of the vast domain of science that can be experienced in the classroom. One cannot experience the astonishingly diverse array of life forms, the power of natural forces, the history of the earth, the behavior of matter in extreme conditions, or the depths of space in the classroom. Texts can deliver science content that is too dangerous or expensive, too big or small, too distant, or occurs over too long a period of time to observe firsthand in the classroom.

There are countless excellent trade texts that deliver information about the natural world. The text *Zipping, Zapping, Zooming Bats* by Earle (1995) provides information about bats and views of bats' internal and external structures—information not readily available for firsthand observation in most classrooms, even in a unit of study about bats.

In our curriculum development work, we encourage students to treat text like an additional source of evidence. Our content-delivery texts emphasize information about unobservable phenomena, like what happens to solids that dissolve in liquids and seem to disappear, and how, over time, the natural forces of wind, water, and ice shape Earth.

Text and the Inquiry Process

We believe that the apparent consensus among inquiry science educators—that text can interfere with experience, and that doing should therefore precede reading—is shaped by a limited view of the specific roles that text can play in supporting inquiry science. Many arguments about the potentials and pitfalls of text in science seem to rest on the assumption that the text is primarily or exclusively a means of delivering content. While it may be that text used in this role alone portrays science largely as a set of facts, text can play a set of dynamic roles in the inquiry process, including setting the context for firsthand investigations, supporting firsthand investigations, providing opportunities for secondhand investigations, and modeling scientific processes and dispositions, as well as the traditional role of content delivery. Each of these roles is authentically connected to the activities of practicing scientists and to ways of learning and communicating science. Figure 5.1 maps the text roles onto the work of scientists.

An expanded view of text in science has had many benefits for the integrated science-literacy program we are developing. Above all, it has helped us to create texts that support students' involvement in inquiry. Texts used in all of the roles described can support students at each stage of the inquiry process, from posing a question to investigating and making sense of their investigations. While inquiry-oriented science educators have typically situated text after firsthand investigations to avoid interference with students' processes of discovery, an expanded view of the roles of text in inquiry invites flexibility in the placement of text with respect to hands-on inquiry. While particular roles are more closely associated with reading before, during, or after firsthand investigations in our curricula, we prefer to be guided in our placement of texts by the unfolding inquiry and the role of the text in that inquiry. For example, we most often situate texts that primarily deliver content after students' firsthand investigations so students can focus first on their own discoveries, but texts that model scientific processes are used before, during, or after firsthand investigations to help students engage in their investigations as scientists do and to reflect on how their experiences are like those of scientists. Texts that set context might support students in the exploration phase of inquiry, or they might help students connect their classroom investigations already underway to natural phenomena and events.

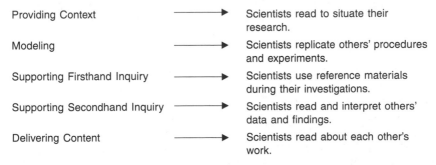

FIGURE 5.1. Examples of text roles mapped onto authentic uses of text in science.

CONSIDERATIONS FOR THE DEVELOPMENT
AND SELECTION OF TEXTS FOR INQUIRY-BASED SCIENCE

The perspective that underlies our design of texts calls for texts to be accessible for students who are often unable to benefit from higher-level science learning. Our intent, in the design and implementation of this project, was to create texts that served critical purposes in the learning of science and in becoming literate and, at the same time, could be read by the students who most depend on schools for academic learning. Our focus in this chapter has been on the functions or roles that texts can have in a science curriculum. However, we want to emphasize that our intent in this project is to ensure that students who often have not been able to read science texts because of their inaccessibility, due to dense content can participate with the texts as readers—not only as listeners. Hiebert (Chapter 1, this volume) has described in detail the model of text accessibility that underlay the design of texts. By developing texts around the core concepts and processes related to a particular conceptual domain in science, we have been able to limit the use of unique, difficult words. The texts use a high percentage of high-frequency and easily decodable words, and the use of difficult words is reserved for a set of core science words that are encountered often. By limiting the introduction of new, difficult words and focusing on core concept and process words that students will encounter repeatedly in their investigations and discussions, we make it more likely that students will be able to independently read and understand the texts, and that they will gain active control over the most conceptually important science vocabulary. In addition, as students proceed through units, the careful unfolding of concepts and associated vocabulary can help them to gain powerful world knowledge and to access subsequent texts.

In closing, we want to offer some considerations for the selection of texts for use in science. These selection guidelines are culled from the design principles that we have used in our development of text. They focus on the selection of accessible texts that support students' involvement in inquiry.

- Does this text address a critical body of information related to the science theme under study?
- Is the information presented best introduced through text?
- Is the genre an authentic representation of the information? That is, are texts of this type used by practitioners and learners within this particular domain?

- Are difficult science words conceptually important, judiciously selected, and repeated sufficiently often?
- Is there in the style or content anything that will distract children from grasping the information that they need to learn?
- Do the visual elements (e.g., illustrations and visual representations of information) support readers in understanding the most important science ideas?
- Can this text be used to complement and support inquiry science (and avoid eclipsing the discovery process)?
- Does this text avoid the misinformation and misrepresentation so common in science trade texts?
- Does the set of texts being used, taken together, avoid mere declaration of fact and instead represent the complexity of the scientific enterprise?

The challenge of developing science texts for use as part of a hands-on science curriculum led us to think through the most appropriate use of text and experience, respectively, to promote students' inquiry into science topics. Considering the ways in which scientists rely on text and experience gave rise to a framework for the roles of text in inquiry science that describes how students can make active and authentic use of text as they inquire about the natural world. Our work in developing, implementing, and evaluating curriculum leads us to believe that a considered use of text in combination with experience can result in a curriculum that is richer, more coherent, and more authentic than hands-on-dominated or text-dominated approaches to teaching science. Further, when these texts are constructed to be accessible to students, students' inquiries can lead to the dual opportunities of learning to inquire through experience and through the use of content-rich nonfiction text.

REFERENCES

American Association for the Advancement of Science. (1993). *Benchmarks for science literacy.* New York: Oxford University Press.

Anderson, T. H., West, C. K., Beck, D. P., Macdonell, E. S., & Frisbie, D. S. (1997). Integrating reading and science education: On developing and evaluating WEE Science. *Journal of Curriculum Studies, 29*(6), 711-733.

Armbruster, B. B. (1992/1993). Science and reading (Reading to learn). *Reading Teacher, 46*(4), 346—347.

Bransford, J. D., Brown, A. L., &, Cocking, R. R. (Eds.). (2000). *How people learn: Brain, mind, experience, and school.* Washington, DC: National Academy Press.

Bruning, R., & Schweiger, B. M. (1997). Integrating science and literacy experiences to motivate student learning. In J. T. Guthrie & A. Wigfield (Eds.), *Reading engagement: Motivating readers through integrated instruction* (pp. 149–167). Newark, DE: International Reading Association.

California Department of Education (2004). *Criteria for Evaluating Instructional Materials in science: Kindergarten through grade eight.* Retrieved April 1, 2007, from *www.cde.ca.gov/ci/sc/cf/documents/scicriteria04.pdf*

Cervetti, G. N., Hiebert, E. H., Barber, J., Pearson, P. D., Bravo, M. A., Arya, D. J., et al. (2007). *Science and literacy learning in an integrated science/literacy program: Effects of a large-scale implementation.* Manuscript submitted for publication (copy on file with author).

Duke, N. K. (2000). 3.6 minutes per day: The scarcity of informational texts in first grade. *Reading Research Quarterly, 35,* 202–224.

Duke, N. K., & Bennett-Armistead, V. S. (Eds.). (2003). *Reading and writing informational text in the primary grades: Research-based practices.* New York: Scholastic.

Glynn, S. M., & Muth, K. D. (1994). Reading and writing to learn science: Achieving scientific literacy. *Journal of Research in Science Teaching, 31,* 1057–1073.

Guthrie, J. T., & Ozgungor, S. (2002). Instructional contexts for reading engagement. In C. Collins Block & M. Pressley (Eds.), *Comprehension instruction: Research based best practices* (pp. 275–288). New York: Guilford Press.

Guthrie, J. T., Wigfield, A., Humenick, N. M., Perencevich, K. C., Taboada, A., & Barbosa, P. (2006). Influences of stimulating tasks on reading motivation and comprehension. *Journal of Educational Research, 99,* 232–245.

Klentschy, M., Garrison, L., & Amaral, O. M. (2001). *Valle imperial project in science: Four-year comparison of student achievement data 1995–1999* [Research report]. Washington, DC: National Science Foundation.

Lemke, J. L. (1990). *Talking science: Language, learning, and values.* Norwood, NJ: Ablex.

McGee, L. M. (1982). Awareness of text structure: Effects on children's recall of expository text. *Reading Research Quarterly, 17,* 581–590.

McKee, J., & Ogle, D. (2005). *Integrating instruction: Literacy and science.* New York: Guilford Press.

Meyer, B. J., Brandt, D. M., & Bluth, G. J. (1980). Use of top-level structure in text: Key for reading comprehension of 9th grade students. *Reading Research Quarterly, 16,* 72–103.

National Research Council. (1996). *National science education standards.* Washington, DC: National Academy Press.

National Research Council. (2000). *Inquiry and the national science education standards: A guide for teaching and learning.* Washington, DC: National Academy Press.

Palincsar, A. S., & Magnusson, S. J. (1997). *The interaction of first and second hand investigations in guided inquiry science teaching.* Paper presented at the annual conference of the National Reading Conference, Austin, TX.

Palincsar, A. S., & Magnusson, S. J. (2000). *The interplay of firsthand and text-based investigations in science education*, Report #2-007. Ann Arbor, MI: Center for the Improvement of Early Reading Achievement, University of Michigan.

Palincsar, A. S., & Magnusson, S. J. (2001). The interplay of firsthand and text-based investigations to model and support the development of scientific knowledge and reasoning. In S. Carver & D. Klahr (Eds.), *Cognition and instruction: Twenty five years of progress* (pp. 151–194). Mahwah, NJ: Erlbaum.

Palmer, R. G., & Stewart, R. A. (2005). Models for using nonfiction in the primary grades. *Reading Teacher, 58*(5), 426–434.

Pratt, H., & Pratt, N. (2004). Integrating science and literacy instruction with a common goal of learning science content. In W. E. Saul (Ed.), *Crossing borders in literacy and science instruction*. Arlington, VA: National Science Teachers Association.

RAND Reading Study Group. (2002). *Reading for understanding*. Santa Monica, CA: RAND.

Romance, N. R., & Vitale, M. R. (1992). A curriculum strategy that expands time for in-depth elementary science instruction by using science-based reading strategies: Effects of a year-long study in grade four. *Journal of Research in Science Teaching, 29*(6), 545–554.

Romance, N. R., & Vitale, M. R. (2001). Implementing an in-depth expanded science model in elementary schools: Multi-year findings, research issues, and policy implications. *International Journal of Science Education, 23*(4), 373–404.

Short, K. G., & Armstrong, J. (1993). Moving toward inquiry: Integrating literature into science curriculum. *New Advocate, 6*(3), 183–200.

Strauss, V. (2004, February 3). Back to basics vs. hands-on instruction. *The Washington Post*, A.12.

Varelas, M., & Pappas, C. C. (2006). Intertextuality in read alouds of integrated science-literacy units in urban primary classrooms: Opportunities for the development of thought and language. *Cognition and Instruction, 24*(2), 211–259.

Walsh, K. (2003). Basal readers: The lost opportunity to build the knowledge the propels comprehension. *American Educator, 27*(1), 24–27.

Wang, J. (2005). *Evaluation of Seeds of Science/Roots of Reading Project*. Los Angeles, CA: National Center for Research on Evaluation, Standards, and Student Testing (CRESST), University of California.

Yager, R. E. (2004). Science is not written, but it can be written about. In W. E. Saul (Ed.), *Crossing borders in literacy and science instruction*. Arlington, VA: National Science Teachers Association.

Yore, L. D. (2000). Enhancing science literacy for all students with embedded reading instruction and writing-to-learn activities. *Journal of Deaf Studies and Deaf Education, 5*(1), 105–122.

Yore, L. D., Hand, B., Goldman, S. R., Hildebrand, G. M., Osborne, J. F., Treagust, D. F., et al. (2004). New directions in language and science education research. *Reading Research Quarterly, 39*(3), pp. 347–352.

CHILDREN'S BOOKS

Barber, J. (2006). *Jess makes hair gel.* Nashua, NH: Delta Education.

Barber, J. (2006). *Handbook of interesting ingredients.* Nashua, NH: Delta Education.

Brady, I. (1976). *Wild mouse.* New York: Scribner.

Branley, F. M. (2000). *What the moon is like.* New York: HarperCollins.

Cervetti, G. (2006). *Snail investigations.* Nashua, NH: Delta Education.

Dendy, L. (1998). *Tracks, scats, and signs.* Minocqua, WI: Northwood Press.

Earle, A. (1995). *Zipping, zapping, zooming bats.* New York: HarperCollins.

Griggs, G., Halversen, C., & Strang, C. (2006). *Gary's sand journal.* Nashua, NH: Delta Education.

Halversen, C., & Parizeau, N. (2006). *Beach postcards.* Nashua, NH: Delta Education.

Henwood, C. (1988). *Snails and slugs* (Keeping minibeasts). New York: Franklin-Watts.

Jenkins, S., & Page, R. (2003). *What do you do with a tail like this?* New York: Houghton Mifflin.

Meadows, G., & Vial, C. (2001). *Introducing frogs and toads.* Lebanon, IL: Dominie Press.

Nyquist, K. B. (2003). *Jane Goodall: Protecting primates.* Washington, DC: National Geographic Books.

Otto, C. (1996). *What color is camouflage?* New York: HarperCollins.

Ryder, J. (1996). *Where butterflies grow.* New York: Puffin.

6

Informational Text Difficulty
for Beginning Readers

NELL K. DUKE
ALISON K. BILLMAN

> Baby Whale looked at her Mommy.
> Whales have live babies, or *young*.

These sentences are similar in several respects: Both have six words; both involve whale mothers and babies; they even have nearly the same number of letters. They are also different in important ways. For example, the former requires children to understand that the text refers to individuals, the latter to whales in general; the former requires processing a third-person possessive pronoun (*her*), and the latter requires processing an appositive (or *young*). Most salient is that the books suggest different genres of text—the former a fictional narrative or storybook text, the latter an informational text.

For some time in U.S. history, fictional narrative has held a privileged place among texts for young readers. Informational text, in contrast, was assumed to be too difficult or inappropriate for use when children are learning to read. This assumption has been reflected in a scarcity of informational texts in young children's classroom environments and experiences (e.g., Duke, 2000), in core reading programs (Moss & Newton, 2002), and in beginning writing education (e.g., Pressley, Rankin, & Yokoi, 1995) (see Duke, Bennett-Armistead, &

Roberts, 2003, for a review). However, research has demonstrated that informational text is appropriate for young children (see later discussion). We elaborate on that point, after defining *informational text*. We then turn to what makes informational texts more or less difficult for young children, and argue that some attempts to make informational text easier may, in fact, make it more difficult. We conclude with a call for research and development in this important and understudied area.

DEFINING INFORMATIONAL TEXT

First, a discussion about what informational text is, as we define it. Informational text is text whose primary purpose is to convey information about the natural or social world, and that has particular linguistic features to accomplish that purpose. A book about Mexico, a website about dragonflies, a magazine article about the melting of the ice caps—all of these are likely to be informational text by our definition. Notably, for us, informational text is not synonymous with "nonfiction." We view nonfiction as a broad category that includes any type of text that is true or purports to be true—not only informational text but also biography, nonfiction narrative (i.e., true stories), procedural or how-to text, and so on. These distinctions are important because these kinds of text have different purposes and different structures and text features to accomplish those purposes (see Duke & Tower, 2004, for further discussion). These different purposes, structures, and text features pose different demands for beginning readers. For example, to comprehend a procedural or how-to text, a child needs to know to look for a section on materials needed, and to understand what that list is conveying, a child needs to know that the steps presented should be read and followed in order, and that he or she can look to the illustrations for further information about how to perform a step and what the finished product looks like (Purcell-Gates, Duke, & Martineau, 2007). None of this knowledge is needed to comprehend what we call an *informational text*, for which different knowledge is needed.

Even within the category of "informational texts" there are, in fact, a number of different text types. For example, some informational texts are what we have called *process* informational texts. These convey information about a process such as how trees are made into paper, how sand is made into glass, or how milk and other ingredients are made into ice cream. These books are not written with the intent to teach children how to make these things on their own—in which case they would have different features and be procedural or how-to texts by our definition (Purcell-Gates et al., 2007)—but rather to teach children about how such things are made. Certain features are expected of process informational texts. For example, they typically follow a chronological structure and thus need to be read in order, from beginning to end, in their entirety; they may have a flow chart at their conclusion that summarizes the process described (e.g., Reid, 1996). In contrast, what we have called *all-about* informational text typically conveys information about different aspects of or categories within a particular topic. For example, a book all about penguins would likely tell what kind of animal penguins are, their physical features, where they live, what they eat, dangers they face, and so on (similarly for a book about any animal). Unlike process informational texts, all-about informational texts typically do not have a chronological structure (the text structure for this type of text is referred to as enumerative) and do not need to be read in order or in their entirety. For example, if children were studying what Arctic animals eat, they might start by consulting an index in the back of the penguins book and then turn to and read only the section that addresses what they eat (and go on to do the same in books about other Arctic animals). Although there likely would be diagrams in an all-about informational text—for example, a diagram of different parts of a penguin's body—a flow chart summarizing the content of the book would likely not be appropriate.

To complicate matters further, there are texts that are in some ways informational texts, as we have defined them, but also meet criteria for other kinds of text. A classic example of this is the *Magic School Bus* books (e.g., Cole, 1992). These books clearly have as one purpose conveying information about the natural world, and they have many text features one would expect given this purpose. But these books also have the purpose of entertaining, with many text features designed to serve this purpose. The books are fantasy fictional narrative on the one hand, while nonfiction informational on the other hand (see Smolkin & Donovan, 2004, for further discussion). Pappas (2006) calls books of the Magic School Bus type *informational-annotated story hybrid texts* and identifies six other types of hybrid informational texts. For the purposes of this chapter, our comments do not refer to these kinds of texts, except when otherwise noted.

INFORMATIONAL TEXTS ARE AMONG THE "RIGHT TEXTS" FOR BEGINNING READERS

Evidence we have to date suggests that informational texts are among the right texts for beginning readers. In one experimental study, some first-grade teachers were randomly assigned to include more informational text in classroom environments and activities throughout the year (Duke, Martineau, Frank, & Bennett-Armistead, 2008). Specifically, experimental-group teachers were asked to aim for approximately one-third informational texts in classroom libraries, on classroom walls and other surfaces, and in any activity during the day that involved text of three or more related sentences. We found no harm to children in the informational-text-enriched classrooms—for example, they were equally strong in their decoding and encoding skills (in fact, they were stronger in the case of the classes that entered the year with relatively low literacy knowledge). Children in the informational-text-enriched classes also had more positive attitudes toward reading and were more effective writers of informational text.

Hiebert has demonstrated that beginning readers' fluency can be developed through repeated reading of informational text (Hiebert, 2005, 2006). In fact, she demonstrated that fluency development was better promoted by repeated reading of informational text than of narrative texts, although the informational texts were written specifically to help in building fluency, whereas the narrative texts were drawn from trade books, so it might have been that, rather than genre, that accounted for the difference. In any case, it is clear that informational text can be a productive text type with which to build fluency, a major area of need for beginning readers.

Research suggests that some young children prefer informational texts as reading material (e.g., Kletzien, 1999; Kletzien & Szabo, 1998). For beginning readers, text interest may be very important, providing them with motivation to struggle through the decoding and other challenges that reading poses for them (Caswell & Duke, 1998; Fink, 1995/ 1996). Indeed, Menon and Hiebert (1999) suggest that the engagingness of text is one of the dimensions that should be considered in characterizing and evaluating texts for beginning readers (see also Hoffman, Christian, et al., 1994). And with older students, with whom more research on issues of interest has been conducted, text interest is shown to influence interactions with texts in a wide variety of ways (e.g., Baldwin, Peleg-Bruckner, & McClintock, 1985), making it more likely that students will set personal goals for their learning and perceive literacy as a lifelong pursuit (Turner, 1997; see Renninger, Hidi, & Krapp, 1992, for an extended discussion of the role of interest in reading). Particularly for beginning readers with a strong interest in informational texts, or topics addressed in them, informational texts are among "the right texts."

WHAT MAKES INFORMATIONAL TEXTS FOR BEGINNING READERS MORE OR LESS DIFFICULT?

There is surprisingly little research available to help in answering this question. The kinds of studies that would be most informative to us in writing a section like this—for example, studies that examine beginning readers' interactions with a wide variety of informational texts, systematically varying characteristics of the texts while holding others constant, or studies that examine characteristics of readers most predictive of their success and failure in reading a given informational text—simply have not been done. So, in writing this section, we relied primarily on extrapolations from research and thinking on text difficulty more generally, and on personal experiences with informational text and young children (sometimes in the context of a research study, but not a research study in which the focus was text difficulty).

In their report on directions for research and development in reading comprehension, the RAND Reading Study Group (2002) considered four elements that contribute to comprehension: (1) the reader, (2) the text, (3) the activity, and (4) the context of the reading event. We use these four elements as a heuristic for discussing difficulties and opportunities that informational texts may present for beginning readers, although for parsimony we combine the activity and context elements. For reasons that become apparent later, we discuss these elements in an unorthodox order: beginning with the text, then discussing the activity and context of the reading event, and concluding by discussing reader factors.

Some Text Factors

Many characteristics that affect the difficulty of other types of text, or text in general, also apply to informational texts for beginning readers. Certainly the difficulty of individual words within the text—their frequency, decodability using commonly known phonograms, and so on—is also relevant with informational texts. So too are general issues such as the size of font, length of sentences, and number of sentences per page. Somewhat more subjective issues also apply, such as the general appeal or engagingness of the text and the degree to which the illustrations support word recognition and decoding, as well as construction of meaning.

Content is a factor we consider with many types of text. For example, with fictional narrative text, we think about whether the themes in a given text may be too mature for beginning readers, or whether children will be able to relate in some way to the experiences of the characters. With informational text, however, content may be of particular importance, given the purpose of informational text to convey information, or content, about the natural or social world. We need to consider the level of sophistication of the content (e.g., a book about dogs is likely to be more accessible from a content perspective than a book about electricity) but also the structure of the content (e.g., a book that describes a process from beginning to end may be easier to follow than one in which the only pieces of the process are referenced), the vocabulary associated with the content (see later discussion), and so on. As we discuss in the paragraphs that follow specific features of informational text, other ways in which content can interplay with text difficulty will become apparent.

An analysis of informational texts in science at a reading level appropriate for children in second and third grade (Purcell-Gates et al., 2007), revealed a number of features of this type of text. These features are likely to affect text difficulty, although, as we argue at the conclusion of this section, this relationship is not likely to be a simple one.

Structurally, informational texts we examined often included an opening statement or general classification (e.g., "Dragonflies are a type of insect") and concluded with a general statement or closing (e.g., "There is so much to learn about this amazing insect!"). Between the opening and closing, we almost always found a description of attributes or components of the subject (e.g., "Dragonflies have six legs and two pairs of wings" and characteristic events of the subject (e.g., "Dragonflies eat flies and other small insects"). We also found compare–contrast structures (how things are alike and different), as well as classifying, either within a sentence (e.g., "Dragonflies are a type of insect") or across sentences (e.g., "Some dragonflies live in forests near streams; Some dragonflies live in fields near marshes; Some dragonflies live in deserts near pools"). Most likely, had our analysis included a wider variety of informational texts—for example, informational texts on social studies topics—we would have found additional text structures typical of informational text, such as problem–solution, cause–effect, and so on (Meyer & Rice, 1984). Indeed, in an analysis of informational texts appropriate for reading aloud to kindergarten children, which included texts on social studies as well as science topics, these additional text structures were observed (Duke & Kays, 1998).

In our analysis, informational texts almost always included timeless verb constructions and generic noun constructions. That is, instead of talking about a specific thing or character at a specific point in time (e.g., "Daisy Dragonfly laid her eggs"), informational texts typically talk about a class of things across time (e.g., "Dragonflies lay eggs"). Notably, generic noun constructions are not always accomplished with a plural form as in the last example. Sometimes a singular form is used (e.g., "A dragonfly lays eggs"). The author intends this to be generic, to refer to all dragonflies, and adult readers will understand it as such. However, young children may not recognize that intended meaning. In our experience, when reading constructions like this, some young children think the construction is specific—for example, referring only to an individual dragonfly in the picture—rather than generic. For these children, use of the singular form may increase text difficulty. The language of informational texts we analyzed was also almost always denotative more than connotative. That is, the language is direct, explicit, and precise, rather than implied, implicit, and "fuzzy." For example, the text might read, "Most dragonflies are between 1 and 4 inches long" rather than "Dragonflies are small creatures." More denotative language may be helpful to beginning readers, requiring fewer inferences and less interpretation. On the other hand, it may also pose challenges, such as understanding measurement (e.g., "between 1 and 4 inches long") and understanding precise terminology that may be unfamiliar.

Having specialized or technical vocabulary has long been noted as a characteristic of informational text (Duke & Kays, 1998), and having some specialized vocabulary was almost always observed in the texts we studied. This vocabulary includes words unlikely to occur in everyday conversation, or words that are specific to a particular topic or set of topics within science or social studies (e.g., *thorax, wingspan, larva*). The rarity of these words is likely important from the perspective of word recognition (with rarer words less likely to be automatically recognized by beginning readers and therefore requiring decoding effort) and from a vocabulary-learning perspective (with readers less likely to have had past experience with the words to help build their understanding). However, there are also some supports for such words in informational text that should be noted. Recent analyses suggest that this potentially difficult vocabulary is more likely to be repeated in informational texts than in narrative texts, in which a rare word—for example, an uncommon adjective used to describe a character—may appear only once in the text (Hiebert, 2007). Repetition of difficult words is an important form of support for beginning readers (Hiebert & Martin, Chapter 3, this volume), particularly for vocabulary learning (e.g., Blachowicz & Fisher, 2000). In addition, the informational texts we analyzed almost always included at least one definition, often many more than that, within the text. Other kinds of support for vocabulary learning, such as graphics (e.g., a diagram of a dragonfly might include an arrow and label for *thorax*) and picture or word-based glossaries, may also be present.

Another cluster of features we identified in our analyses are features that might be characterized as navigational—features that help readers to locate particular portions of the text or to identify the focus of the text in a given section. These include the index and headings, which were often observed in the texts we analyzed, and the table of contents, which was observed somewhat less often. Notably, these features are sometimes present in texts for beginning readers "in name only." That is, there is a table of contents, heading, and/or index, but the book is so short, and information so light, that they really are not actually needed. For example, an 8-page book with a single sentence on each page is unlikely to give rise to an authentic purpose for using an index. The opposite situation is also observed, in which a text would benefit from having such navigational features and does not. This too can be problematic for beginning readers, as discussed later in this section.

Finally, our analyses found features related to the graphics of the informational texts. First, the illustrations in these texts were almost always realistic in nature or actual photographs. Given that some reading series contain selection after selection of illustrated tales of talking animals, realistic illustrations may be a jarring characteristic for some beginning readers. Second, we often found labels and/or captions within the informational texts we examined. While not graphics per se, the primary referent and purpose for this text is the graphics. Third, our analyses revealed the use of a number of different graphical devices, such as diagrams, charts, maps, tables, graphs, boldface and italicized vocabulary, and so on. In many informational texts for beginning readers that we have examined, it could be reasonably argued that most of the information being conveyed is indeed being conveyed through the graphics rather than the running text.

Researchers have also examined the characteristics of informational texts appropriate for reading aloud to young children—specifically kindergartners (Duke & Kays, 1998; Pappas, 1986, 1987) or primary-grade children (Pappas, 2006). Many of the features identified in these analyses overlap with those discussed above. However, there are some additional features identified that should be noted. One is the frequent repetition of the topical theme of the text (Duke & Kays, 1998). For example, a text on dragonflies would begin many sentences with this term and have it elsewhere in sentences, as well. Another, identified by Pappas (2006), is the presence of a prelude (a short narrative or comment designed to capture readers' attention and draw them into the text, such as an anecdote about a sneeze at the outset of a book about germs), an afterword (additional information about the topic in a section at the end of the text), and/or an addendum (such as excerpts of the journal of a beekeeper in an informational text about beekeeping). None of these elements were found in all information books studied, but each was found in a number of books. Pappas (2006) also found examples of information books with short historical vignettes within them—for example, the relaying of a Greek legend about Arachne in a book about spiders, and short sections about an experiment readers could try to illustrate or test out a concept. The degree to which such features are present in texts designed for beginning readers to read themselves, rather than for read-aloud, has not been investigated.

The relationship between the text features we have discussed and text difficulty is likely highly complex. We cannot generalize that the more informational text features a text has the more difficult it is, because sometimes features are going to be of great aid to the reader in both word recognition and in comprehension, such as with graphics that support and elaborate the running text, or table of contents and headings that make the structure of the topic and main ideas more plain. We also cannot generalize, however, that more informational text features are necessarily better for readers. If the features are used inauthentically (see example of navigational features "in name only" discussed earlier) or of poor quality, they can be more confusing and distracting than actually helpful. For example, we have seen informational texts for beginning readers that seem to be written with more interest in using a compare–contrast structure (probably due to demands of a scope and sequence of skills in the program) than in whether and when that structure is actually a good match to the information being conveyed. Moreover, of course, all of this interacts with reader factors. Children who are more attentive to and better at identifying text structures may be less affected by poorly applied or poorly signaled text structures. The activity and context factors interact with text factors, as well. For example, in a classroom in which the teacher is supporting children's comprehension of diagrams, diagrams in informational texts may support understanding. However, in classrooms in which instructional attention is not paid to diagrams, readers unfamiliar with them will likely find their presence in informational texts, at best, unhelpful and, at worst, frustrating and distracting. We turn now to some of these other factors in informational text difficulty.

Some Activity and Context Factors

The context around the reading of a text may impact text difficulty in a number of ways. One factor is likely whether the text is read in isolation or as part of a larger unit of informational study. For example, if a child is reading a book about weather at the same time that the teacher and the class are engaging in a study of weather, it will probably be easier. The unit may include hands-on experiences with weather instruments like thermometers, barometers, or windsocks, or a visit from a local meteorologist. The readers are participating in a wide array of activities that are developing vocabulary and background knowledge that will support their reading of texts about weather (see later discussion about vocabulary and background knowledge as important reader factors). Research also suggests that children who have access to both hands-on experiences and texts on a topic learn more about the topic than children who have access to only one or the other (Anderson & Guthrie, 1999; Pearson, 2006).

Similarly, having available a collection of related informational texts may make reading less difficult for children. For example, if a child is reading a collection of books about weather, the books themselves can build vocabulary and background knowledge that can support or scaffold understanding. The set may include texts written at different levels, allowing the child to begin with easier texts and progress to more complex texts. Additionally, books may present the same or similar information in different ways. For example, one text may only mention the names of weather instruments that a meteorologist may use, while another may have a whole section that describes the weather instruments in detail, explains how they are used, and provides photographs of each. In this sense, the books become cross references. Reading a collection of informational texts on different topics but with similar characteristics may also be supportive to young readers. This may be accomplished through books by the same author or in the same format (e.g., question–answer) or with similar features (e.g., maps, map keys). Many scholars place a premium on the kinds of intertextual or text-to-text links that may be encouraged by reading multiple related texts (Hartman, 1992), and we are increasingly seeing items that require some degree of text-to-text comparison or integration on large-scale assessments.

The authenticity of the reading event is also likely a factor in text difficulty. Following Purcell-Gates (e.g., Purcell-Gates, Degener, Jacobson, & Soler, 2002), we view authenticity as the degree to which texts are read or written for the reasons people read and write in the world outside of schools, and the degree to which the texts being read or written are like those that are read or written outside of schools. Authentic reading of informational text involves reading for the purpose of obtaining information that you want or need to know, and reading texts that are the same as or much like those you would find in bookstores or libraries, at newsstands, or in similar locations (Duke, Purcell-Gates, Hall, & Tower, 2006/2007). Having children read an information book about snakes to settle an argument they are having regarding whether a snake can eat a dog, having children read an informational website about recycling to inform an initiative they are involved in to reduce waste at their school, or helping children read a children's magazine article they selected about chocolate because "We love chocolate!" would likely constitute authentic reading events by our definition. In contrast, having children read an informational selection in their reading program solely because it was the next selection or because you thought they should, or having children read an informational paragraph on a worksheet and then answer the worksheet's questions about it would be "school only" reading events. (See Duke et al., 2006/2007, for many examples of more and less authentic literacy events with science informational text in the context of second- and third-grade classrooms.) We suspect that informational reading is less difficult, more educational, or both, in the context of more authentic reading activities because there is likely to be greater alignment between children's purpose for reading and the purpose for which the text was written to be read. Over time, second- and third-grade children engaged in more authentic literacy activities in science did show greater growth in reading comprehension (Purcell-Gates, Duke, & Martineau, 2007). The Concept-Oriented Reading Instruction (CORI) approach shown to be so effective with third-grade students also engages students in many authentic literacy events (Guthrie, Wigfield, & Perencevich, 2004).

The nature and degree of instructional support that teachers provide also impacts informational text difficulty. Teachers who help students approach the decoding of unfamiliar words in informational text, who scaffold students' application of appropriate comprehension strategies, and who use a variety of techniques to aid students in understanding key vocabulary and concepts in informational texts are likely to have students who experience less difficulty with informational texts. We also suspect, though we admittedly do not have even indirect research support for this, that teachers who know more about informational texts, and the challenges and opportunities it poses for beginning readers, will be more effective at helping children develop their ability to read this type of text.

Some Reader Factors

Finally, there are a host of important reader factors that affect the difficulty of informational text for beginning readers. Beginning readers are, by definition, beginners. Their lexicon of known words in print is limited, and their decoding abilities are just beginning to develop. Their reading is likely to be slow and choppy and may not yet be attentive to punctuation or other indicators of expression. As language learners, they are also just developing their vocabularies, with many words they encounter in informational text potentially unfamiliar to them semantically as well as orthographically. They have had little practice attending to meaning while simultaneously processing the print on the page. And they may be at the early stages of developing their ability to be strategic meaning-makers with text. Most likely, these factors are at least as salient with informational text as with other kinds of text beginning readers encounter.

There are also many reader factors that are specific to informational text, or at least more salient with this type of text. Because the purpose of informational text is to convey information, or knowledge, one such factor is the reader's background knowledge. The collections of experiences children have with the world and with different kinds of texts contribute to the background information that a reader draws on when making meaning from text. Children are in the process of building this background. In some cases, children will not have had the experiences necessary to support their understanding of an informational text, and some children will certainly have had more such experiences than others. As a case in point, we know of a 6-year-old girl who had good decoding skills and so, pronounced the word *pulp* when reading a text about growing pumpkins. However, this same child had trouble making sense of the word *pulp* or using it in a writing activity. Although she knew it was something inside a pumpkin, she did not know how to describe or make sense of pumpkin pulp. When asked, she had never carved a pumpkin. Children, like this girl, who lack experiences and knowledge related to the informational texts they are reading, are more likely to have difficulty with informational texts. Indeed, every indication is that there is a strong relationship between background knowledge, vocabulary knowledge, and reading success (Stanovich, 2000).

A second category of background knowledge regards reading and learning from informational texts. Although we believe the situation is beginning to change, as noted earlier, children in primary grades are less likely to have reading experiences that include informational texts. For this reason, they are often less familiar with the function, structures, or features of informational text than they are with other forms of text. We suspect that the more experience children have reading and learning from informational texts, and thus the more familiar they are with the purpose and features of this genre, the more likely they will be efficient and effective readers of this type of text. It seems reasonable to assume that a child who knows how to use features like the table of contents and the index, or who is able to glean information from the graphical features of informational texts (e.g., tables, diagrams), will be more successful when reading informational texts. Beyond the text features that are commonly associated with informational text, certain authors or publishers have particular styles or formats that cross their texts (e.g., author Gail Gibbons has a distinct style). A child who is familiar with those formats will be able to draw on them when reading a new text by the same author or publisher.

Despite limited background and skills, beginning readers may be passionately interested in reading informational texts on a particular topic or theme. As noted earlier, this passion fuels the motivation to persist even when the texts present challenges that we might consider daunting for a beginning reader (again, see earlier discussion). With respect to informational text specifically, children who are passionate about one topic may become mini-experts whose familiarity with the content and vocabulary, as well as their interest, helps them manage the complexities of informational text. A particular first-grade boy one of us (Billman) worked with was fascinated with mathematics—to the point he would only read books that explained mathematics. Not surprisingly, he gradually became sufficiently familiar with terms and concepts to allow him to read books that were written for students at much higher grade levels. Of course, interest does not lie solely within the individual. The activity and context in which a text is read can affect how interested children are in it; some teachers appear to have the ability to motivate children to read any text (Pressley et al., 2003), and some texts are almost inherently interesting to children. So, we see how reader, activity, context, and text factors interact to affect the difficulty of informational text for beginning readers.

SOME ATTEMPTS TO MAKE INFORMATIONAL TEXT EASIER MAY IN FACT MAKE IT MORE DIFFICULT

Repeating our caveat of earlier that many of the studies that would inform our understanding of text difficulty for beginning readers have yet to be done, our best guess is that some attempts to make informational text easier for beginning readers may, in fact, make it more difficult. We have addressed a number of these in our discussion already:

- Including an informational text feature such as an index or table of contents for which there is no need may be more confusing and distracting than helpful.
- On the other hand, avoiding an informational text feature that might help children make meaning is also problematic.
- Content should drive the structure rather than the structure driving the content.
- Some young children do not appear to understand a singular construction generically (e.g., "a shark" is meant to mean *all sharks*).

In this section we briefly identify a few other moves that may in fact make informational text more difficult for young readers. We include this discussion in hopes that it might be informative to writers and publishers working on informational texts, and also in hopes that it might help educators in making decisions about selecting informational texts for beginning readers and scaffolding their interactions with them.

Some information books ascribe human characteristics to the animal or thing being discussed, as in Marzollo's book *I'm a Seed* (1996), or in any number of books with an animal named Bill, Sally, Joe, or the like, in which the story is meant to convey information about the species as a whole. While some may view this personifying or anthropomorphizing as a way to reduce the decoding demands of a text and/or help children relate to the content, we suspect that it may make the text more difficult because it requires some understandings (e.g., that a seed is talking) or inferences (e.g., when it says, "Joe the Shark ate some plankton," it is really saying that at least some kinds of sharks eat plankton) that may be difficult for young children. Moreover, such an approach can cause misconceptions—one reason why the National Science Teachers Association (NSTA) has taken a position against this device (National Science Teachers Association, nd). Of course, misconception-promoting or inaccurate informational texts are not limited to those with personalizing or anthropomorphizing, but we will not address that issue in this chapter.

Closely related to this is fictionalizing in an informational text—that is, having some fictional and some nonfiction, informational elements within the same text. As noted earlier, there are many different ways that this is approached (Pappas, 2006), and we suspect some are not problematic. For example, a story of what two fictional children learn on their field trip to a post office might work just fine, particularly if information is conveyed in generic and timeless terms when appropriate. Other times, however, it may be problematic. For example, in Packard's book *I Am Not a Dinosaur* (1997), a cartoon-looking dinosaur makes a series of statements about characteristics he does not have (e.g., "I do not have horns," "I do not roar"), finally concluding that a characteristic he does have—wings—is quite nice itself. Read as a fictional narrative text, there is no problem. But read as an informational text, we can see misconceptions result—for example, that all dinosaurs had horns and roared.

A related problem is when the informational text does not, in fact, convey information (in which case, of course, it is debatable whether it should be called an informational text). We have seen a surprising number of examples of this. For example, we see some books for beginning readers that appear on the surface to be informational but, in fact, teach something so fundamental that most beginning readers would have learned it years previously (e.g., names of basic colors). At the least, offering children texts like these, rather than texts from which they really could learn about the natural and social world, constitutes a missed opportunity to build the knowledge base of beginning readers and to model authentic informational text.

Publishers and writers sometimes use devices to stimulate children's interest in informational text that actually can get in the way of the information they are trying to convey. Allen and Tudor's book *Are You a Ladybug?* (2003) is one of a series of books that asks the reader if he or she is a specific animal. When confronted with the question, "Are you a ladybug?" we assume that most children would answer "no," making the follow-up statement, "If you are, your parents look like this and eat aphids," irrelevant. Another device often used to catch readers' interest is the inclusion of sensational information that is secondary to the main topics of the text. Schraw and Lehman (2001) explain that research with older students found that these seductive details result in the readers losing track of the main ideas they are reading while remembering the sensational, less important details.

As previously noted, vocabulary in informational text is complex and technical. In the interest of making a text more accessible for young readers, some authors will substitute more common or less technical vocabulary (e.g., *sleep* for *dormant*). These substitutions can lead to misconceptions, depending on the nature of the material and the specific background knowledge the child draws upon. As a case in point, consider the case of substituting the word *sleep* for *dormant* when describing the wintering state of an acorn in the ground; the word *dormant* means not actively growing and is much different from how a child might understand *sleep* as meaning to rest after being tired. Using the term *sleep* would be misleading to the child and would potentially create misconceptions, in addition to constituting a missed opportunity to expose the child to academic vocabulary. That said, the word *dormant* is likely unfamiliar to many beginning readers—a word they have neither decoded before nor know from a vocabulary perspective. In situations like this, the author should consider supporting children's understanding within the text. One way this can be accomplished is by embedding a definition within the text (e.g., "When acorns are dormant it means the acorns are not growing"). The author should also repeat the word whenever appropriate as children need multiple encounters with words in order to learn them both conceptually and from a word-recognition perspective.

CONCLUDING REMARKS AND RECOMMENDATIONS

As previously noted, informational text and its use in the primary grades is an understudied area. In the absence of extensive research on the matter, we suggest that publishers and writers of informational texts for beginning readers avoid the strategies that we have suggested may not make informational text less difficult, or that may even make it more difficult. Instead, we suggest focusing heavily on the reader, text, activity, and context factors discussed earlier with respect to informational text difficulty:

- Create texts that are likely to be of high interest to students.
- Do not assume too much background knowledge, and rather, write the text as a vehicle to build that knowledge.
- Provide text features that will support understanding—definitions of words, illustrative graphics, clearly signaled structures, useful navigational features; do not use features just for the sake of using them.
- When possible, provide multiple texts that are related by topic, author, features, or other factors.
- When appropriate, provide notes or supplementary materials that suggest authentic contexts in which the texts can be used, and productive instructional supports that can be used with them.
- Do not avoid vocabulary that is important to understanding and knowledge building, but do not use unfamiliar vocabulary unnecessarily either. Provide support for children to learn the meaning of the vocabulary—for example, through graphics and a definition.

Paralleling this list of recommendations for authors and publishers are some considerations for teachers interested in providing the best opportunities for children to learn with and from informational texts.

- Select texts carefully, avoiding those that seem to be based on questionable assumptions about whether young children can handle informational text and what makes informational text easier and more difficult for young children.
- Choose texts that are likely to be of high interest to students, as well as conveying important content or providing important instructional opportunities.
- Be cautious in making assumptions about students' background knowledge. Whenever possible, assess their knowledge and, as appropriate, provide opportunities for building background through activities and experiences that are related to the topics they are reading about.
- Choose texts that use text features that support understanding—

definitions of words, illustrative graphics, clearly signaled structures, useful navigational features (though not to an extreme, as
overly structured or feature-ful text may present its own difficulties).

- When possible, build libraries of multiple texts that are related
  by topic, author, features, and other factors.
- Support readers by providing authentic contexts in which the
  texts can be used.
- Focus on and teach vocabulary that is important for understanding and knowledge building across texts and topics.

Throughout this chapter, we have identified a number of areas in
which more research in this area is needed. We encourage the research
community to conduct those studies that will contribute to the field's understanding of informational text and beginning readers. Some studies
that we believe are needed include examinations of:

- Beginning readers' interactions with a wide variety of informational texts where certain characteristics of texts are varied and
  others are held constant.
- Characteristics of readers that are most predictive of their success
  and difficulties in reading a given informational text.
- What makes informational text more or less difficult for beginning readers—for example, the relationship of text features and
  text difficulty for beginning readers.
- How exemplary teachers of informational literacy support beginning readers.

Finally, we encourage everyone who is involved with informational
text with young readers—practitioners and researchers—to be attentive
to text difficulty issues. It is clear that both the wisdom of practice and
the guidance of research will be needed to move forward in this important area of work.

REFERENCES

Allen, J., & Tudor, H. (2003). *Are you a ladybug?* New York: Kingfisher.
Anderson, E., & Guthrie, J. T. (1999). *Motivating children to gain conceptual
knowledge from text: The combination of science observation and interesting
texts*. Paper presented at the Annual Meeting of the American Educational
Research Association, 19–23 April, in Montreal, Canada.
Baldwin, R. S., Peleg-Bruckner, Z., McClintock, A. H. (1985). Effects of topic in-

terest and prior knowledge on reading comprehension. *Reading Research Quarterly, 20,* 497–504.

Blachowicz, C. L. Z., & Fisher, P. (2000). Vocabulary instruction. In M. L. Kamil, P. B. Mosenthal, P. D. Pearson, & R. Barr (Eds.), *Handbook of reading research* (Vol. 3, pp. 503–524). Mahwah, NJ: Erlbaum.

Caswell, L. J., & Duke, N. K. (1996, March). Non-narrative as a catalyst for literacy development. *Language Arts, 75,* 108–117.

Cole, J. (1992). *The Magic School Bus lost in the solar system.* Illustrated by B. Degen New York: Scholastic.

Duke, N. K. (2000). 3.6 minutes per day: The scarcity of informational texts in first grade. *Reading Research Quarterly, 35,* 202–224.

Duke, N. K., Bennett-Armistead, V. S., & Roberts, E. M. (2003). Filling the great void: Why we should bring nonfiction into the early-grade classroom. *American Educator, 27*(1), 30–35.

Duke, N. K., & Kays, J. (1998). "Can I say 'once upon a time'?": Kindergarten children developing knowledge of information book language. *Early Childhood Research Quarterly* 132, 295–318.

Duke, N. K., Martineau, J. A., Frank, K. A., & Bennett-Armistead, V. S. (2008). *The impact of including more informational text in low-SES first grade classrooms.* Unpublished manuscript. East Lansing: Michigan State University.

Duke, N. K., Purcell-Gates, V., Hall, L. A., & Tower, C. (2006/2007). Authentic literacy activities for developing comprehension and writing. *The Reading Teacher, 60,* 344–355.

Duke, N. K., & Tower, C. (2004). Nonfiction texts for young readers. In J. Hoffman & D. Schallert (Eds.), *The texts in elementary classrooms* (pp. 125–144). Mahwah, NJ: Erlbaum.

Fink, R. P. (1995/1996). Successful dyslexics: A constructivist study of passionate interest reading. *Journal of Adolescent and Adult Literacy, 39,* 268–280.

Guthrie, J. T., Wigfield, A., & Perencevich, K. C. (2004). *Motivating reading comprehension: Concept-oriented reading instruction.* Mahwah, NJ: Erlbaum.

Hartman, D. K. (1992). Eight readers reading: The intertextual links of able readers using multiple passages. *Reading Research Quarterly, 27,* 122–123.

Hiebert, E. H. (2005). The effects of text difficulty on second graders' fluency development. *Reading Psychology, 26,* 1–27.

Hiebert, E. H. (2006). Becoming fluent: What difference do texts make? In S. J. Samuels & A. E. Forstrup (Eds.), *What research has to say about reading fluency* (pp. 204–226). Newark, DE: International Reading Association.

Hiebert, E. H. (2007). The word zone fluency curriculum: An alternative approach. In M. R. Kuhn & P. J. Schwanenflugel (Eds.), *Fluency in the classroom* (pp. 154–170). New York: Guilford Press.

Hoffman, J. V., McCarthey, S. J., Abbott, J., Christian, C., Corman, L., Curry, C., et al. (1994). So what's new in the basals?: A focus on first grade. *Journal of Reading Behavior, 26*(1), 47–73.

Kletzien, S. B. (1999, December). *Children's reading preferences and information books.* Paper presented at the National Reading Conference, Orlando, FL.

Kletzien, S. B., & Szabo, R. J. (1998, December 1–4). *Information text or narrative text?: Children's preferences revisited.* Paper presented at the National Reading Conference, Austin, TX.

Marzollo, J. (1996). *I'm a seed.* New York: Cartwheel.

Menon, S., & Hiebert, E. (1999). *Literature anthologies: The task for first grade readers.* Ann Arbor: Center for Improvement of Early Reading Achievement, University of Michigan.

Meyer, B. J. F., & Rice, G. E. (1984). The structure of text. In Pearson, P. D., Barr, R., Kamil, M. L., & Mosenthal, P. B. (Eds.), *Handbook of reading research*, Vol. I (pp. 319–352). New York: Longman.

Moss, B., & Newton, E. (2002). An examination of the informational text genre in basal readers. *Reading Psychology, 23*(1), 1–13.

National Science Teachers Association. (n.d.). *Outstanding science trade books for children: About the books and selection process.* Retrieved July 4, 2007, from *www3.nsta.org/ostbcprocess.*

Packard, M. (1997). *I am not a dinosaur.* New York: Cartwheel.

Pappas, C. C. (2006). The information book genre: Its role in integrated science literacy research and practice. *Reading Research Quarterly, 41*(2), 226–250.

Pearson, P. D. (2006, July). Toward a model of science-literacy integration. Presentation at the National Geographic Society Literacy Achievement Research Center Summer Institute, Washington, DC.

Pressley, M., Dolezal, S. E., Raphael, L. M., Mohan, L., Roehrig, A. D., & Bogner, K. (2003). *Motivating primary-grade students.* New York: Guilford Press.

Pressley, M., Rankin, J., & Yokoi, L. (1995). *A survey of instructional practices of primary teachers nominated as effective in promoting literacy* (Reading Research Report No. 41). Athens, GA, & College Park, MD: Universities of Georgia & Maryland, National Reading Research Center.

Purcell-Gates, V., Degener, S. C., Jacobson, E., & Soler, M. (2002). Impact of authentic adult literacy instruction on adult literacy practices. *Reading Research Quarterly, 37*(1), 70–92.

Purcell-Gates, V., Duke, N. K., & Martineau, J. A. (2007). Learning to read and write genre-specific text: Roles of authentic experience and explicit teaching. *Reading Research Quarterly, 42*, 8–45.

RAND Reading Study Group. (2002). *Reading for understanding: Towards an R&D program in reading comprehension.* Santa Monica, CA: RAND Education.

Reid, M. E. (1996). *Let's find out about ice cream.* New York: Scholastic.

Renninger, K. A., Hidi, S., & Krapp, A. (Eds.). (1992). *The role of interest in learning and development.* Hillsdale, NJ: Erlbaum.

Schraw, G., & Lehman, S. (2001). Situational interest: A review of the literature and directions for future research. *Educational Psychology Review, 13*(1), 23–52.

Smolkin, L. B., & Donovan, C. A. (2004). How not to get lost on *The Magic School Bus*: What makes high science content read-alouds? In E. Saul (Ed.), *Crossing borders in literacy and science instruction* (pp. 291–313). Newark, DE: International Reading Association.

Stanovich, K. E. (2000). *Progress in understanding reading: Scientific foundations and new frontiers*. New York: Guilford Press.

Turner, J. C. (1997). Starting right: Strategies for engaging young literacy learners. In J. T. Guthrie & A. Wigfield (Eds.), *Reading engagement: Motivating readers through integrated instruction* (pp. 183–204). Newark, DE: International Reading Association.

7

Text Modification

Enhancing English Language Learners' Reading Comprehension

YOUNG-SUK KIM
CATHERINE E. SNOW

Too many English language learners (ELLs) struggle with reading comprehension in English. Clearly, the reasons for their struggles are multiple and heterogeneous. Taking as a starting point the heuristic for studying reading comprehension developed by the RAND Reading Study Group (2002) (see Figure 7.1), we might locate their difficulties in any of four primary areas: the sociocultural context for the reading activity, the activity the reader is asked to engage in, the reader's skills and capabilities, or features of the text being read. Any of these can by itself be a source of difficulty, but it is mismatches between them that are particularly potent in generating comprehension struggles. For example, asking competent third-grade readers to comprehend sixth-grade text generates such a mismatch, and so does asking students to read in a language they do not fully command, or to engage in school-assigned activities they have not been taught about. As this model represents reading comprehension, it is not surprising that ELLs might struggle with English reading: Their language (and perhaps literacy) skills are limited, the

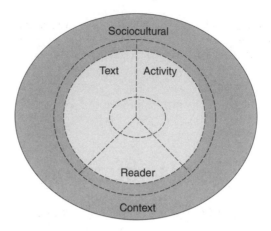

FIGURE 7.1. A heuristic for understanding reading comprehension. From RAND Reading Study Group (2000).

sociocultural context in which they are reading is likely to be unfamiliar, school-assigned reading may well presuppose background knowledge or specific skills they do not have, and assigned texts were designed for native speakers rather than second-language learners. Improvement in ELLs' reading abilities might derive from attention to any component of the model—for example, giving reading materials and activities that are more socioculturally familiar, or providing instruction focused on learners' language and literacy skills. In this chapter, though, we emphasize the role of the text, and the possibilities of modifying texts being read as one approach to improving comprehension.

Why focus on the text? For one reason, text modifications are relatively inexpensive and easy to do; in an era of computer-mediated instructional materials, in particular, the text is a site for applying "universal design" principles (Rose & Meyer, 2002; Rose, Meyer, & Hitchcock, 2005) that promote educational success without categorizing or tracking students. Furthermore, understanding which text modifications benefit ELLs might give us insights into the comprehension process more generally, with consequences for the better design of texts for all learners. Finally, while there has been almost no research examining the impact of text modifications on ELLs in U.S. K–12 settings, there is a more robust knowledge base derived from studies of text modification with English-only (EO) students, and with older foreign- or second-language learners. Thus, we have a basis both for some well-justified instructional recommendations in the short run, and for a promising research agenda to improve text modifications in the long run.

In this chapter, we first review research on methods that have been used in attempts to make text more comprehensible to second-language (L2) learners and native speakers, and their effects on reading comprehension. Then, we present examples of modified text consistent with suggestions made in the research. Subsequently, we discuss some larger considerations to be taken into account when contemplating the use of modified texts in the classroom. Finally, we offer suggestions for future research.

MODIFYING TEXT: TWO ROUTES

There are two primary ways of modifying or adapting reading materials for L2 learners: simplification and elaboration (Oh, 2001; Ragan, 2006; Young, 1999). Simplification involves reducing the challenge of vocabulary and sentence structure (syntax) in text—for example, by selecting words from a limited list (to reduce the "type-token ratio," or ratio of different words to all words), by limiting the text to high-frequency vocabulary likely to be known to L2 learners, by shortening sentences, by restricting syntactic structures used to those showing canonical word order (subject-verb-object), and/or by avoiding complex constructions (nominalizations, embedded relative clauses, etc.) (Oh, 2001; Parker & Chaudron, 1987). Simplification of text is a prevalent strategy used to adapt or modify reading materials for L2 learners to improve comprehensibility of input (Oh, 2001; Parker & Chaudron, 1987; Young, 1999), reflecting the fact that many educators believe vocabulary and complex syntax are primary obstacles to comprehension for L2 learners (Blau, 1982) and vocabulary, in particular, is a major factor (Graves, 2006). Of course, linguistic complexity is an important determinant of comprehensibility for EO readers as well, and readability formulas (which reflect the level of syntactic and lexical complexity in texts) have been widely used as guidelines for text-selection and text-revision for native speakers of English (Davison, 1984; Duffy et al., 1989) as well as for L2 learners (Yano, Long, & Ross, 1994).

In contrast to simplification of text, elaboration of text involves increasing redundancy and enhancing explicitness (i.e., describing underlying thematic relationships more explicitly). In other words, elaboration involves "clarifying, elaborating, explaining, and providing motivation for important information and making connections explicit" (Beck, McKeown, Sinatra, & Loxterman, 1991, p. 256). The goal of elaboration is to improve text coherence through clarification, repetition, and explicit connections; as a consequence, elaboration may not reduce linguistic complexity as measured by readability formulas (Oh, 2001; Ragan, 2006; Yano et al., 1994).

Effectiveness of Simplification and Elaboration in Improving Reading Comprehension

Studies of the effects of text modification on reading comprehension have revealed that L2 learners perceive modified texts, both simplified and elaborative, to be easier to read; they report feeling that they understand modified texts better than unmodified texts (Blau, 1982; Lotherington-Woloszyn, 1993; Oh, 2001). Given the importance of practice in improving reading, these perceptions might be significant because they suggest, at least, that learners might be more motivated to persist in reading modified texts.

However, findings about the actual effects of modified texts on L2 learners' reading comprehension are somewhat inconsistent. For example, Yano and his colleagues (1994) showed that simplified text was effective in increasing Japanese (English as a Foreign Language) (EFL) college students' (intermediate to high proficiency) reading comprehension, but there was no difference in their comprehension of simplified vs. elaborative texts, after controlling for students' overall English proficiency. In contrast, other studies have failed to find positive effects of simplified texts in comparison to either authentic or elaborative texts (Blau, 1982; Lotherington-Woloszyn, 1993; Oh, 2001; Young, 1999). Blau (1982) showed that eighth-grade students in Puerto Rico did not benefit from syntactically simplified texts. In addition, Lotherington-Woloszyn (1993) reported that English as a Second Language (ESL) college students of intermediate proficiency in the United States did not comprehend simplified texts better than unmodified texts.

Other studies indicate that both elaboration and simplification of text help L2 learners' reading comprehension. Both elaborative text (those provided with paraphrases and synonyms, for example) and text with simplified syntax facilitated reading comprehension for English learners (8th through 11th grades) of diverse first-language (L1) backgrounds in an international community in Taiwan (Brown, 1987). Oh (2001) reported that Korean 11th-grade students with high English proficiency benefited from both elaborative and simplified texts, while students with low English proficiency benefited only from elaborative texts, not from the original, unmodified texts or from simplified texts.

Furthermore, simplified and elaborative text may have differential effects on different types of comprehension—literal (or factual), synthetic, or inferential. In a study with Japanese college EFL students, Yano et al. (1994) showed that, after controlling for students' overall

English proficiency, students who read simplified and elaborative texts were able to answer more literal (or factual) questions correctly than those who read unmodified texts. In addition, students who read elaborative texts outperformed students who read simplified and unmodified texts in making inferences from texts. These results suggest that both simplified and elaborative texts help students extract surface factual information, while elaborative text is more effective in promoting higher levels of understanding.

The inconsistent findings about the effects of simplified text on reading comprehension may be attributable to the potential disadvantages of simplifying vocabulary and syntax in texts. First, sentences with limited (simplified) vocabulary and syntax tend to be choppier and less natural than authentic discourse materials, and this may interfere with readers' construction of meaning (Blau, 1982). Second, simplified text may lack coherence and cohesion, leaving the relationship between pieces of information unclear (Honeyfield, 1977), and thus making appropriate inferences more challenging. Third, simplification of the language may lead to simplification of content. For example, compare the following unmodified sentence with the simplified version (Yano et al., 1994).

[Unmodified text]
Because he had to work at night to support his family, Paco often fell asleep in class.

[Simplified text]
Paco had to make money for his family. Paco worked at night. He often went to sleep in class.

The unmodified sentence is longer and more complex but also more natural and authentic; most importantly, it makes explicit the relationship among the three claims. In contrast, the simplified sentences are awkward and lack explicit indication of relationships between the propositions in the sentences. Furthermore, simplified texts may have undesirable consequences for language acquisition if learners develop reading strategies that are difficult to transfer to unsimplified target language materials (Honeyfield, 1977). Thus, while simplification might, under some conditions, promote comprehension of specific texts, it also limits learners' exposure to the complex and sophisticated language structures they will ultimately need to process (Yano et al., 1994).

Although evidence about the effect of simplification of text on L2 learners' reading comprehension is mixed, it seems unambiguous that elaborative modification of text facilitates native speakers' (Beck, McKeown,

Omanson, & Pople, 1984; Beck, McKeown, Sinatra, & Loxterman, 1991) and L2 learners' reading comprehension (Oh, 2001; Parker & Chaudron, 1987) and listening comprehension (Chaudron & Richards, 1986). In a review of studies on text modifications and comprehension for L2 learners, Parker and Chaudron (1987) concluded that elaborative modifications and clear segmenting of thematic structure helped L2 learners' comprehension. Furthermore, Korean L2 learners of both low and high proficiency in English showed better reading comprehension when texts were modified with elaborative techniques (Oh, 2001). Despite their linguistic complexity, elaborative texts may provide better reading materials because comprehension depends more on "the availability of comprehensible information within the text" (Brown, 1987, p. 60) and "the frequency with which the reader comes across the information" (Oh, 2001, p. 86). Increased redundancy (through exemplification, repetition, paraphrase, definition, and synonym), clarification, and clearer thematic structure may provide L2 learners with an enriched semantic context which they can use in drawing inferences about the content, helping them to glean more critical information from even linguistically complex texts (Oh, 2001). In one study, L2 learners reported that redundancy in the unmodified text was helpful for their comprehension, while reduction of redundancy in the simplified text posed difficulty for them (Lotherington-Woloszyn, 1993).

Mechanisms of Action

What are specific ways that elaborative modification may help readers' comprehension? Findings from previous studies with both native speakers of English and L2 learners suggest that the key to effective elaborative modifications is improving text coherence (e.g., making causal sequence or temporal relationships explicit) and cohesion (e.g., preventing referential confusion and making referential repairs) (Beck et al., 1984; Beck et al., 1991; Linderholm et al., 2000; Vidal-Abarca, Martinez, & Gilabert, 2000).

Studies of cognitive processing during comprehension indicate that text difficulty depends not only on lexical and syntactic complexity but also on text structures (e.g., sequential, causal, or contrastive structure) (Britton & Gülgöz, 1991; Linderholm et al., 2000; van Dijk & Kintsch, 1983). Therefore, one critical way to support the construction of coherent mental representations of texts is to facilitate the inferential process by making connections between text events more explicit, and by improving text coherence. This can be achieved by clarifying information in text, supplying transitions, and adding or deleting information to make the text follow a coherent plan (Britton, Van Dusen, Gűlgőz, & Glynn, 1989).

Much evidence from studies with EO students shows that improved text coherence facilitates readers' comprehension (Beck et al., 1984, 1991; Vidal-Abarca et al., 2000). For example, Beck, McKeown, Omanson, and Pople (1984) improved text coherence by revising text features such as ambiguity of content, background knowledge required for comprehension, and surface form of the text. Their study showed that although revision of texts increased the readability indexes, revised texts resulted in better comprehension for more- and less-skilled third-grade readers. In another study, Beck, McKeown, Sinatra, and Loxterman (1991) improved text coherence by making the causal sequence more explicit in four social studies passages, resulting in improved free recall and comprehension of texts for fourth- and fifth-grade students. Similarly, Vidal-Abarca, Martinez, and Gilabert (2000) showed that making the causal structure of text explicit improved eighth-grade students' recall and comprehension as indicated by responses to inference questions.

Similar findings have emerged in studies of L2 readers. In their study of Dutch-speaking college students reading in English, Linderholm et al. (2000) concluded that text comprehension is improved when causal connections are explicit (i.e., temporal order is simple [cause followed by consequent], goals are explicitly stated, and coherence breaks caused by inadequate explanation, multiple causal connections, and distant causal relations are repaired). In particular, less-skilled readers benefited from explicit causal structure in texts, performing as well as skilled readers on reading comprehension. However, when the text became more complex, or the causal connections were more implicit, less-skilled readers continued to have more difficulty comprehending content (Linderholm et al., 2000).

Another way to improve text coherence and help a reader in making connections between events is an explicit focus on clarifying cohesion, or modifying referents in the text (Blau, 1982; Pretorius, 2005). Implicit referents and anaphoric inferencing pose challenges and interfere with reading comprehension for native speakers (Gernsbacher, 1989) and even more for L2 learners (Pretorius, 2005). For example, college students who were English learners found it difficult to correctly identify the correct referents when they encountered anaphoric paraphrases and determiners, whereas the referents of pronouns were easier for them to identify. In addition, determiners that referred back farther (the anaphoric ties stretch over a longer section of discourse) and to more complex antecedents were more ambiguous and difficult to resolve for ESL college students (Parish & Perkins, 1985) even for native speakers (Beck et al., 1991; Cirilo, 1981). In his study of 68 first-year college L2 learners of English in South Africa, Pretorius (2005) found that the learners' ability to resolve or understand anaphoric referents (e.g., pronouns and determiners) was related to their reading ability in English. In addition, the amount of anaphoric inferencing the text demands appears to be an important determinant of ease of comprehension, particularly for L2 learners of low reading ability (Pretorius, 2005). Therefore, modifications of several elements in texts may improve comprehensibility (i.e., explicit marking of anaphoric referents; reducing the distance between antecedent and anaphoric devices; shortening antecedents; ensuring more featural (morphological and semantic) overlap among anaphoric referents may improve comprehension. See Table 7.1 for examples of modifications. For example, college English L2 learners found it easier to comprehend simplified texts when texts had *explicit* surface clues for understanding relationships (e.g., relative pronouns, subject and finite verbs retained in subordinate clauses; conditional sentences explicitly expressed) despite the fact that these generated longer sentences and more complex syntactic structures (Blau, 1982).

Britton and Gülgöz (1991) made relationships between ideas more explicit in expository texts by making the implicit referents explicit, repeating a linking word from the previous sentence and using the same terms for concepts introduced recurrently, and presenting given information first in the sentences, followed by new information. College students were able to recall more and learned more idea units from text modified in these ways.

Finally, it may be helpful to teach L2 learners to attend to textual cues—keeping track of referents in the text—particularly for expository texts (Pretorius, 2005), given that these anaphoric devices are prevalent in expository texts and attention to text cues is even more necessary for reading texts on unfamiliar topics and context (Allen, 1985).

In summary, a substantial body of research suggests that, although linguistic complexity of the text is an important factor in determining the ease of reading comprehension for L2 learners (Garcia, 1991; Graves, 2006), simplifying linguistic complexity by limiting vocabulary and syntactic structure in text does not appear to be an effective way to enhance L2 learners' reading comprehension (at least for the late adolescent and adult L2 learners who have been the subject of most studies). In contrast, research suggests that the comprehensibility of text is improved when rich, elaborative scaffolding of both vocabulary and syntax are provided, and when text coherence and cohesion are improved. In addition, it appears that a combination of different types of modifications, rather than single adjustments of one type or another (e.g., repetition or making topics salient), results in enhanced comprehensibility (Beck et al., 1991; Parker & Chaudron, 1987; Yano et al., 1994).

TABLE 7.1. Examples of Making Anaphoric Repairs to Enhance Comprehensibility of Text

Types of anaphoric modifications	Examples		Changes made
	Unmodified text	Modified text	
Explicit marking of anaphoric referents	Ann predicted that Pam would lose the track race, but *she* came in first very easily. (Gernsbacher, 1989)	Ann predicted that Pam would lose the track race, but *Pam* came in first very easily. (Gernsbacher, 1989)	The ambiguous pronoun *she* is replaced by a proper noun, *Pam*.
Reducing the distance between antecedent and anaphoric devices	By comparison, *working class jobs* reach full earning capacity relatively quickly but provide fewer promotion prospects and less income for investment. In addition, *they* are less secure. (Pretorius, 2005)	By comparison, *working class jobs* reach full earning capacity relatively quickly, but *these jobs* are less secure, provide fewer promotion prospects, and less income for investment.	In the original text *they* refers back to *working class jobs*, which is two propositions away. In the modified text, the pronoun *they* is replaced by *these jobs* and moved closer to the antecedent.
Making antecedents shorter	*One study found that female aspirations for high-status jobs rose by 7% between 1970 and 1976. During the same time, male aspirations for such jobs declined 5%. A second study found a similar decline in gender-typed occupational choices when high school seniors of 1964 were compared to high school seniors of 1975. Although such evidence* is encouraging, we must bear in mind that women still tend to be heavily overrepresented in traditional female jobs. (Pretorius, 2005)	*Studies have shown that female aspirations for high-status jobs rose while gender-typed occupational choices declined. Although such evidence* is encouraging, we must bear in mind that women still tend to be heavily overrepresented in traditional female jobs.	In the unmodified text, the determiner, *such*, is followed by a single noun, *evidence*, that paraphrases or summarizes the contents of the antecedent, which is the entire four sentences. In the modified text, the long antecedents are summarized more concisely.

More morphosyntactic and semantic clues in the anaphoric tie	John threw *the stone*. It was heavy. John fed *the robin*. *It* was hungry. People are *hostile* to other social groups who are easily identifiable because they are different racially, religiously, or politically. In fact, modern history is full of examples that show how politicians, to divide people and realize their own selfish ambitions, have exploited *this*.	John threw *the stone*. *The rock* was heavy. (Gernsbacher, 1989) John fed *the robin*. *The bird* was hungry. (Gernsbacher, 1989) People are *hostile* to other social groups who are easily identifiable because they are different racially, religiously, or politically. In fact, modern history is full of examples that show how politicians, to divide people and realize their own selfish ambitions, have exploited *this hostility*. (Pretorious, 2005)	The modified text used a synonym and semantic superordinance in order to relate the two nouns semantically (e.g., the stone and the rock; the robin and the bird). The third sentence employs repetition of a word, *hostility*, which contains explicit morphosyntactic clues for *hostile*.

EXAMPLES OF ELABORATIVE MODIFICATIONS OF TEXT

We provide examples of modified texts to make clear the kinds of elaborations that work well. The first example comes from Beck and her colleagues' work with native English speakers who were in upper-elementary school (Beck et al., 1991). They modified expository texts (social studies) to improve coherence by clarifying relationships among ideas, making implicit information explicit, and elaborating and explaining concepts.

For example, compare the following original sentences with the modified ones about the French and Indian War as initiating events of the American Revolution (see Beck et al., 1991, for more examples).

[Unmodified text]
As a result of this war, France was driven out of North America. Britain would now rule Canada and other lands that had belonged to France. This brought peace to the American colonies. The colonists no longer had to fear attacks from Canada.

[Modified text]
Britain won the war. Now Britain had control of North America, including Canada. The French had to leave North America. The colonists were very glad that Britain had won. They now felt safer in their homes. Before the war, Indians had often attacked colonists who lived near the borders. Now Britain owned these lands where the Indians lived. The colonists were sure that Britain would protect them.

In the original text, the normal expectation that the phrase *as a result of this war* will be followed by a statement about the winner of the war is not fulfilled; the defeated party is taken as the focal point and described using the relatively uncommon expression *driven out of North America*. In the modified text, it is explicitly stated who the winner of the war was, shifting the emphasis to Britain; this is more relevant to the purposes of this passage, setting the stage for subsequent pre-Revolution conflict. Second, the revised text made implicit information explicit and provided the kind of knowledge and information necessary for comprehension—lack of peace before the war. The original sentence "This brought peace to the American colonies" presumes that readers are aware of the problem or a contrasting situation (unrest), but this has not been explicitly stated in the text. Furthermore, in the original text new information about the colonists' fear of attacks was presented as given information. The modified version clearly states colonists' fear of attacks in relation to the information already provided, rather than treating it as presupposed. Finally, the modified text used temporal markers such as *Before* and *Now* to explicitly signal the temporal sequence of events.

A second example comes from a middle school vocabulary intervention project specifically targeted for urban middle schoolers, including many ELLs. This intervention uses a program called Word Generation. Word Generation texts present a dilemma or controversy selected for optimal interest and cultural relevance to urban adolescents. Furthermore, as a vocabulary intervention program, it places emphasis on providing support for core vocabulary through presentation of the words in rich semantic contexts, provision of student-friendly definitions, multiple exposures to the words in a variety of contexts, repetition of concepts, and provision of appropriate background knowledge.

The following are examples of texts used to introduce the week's topic and new focal words before and after modification for ELLs.

[Unmodifed text]

Why do we go to school? One prime goal of education is to transmit knowledge. Another is to enhance students' capacities to earn a good living. Some would argue that schools should orient students toward a set of shared values in order to facilitate the maintenance of a democratic state. Others contend that schools should help students develop an understanding of the perspectives of others to promote social harmony. Still others think schools should teach students to challenge authority, reject received opinion, and think for themselves. Of course, if we accept this last version of what schools should do, then we will have to expect that the curriculum will be massively adjusted and classroom activities radically altered. Whereas thinking for themselves is something we say we want students to do, we don't always give them the license to do so in the classroom.

[Modified text]

Why do we go to school? One goal of education is to transmit knowledge. Another is to enhance students' capacities to get a good job. Some say that schools should orient students toward a set of shared values in order to facilitate the continuation of a democratic nation. Others say that schools should help students develop an understanding of the perspectives of others to promote a peaceful and better society. Still others think schools should teach students to challenge authority, reject accepted opinion, and think for themselves. Of course, if we agree with this last version of what schools should do, then we will expect that lessons will be greatly adjusted and that classroom activities will be changed. Whereas thinking independently is something everybody thinks students should do, they don't always have the opportunity to do so in the classroom.

While maintaining the main ideas and sophisticated language and content of the original text, in the modified text many idiomatic expressions, which are likely to be less familiar to ELLs, are paraphrased (e.g., *to get a good job* for *to earn a good living*; *the continuation of a democratic nation* instead of *the maintenance of a democratic state*; *a peaceful and better society* for *social harmony*; *have the opportunity* for *give them the license*). Furthermore, in the modified text grammatical elements are made more explicit; for example, the auxiliary verbs *will be* are explicitly retained (i.e., *classroom activities will be changed* as compared to *classroom activities radically altered* in the unmodified text). In addition, some sentences were syntactically restructured; for example, depth of embedding of complement clauses was reduced by substituting (e.g., *something everybody thinks students should do instead of something we say we want students to do*.) Finally, some vocabulary words were modified (e.g., *massively* is replaced with *greatly*; *would argue* or *contend* are replaced with *say*).

WHO, WHY, HOW, AND WHEN TO USE MODIFIED TEXTS

Text modification has been used in many L2 contexts in order to provide linguistic input that is more comprehensible to L2 learners. However, like any educational innovation, the conditions of implementation are crucial to generating the desired results. Text modifications should also be introduced with a full awareness of the advantages and disadvantages they offer (Ragan, 2006).

First, the goal of the reading activity needs to be taken into account. Modified text may be appropriate to help achieve certain specific short-term goals, such as learning specific content, but at some cost to the long-term advantages for language learning and comprehension skills, that is, exposure to authentic unmodified text. In other words, if the goal is to prepare for a social studies or science test, modified text can be helpful, but if the goal is to support L2 development, then modified text must be designed to "increase comprehensibility while maintaining essential features typical of unmodified text" (Oh, 2001, p. 91).

Second, it is important to recognize that many learner factors determine whether modified texts will generate improved comprehension. Learners' L2 proficiency levels, learning needs, and background knowledge can all interact with the nature and intensity of text modification. It is particularly important not to continue to offer modified texts to advanced learners who should be learning to deal with authentic texts. It may in some cases be helpful to use modified texts *in addition to* original texts, as a support rather than a substitute.

Third, the context of instruction has to be considered. Modified text may be more helpful when students are learning on their own or working in a group than during guided reading, where the teacher is available to fill in the gaps in background knowledge and to make text more explicit and accessible.

Fourth, the specific goals of a literacy-instruction program can determine whether modified texts will be helpful. For example, if the goal of a lesson is to teach students how to make inferences across several paragraphs, elaborative text with highly explicit text structure and referential repairs may not serve the purpose. However, if the goal is teaching students how to make appropriately constrained inferences about the meanings of unknown vocabulary items, then semantically enriched texts work well. Similarly, if the goal is to help students build fluency by reading with ease and comprehension on their own, then highly motivating simplified or predictable texts may be very valuable, especially for younger learners.

Finally, it is also important to consider whether other instructional strategies can be used instead of modification to achieve the same goal. For example, systematic instruction in reading comprehension strategies and approaches (e.g., *Questioning the Author* by Beck, McKeown, Hamilton, and Kucan, 1998) may help students learn how to engage with the text actively and effectively without the need for modified text.

FUTURE DIRECTIONS IN RESEARCH

Despite the ever-increasing number of ELLs in K–12 settings in the United States, hardly any research has examined the effectiveness of text modification for these students. In particular, a large program of research is needed to generate a nuanced understanding of the relationship between text modification and reading comprehension for students of different developmental stages. Although previous studies have shown that simplification of syntax and vocabulary may not enhance reading comprehension for L2 learners of low English proficiency, these results derive primarily from work with adult L2 learners. Thus, the results of these studies might be limited to readers who are cognitively sophisticated and fluent readers in their native language; furthermore, these previous studies focused on comprehension as the outcome of interest rather than on building early reading skills (word recognition accuracy and fluency, targets of early reading instruction).

It is entirely possible, and indeed seems likely, that text with simplified vocabulary and syntax may facilitate young ELLs' acquisition of basic reading skills (including comprehension) in the early stages of reading development before they have achieved automaticity in recognizing the 2,000-plus most frequently occurring English words. We know very little about what types of text will be most effective for ELLs in primary grades who are learning to read and write for the first time in a language they do not speak proficiently. One framework that involved texts designed to develop reading fluency for primary-grade students is Text Elements by Tasks (TExT) (Hiebert, 2005; Hiebert, Brown, Taitague, Fisher, & Adler, 2003). The TExT framework includes a number of features to support students' development: use of high-interest words that are also highly imageable; systematic introduction of high-frequency and phonetically regular words; texts with words that represent familiar concepts; and repetition of critical content and vocabulary. Though this framework has yet to be tested with young ELLs, its features seem likely to support their reading development, as they do for EO readers. It is not clear, though, whether these same features will support comprehension of slightly more advanced readers, whether ELL or EO.

Therefore, systematic investigation is needed to clarify the interaction between the students' levels and the difficulty of the text. Effectiveness of various modifications may well vary as a function both of the developmental level and of the proficiency of particular readers.

Future studies should expand our understanding of how elaborative modification of text works for ELLs. Our understanding about the effects of text coherence on reading comprehension comes primarily from work with native English speakers. Although what works for native English speakers is likely to work for ELLs, there may be additional modifications that address the specific difficulties and challenges that ELLs face in their comprehension. For example, vocabulary acquisition has shown to be highly critical but very challenging for ELLs. Are there effective ways that elaborative text can foster ELLs' vocabulary knowledge without hampering their reading comprehension? Furthermore, the relationship between students' understanding of anaphoric references and their reading comprehension should be investigated with ELLs of various developmental stages. Future studies also should investigate tradeoffs between instruction and text modification. For example, students can be instructed to pay attention to cohesive devices in order to relate new information to already given information in the text; instruction in recovering anaphoric referents in text may have as much impact on their reading comprehension as strengthening the textual cues to the anaphoras.

Finally, systematic efforts to investigate the effects of text modifications on reading comprehension for ELLs should enable theories of reading comprehension to expand to incorporate L2 and well as L1 readers. Most studies on cognitive processing in comprehension have been limited to native speakers. Studies of ESL or EFL readers have mostly been attempts to solve problems of practice, and thus have typically omitted any theoretical framework explaining how text structure interacts with readers' cognitive processes. Future studies will benefit from systematic, testable, comprehensive models of reading development that provide guidance about the most important points of comparison between first- and second-language readers.

NOTE

1. The order of the authors is alphabetical, indicating the difficulty of determining who contributed more to the writing of the paper.

REFERENCES

Allen, J. (1985). Inferential comprehension: The effects of text source, decoding ability, and mode. *Reading Research Quarterly, 20,* 603–615.

Beck, I. L., McKeown, M. G., Hamilton, R. L., & Kucan, L. (1998). Getting at the meaning: How to help students unpack difficult text. *American Educator, 22*(1 & 2), 66–71, 85.

Beck, I. L., McKeown, M. G., Omanson, R. C., & Pople, M. T. (1984). Improving the comprehensibility of stories: The effects of revisions that improve coherence. *Reading Research Quarterly, 19,* 263–277.

Beck, I. L., McKeown, M. G., Sinatra, M., & Loxterman, A. (1991). Revising social studies from a text-processing perspective: Evidence of improved comprehensibility. *Reading Research Quarterly, 26,* 251–276.

Blau, E. K. (1982). The effect of syntax on readability for ESL students in Puerto Rico. *TESOL Quarterly, 16,* 517–526.

Britton, B. K., & Gülgöz, S. (1991). Using Kintsch's computational model to improve instructional text: Effects of repairing inferences calls on recall and cognitive structures. *Journal of Educational Psychology, 83,* 329–345.

Britton, B. K., Van Dusen, L., Gülgöz, S., & Glynn, S. M. (1989). Instructional texts rewritten by five expert teams: Revisions and retention improvements. *Journal of Educational Psychology, 81,* 226–239.

Brown, R. (1987). A comparison of the comprehensibility of modified and unmodified reading materials for ESL. *University of Hawaii Working Papers in ESL, 6*, 49–79.

Chaudron, C., & Richards, J. C. (1986). The effect of discourse markers on the comprehension of lectures. *Applied Linguistics, 7*, 113–127.

Cirilo, R. K. (1981). Referential coherence and text structure in story comprehension. *Journal of Verbal Learning and Verbal Behavior, 20*, 358–367.

Davison, A. (1984). Readability—Appraising text difficulty. In R. C. Anderson, J. Osborn, & R. J. Tierney (Eds.), *Learning to read in American school: Basal readers and content texts* (pp. 121–139). Hillsdale, NJ: Erlbaum.

Duffy, T. M., Higgins, L., Mehlenbacher, B., Cochran, C., Wallace, D., Hill, C., et al. (1989). Models for the design of instructional text. *Reading Research Quarterly, 14*, 434–437.

Garcia, G. E. (1991). Factors influencing the English reading test performance of Spanish-speaking Hispanic children. *Reading Research Quarterly, 26*, 371–392.

Gernsbacher, M. A. (1989). Mechanisms that improve referential access. *Cognition, 32*, 99–156.

Graves, M. F. (2006). *The vocabulary book: Learning and instruction.* New York: Teachers College, Columbia University.

Hiebert, E. H. (2005). The effects of text difficulty on second graders' fluency development. *Reading Psychology, 26*, 183–209.

Hiebert, E. H., Brown, Z. A., Taitague, C., Fisher, C. W., & Adler, M. A. (2003). Texts and English language learners: Scaffolding entrée to reading. In F. Boyd, C. Brock, & M. Rozendal (Eds.), *Multicultural and multilingual literacy and language practices.* New York: Guilford Press.

Honeyfield, J. (1977). Simplification. *TESOL Quarterly, 11*, 431–440.

Linderholm, T., Everson, M. G., van den Broek, P., Mischinski, M., Crittenden, A., & Samuels, J. (2000). Effects of causal text revisions on more- and less-skilled readers' comprehension of easy and difficult texts. *Cognition and Instruction, 18*(4), 525–556.

Lotherington-Woloszyn, H. (1993). *Do simplified texts simplify language comprehension for ESL learners?* ERIC ED 371-583.

Oh, S. (2001). Two types of input modification and EFL reading comprehension: Simplification versus elaboration. *TESOL Quarterly, 35*(1), 69–96.

Parish, C., & Perkins, K. (1985). Factors influencing anaphoric processing in ESL reading comprehension. *Journal of Research in Reading, 8*, 106–115.

Parker, K., & Chaudron, C. (1987). The effects of linguistic simplification and elaborative modifications on L2 comprehension. *University of Hawaii Working Papers in ESL, 6*, 107–133.

Pretorius, E. J. (2005). English as a second language learner differences in anaphoric resolution: Reading to learn in the academic context. *Applied Psycholinguistics, 26*, 521–539.

Ragan, A. (2006). Using adapted texts in ELL classrooms. *ELL Outlook.* Retrieved May 10, 2007, from *www.coursecrafters.com/ELLOutlook/2006/mar_apr/ELLOutlookITIArticle1.htm.*

RAND Reading Study Group. (2002). *Reading for understanding: Toward an*

R&D program in reading comprehension. Santa Monica, CA: RAND. Available at *www.rand.org/multi/achievementforall/reading/readreport.html*.

Rose, D. H., & Meyer, A. (2002). *Teaching every student in the digital age: Universal design for learning*. Alexandria, VA: Association for Supervision and Curriculum Development.

Rose, D. H., Meyer, A., & Hitchcock, C. (2005). *The universally designed classroom: Accessible curriculum and digital technologies*. Cambridge, MA: Harvard Education Press.

van Dijk, T. A., & Kintsch, W. (1983). *Strategies of discourse comprehension*. New York: Academic Press.

Vidal-Abarca, E., Martinez, G., & Gilabert, R. (2000). Two procedures to improve instructional text: Effects on memory and learning. *Journal of Educational Psychology, 92,* 1–10.

Yano, Y., Long, M. H., & Ross, S. (1994). The effect of simplified and elaborated texts on foreign language reading comprehension. *Language Learning, 44,* 189–219.

Young. D. J. (1999). Linguistic simplification of SL reading material: Effective instructional practice? *The Modern Language Journal, 83,* 350–366.

Part III

Instructional Strategies for Adapting Texts for Beginning and Struggling Readers

8

Text–Reader Matching

Meeting the Needs of Struggling Readers

HEIDI ANNE E. MESMER
STACI CUMMING

In 2005, Allington identified text–reader matching as one of the pillars missing from the five forwarded in the National Reading Panel (NRP) Report (NICHD, 2000). He argued that in addition to phonics, phonemic awareness, comprehension, fluency, and vocabulary instruction, text–reader matching was an essential element of literacy instruction. We agree. In beginning this section of chapters on choosing and adapting texts for readers, we have focused specifically on struggling readers for four reasons. First, many struggling readers are being asked to read books that are simply too hard (Allington, 2001; Atkinson, Wilhite, Frey, & Williams, 2002; Biancarosa & Snow, 2004; O'Connor et al., 2005). Second, for struggling readers, the consequences of text–reader mismatches are disastrous and far-reaching. Often these students fall further and further behind their peers until they are eventually (and possibly inappropriately) identified as having specific learning disabilities (Stanovich, 1985). Making sure that struggling readers have books that they can read is an absolute imperative. Third, we have noticed that struggling readers often do not have access to the powerful textual scaffolds that are appropriate to their stages of developments, like decodability (Jager Adams, Chapter 2, this volume) or pacing (Hiebert & Martin, Chapter 3, this volume). However, our fourth and most important reason for addressing text choices for struggling readers is that text–reader matching is often overlooked.

As a school psychologist and literacy professor working intensely with a school under the auspices of a No Child Left Behind (NCLB) professional development grant, we could not ignore the larger context within which text–reader matching takes place in schools. Reading First has situated reading interventions front and center through the use of literacy-screening and progress-monitoring assessments. The purpose of assessments like the Dynamic Indicators of Basic Early Literacy Skills (DIBELS; Good & Kaminski, 2002), Phonological Awareness Literacy Screening (PALS; Invernizzi, Juel, Swank, & Meier, 2005), or Texas Primary Reading Inventory (TPRI; Texas Education Agency & University of Texas System, 2006), is to identify children who will likely struggle in reading and to provide these children with targeted early-intervention instruction in specific areas (e.g., phonemic awareness, decoding, fluency). Although we agree with strong, targeted intervention instruction in specific skills, one of the simplest and most overlooked forms of intervention for struggling readers is substantial reading practice (Allington, 2001; O'Connor et al., 2002). Specifically, struggling readers need a high volume of on-level reading in materials that match their developmental needs. When we work with struggling readers, we often discover that they do not read materials at their reading levels. Thus, many of the struggling readers that we identified using literacy-screening devices, needed targeted interventions that focused on connected reading in appropriate materials, more so than specific-skills instruction.

We also could not ignore the link between the early-intervention instruction forwarded by Reading First and response to intervention (RTI) (Fuchs & Fuchs, 2006; International Reading Association, 2007), a new option for identifying children with specific learning disabilities under the Individuals with Disabilities Education Act (IDEA). Essentially, RTI asserts that struggling readers should be identified as possessing a specific learning disability based on the degree to which they respond to appropriate, scientifically based instruction. Children who respond slowly, or not at all, to instruction are likely to possess specific learning disabilities and require the most intensive and explicit types of instruction. Fuchs and Fuchs (2006) describe the connections between Reading First policies and RTI, "Many of the same policymakers behind RTI were also responsible for Reading First . . . which requires school to use scientific knowledge to guide selection of core curricula and to use valid screening measures. . . . In a sense, RTI may be understood as an important aspect of Reading First and current educational policy" (p. 94). Thus, RTI is inextricably linked to the screening and progress-monitoring instruments that we now see in schools because these assessments essentially establish the system for using an RTI model. Furthermore, literacy professionals are noting the importance of RTI (International Reading Association, 2006). In the February/March issue of *Reading Today*, 75% of leading literacy professionals believed that RTI should be a "hot topic" (Cassidy & Cassidy, 2007). In July of 2007, the International Reading Association (IRA) issued additional recommendations for reading teachers, schools, and administrators using an RTI model. Because text choices for struggling readers often occur within the context of intervention instruction, and sometimes coincide with special education considerations, we have framed the text interventions in this chapter using an RTI model. There are many forms of appropriate intervention instruction, but in this chapter we will focus on appropriate text–reader matching. Our purposes are to (1) briefly describe RTI; (2) affirm text–reader matching as imperative instructional intervention; (3) provide a theoretical framework for matching struggling readers to appropriate texts; and (4) illustrate how to select texts for different struggling readers.

RESPONSIVENESS TO INTERVENTION

Traditionally, students with learning disabilities (LD) have been identified through the application of the "discrepancy model" forwarded by the 1977 federal definition of LD (Francis et al., 2005). Under this model, students were identified as having a reading disability when their IQ and reading achievement test scores differed significantly. Criticism of the discrepancy model has been extensive and has culminated in three major points of contention (e.g., Aaron, 1997; Fletcher et al., 1998; Francis et al., 2005; O'Malley, Francis, Foorman, Fletcher, & Swank, 2002; Vellutino, Scanlon, & Lyon, 2000). First, struggling readers possessing a discrepancy between IQ and achievement and struggling readers who do not demonstrate such a discrepancy do not qualitatively differ in their abilities or instructional needs (Fletcher et al., 1998; Vellutino et al., 2000). Second, the discrepancy model fails to provide information about the type of instruction that would benefit the learner (Aaron, 1997). Third, the discrepancy model is not proactive and it in fact requires that the problem becomes significantly severe in terms of an IQ/achievement discrepancy before the student can receive special services (Vaughn & Fuchs, 2003). This criticism is called *wait to fail*.

   In 2004, after years of research and scrutiny, the federal government amended the special education law (IDEA: Public Law 108-446) and its guidelines for identifying children with specific learning disabilities. The new regulations permit schools to used RTI procedures as an alternative to the discrepancy model in identifying students for special education. Specifically, the law states that schools "Must permit the use of a process that determines if the child responds to scientific, research-based intervention as a part of the evaluation procedures (300.307 (a) (3))."

The notion underlying RTI is that a student is identified as learning disabled when he or she responds poorly, or fails to respond, to a reliably implemented, research-based intervention (Fuchs, Mock, Morgan, & Young, 2003; Gresham, 2002; Vaughn & Fuchs, 2003; Vellutino & Scanlon, 1987). In the RTI model, interventions and services are provided for students in a three-tiered approach with intensity of intervention increasing at each tier (Fuchs, Fuchs, & Speece, 2002; Marston, 2005; Vaughn & Fuchs, 2003). All students participate in Tier 1, which consists of evidenced-based reading instruction in the regular classroom. As individual-reading progress is monitored, those students who are *not* demonstrating adequate growth are targeted for Tier 2 intervention. In Tier 2, students participate in intensive, small-group or one-on-one interventions aimed at preventing reading difficulties. Also taking place during this tier is the assessment of "responsiveness" to these interventions. The majority of students are expected to "respond" to the interventions in this tier, and once this growth has taken place they are dismissed from the intervention group. Special education eligibility is considered for those students who fail to respond to intervention, and they are transitioned to Tier 3, which is the equivalent of special education (Fuchs & Fuchs, 2006; Gersten & Dimino, 2006; Gresham, 2002).

This chapter describes text–reader matching within an RTI context because over 80% of students with learning disabilities struggle in reading, and we believe, as does the IRA, that classroom and reading teachers must be involved with forming interventions for these struggling readers (Fuchs & Fuchs, 2006; International Reading Association, 2006; Lyon, 1995a, 1995b). If we can provide students with brief interventions in Tier 2, we increase the number of proficient readers and reduce the number of students who are identified as LD. Furthermore, under the current system, many children who are identified for special education may not in fact possess specific learning disabilities but may be "instructionally disabled" (Vellutino, Scanlon, & Sipay, 1996) or disabled by a lack of experience in reading (Cunningham & Stanovich, 1997; O'Connor et al., 2002). One of the best outcomes of RTI work is that researchers have been able to establish whether struggling readers are learning disabled.

By implementing RTI procedures, intensive instruction would be provided to these students in Tier 2, and they would be brought up to speed without being inappropriately labeled as LD. The RTI model will require special educators, classroom teachers, reading specialists, speech/language pathologists, and school psychologists to work together to help children (International Reading Association, 2007). Thus, reading and classroom teachers must possess a basic working knowledge of RTI to work effectively within this model (International Reading Association, 2006).

TEXT–READER MATCHING AS AN INTERVENTION

Intervention instruction is different from other forms of literacy instruction. From the perspective of RTI, intervention instruction differs from classroom instruction in that it is likely to be more intense and specific, more individualized, linked to more frequent assessment, and it is likely to require more data-based documentation and continuous progress monitoring (Fuchs & Fuchs, 2006; Gersten & Dimino, 2006; International Reading Association, 2007). For instance, classroom instruction in first grade might include a focus on decoding words along with guided reading, independent reading, word study, writing, vocabulary, and comprehension; however, intervention instruction for a small group of students in a first-grade classroom might focus almost exclusively on decoding. Teachers using an RTI model collect data as they are implementing their intervention instruction to evaluate the effectiveness of their teaching. The teacher implementing this decoding intervention would assess student progress weekly and maintain records of progress.

For some, the term *intervention* might summon one of several early-intervention programs created in the late 1980s that integrated phonics, writing, sight word learning, and text reading (see Clay 1985; Morris, 2006; Roller, 1998). These tutoring interventions all included text–reader matching but not in the same way that we propose. Many of the aforementioned interventions favored one specific type of text, qualitatively leveled text, a finding supported in a recent survey (Mesmer, 2006). Qualitatively leveled texts are books ordered by assigning holistic difficulty labels that integrate many different text features, including those related to language, content, and format (see Mesmer, 2008). Like other authors, we propose using many different types of texts (e.g., decodable, vocabulary-controlled) to coincide with particular developmental needs, as opposed to relying on one type of material (Brown, 1999; Cole, 1998; Mesmer, 1999, 2004; Hicks & Villaume, 2000; Hiebert, 1998; Vadasy, Sanders, & Peyton, 2005).

We align our work with what is called the *problem-solving method*, an approach to RTI that involves creating individualized interventions for struggling readers (Fuchs & Fuchs, 2006). Like IRA (2007), we note, that there is no "one size fits all" model for RTI. Problem solving begins with a careful analysis of key diagnostic information and then builds instruction based on that data. Teachers determine the magnitude of the problem, analyze the causes, and design a goal-oriented intervention. Then, they measure their goal throughout the intervention. The data that are collected throughout the intervention indicate the degree to which the intervention is meeting the student's needs and allows the teacher to alter instruction. In this chapter, we contend that text–reader matching is, itself, an intervention for use within an RTI context and one that should be implemented frequently for struggling readers. In using a problem-solving approach to choose texts for struggling readers, we note that no one text will work for all students. Instead, we choose different texts, matched to different developmental needs to help struggling readers, and then we document the progress that readers make with appropriate texts.

Text–Reader Matching: A Theoretical Framework

We assert that text–reader matches that are in line with development form an important intervention for struggling readers. Our goal in this chapter is show teachers, administrators, literacy coaches, and reading specialists how to match struggling readers with appropriate texts and how to document progress in those texts. Matching readers with texts involves understanding texts, understanding readers, and understanding when a good match has been made. [*Note.* To avoid awkward prose, we refer to the process of matching readers with appropriates texts as "text–reader" matching. By putting the term *text* before *reader* we do not mean to imply that the reader is of secondary importance. In fact, the reader is the central factor in making a match.]

Text

We begin by defining what we mean by *text*. The word *text* can mean a body of a work, a book, a manuscript, a passage, a textbook, content, or even wording. Literally, *text* derives from the Middle English word *texte*, meaning written account (Houghton Mifflin, 2006). While it is true that a single word, or even a single character, can give a written account, in this chapter we use the term *text* to describe connected pieces of print in continuous formats, like books or passages. From our perspective, a text is an extended piece presented with its complete context. Text is not an isolated word, sentence, or other part presented away from its larger context. For example, we would consider a simple 8-page preprimer with 75 words to be a text, but we would not consider a 75-word excerpt from a lengthier work to be a text.

For quite some time, researchers have investigated which text elements to consider in making text–reader matches (see Chall & Dale, 1995; Harrison, 1980; Hoffman, 2002; Klare, 1963; Mesmer, 2008; Zipf, 1935). From our perspective, this chapter does not permit a full discussion of these. Instead, we will briefly address three types of texts that we have found to be useful in working with struggling readers. These are decodable texts, materials with vocabulary control, and high-interest, low-readability (high-low) materials.

Teachers reportedly use decodable text judiciously for specific purposes like teaching decoding or working with struggling readers (Mesmer, 2006). Decodable text supports readers in sounding out words and is characterized by (1) regular relationships between letters and sounds and (2) a correspondence between the letter–sounds appearing in text and those that the reader has been taught (Mesmer, 2001a, 2001b). Consistently, researchers find that decodable texts repeat particular word parts such as rimes or phonograms (e.g., *-at, -ack, -ash*), keeping the vowel patterns consistent (Cunningham et al., 2005; Hoffman, Roser, Salas, Patterson, & Pennington, 2001; Juel & Roper/Schneider, 1985; Menon & Hiebert, 2005). In decodable texts, the presented letter-sounds consistently map onto a focal pattern and representations that do not conform to this focal pattern, are not presented. For instance, if the focus of a book is short /o/, then words containing *o*s would represent the short /o/ sound (e.g., *hot, stop, box, shop*) and not other sounds (e.g., *boot, fort, hope, boat, broil*). Decodable texts assist readers when they are ready to fully sound out and blend words but have not yet gained control over the many vowel patterns in English.

Instructional consistency is the match between the words in text and the phonics instruction or letter–sound knowledge of the reader (Foorman, Francis, Davidson, Harm, & Griffin, 2004; Mesmer, 2001a; Stein, Johnson, & Gutlohn, 1999). If words are to be "decodable," then a reader must possess the required letter–sound knowledge to decode the words. If a reader has received instruction in the sounds /a/ and /e/ or demonstrates knowledge of these sounds, then instructional consistency would be high in decodable materials focusing on these patterns (e.g., *has, pat, get, fat*). High-quality decodable books combine rhyming, repetition, engaging pictures, and letter–sound consistency in materials that are both engaging *and* decodable.

Vocabulary control is defined by *The Literacy Dictionary* (Harris & Hodges, 1995) as, "the practice of limiting the rate of introduction of new words, as in basal reading texts" (p. 275). Vocabulary-controlled materials pace the introduction of new words within and across stories (Cunningham et al., 2005; Hiebert, 1999; Hoffman, 2002). For example, Book A might introduce the words, *come, at*, and *go*, and Book B would repeat these and then introduce the new words, *like* and *see*. Often, vocabulary-controlled materials systematically introduce and repeat high-frequency words, the most frequently occurring words in English. In our second case, we will show materials that control science vocabulary. Vocabulary-controlled materials maintain tight ratios between new and total words (Hiebert, 1998; Hiebert & Mesmer, 2006). To properly use vocabulary-controlled materials, teachers should use the stories sequentially.

As Hiebert (Chapter 1, this volume) discusses, vocabulary control has almost faded from beginning reading materials (Foorman et al., 2004; Hiebert et al., 2005; Hiebert, 2005). These materials seem to be underutilized and may have particular benefits for struggling readers (Hiebert & Fisher, 2002; Rashotte & Torgeson, 1985). Struggling students in one study were more fluent when rereading materials with vocabulary control than when rereading other materials (Rashotte & Torgeson, 1985). In another study, second graders were more fluent in the vocabulary-controlled materials than in other materials (Hiebert & Fisher, 2002). Vocabulary-controlled text builds confidence because it builds on the basic learning principles of repetition and practice. Both vocabulary-controlled and decodable materials are frequently present in primary classrooms, but many struggling readers are developmentally at the beginning stages of reading and would benefit from the use of these materials.

The last text type that we have found helpful with struggling readers is high-interest, low-readability (high-low) materials. These materials contain topics that interest students in the intermediate grades, but difficulties that match below-grade-level performance (Spadorcia, 2005). These texts are written at lower levels but contain content that would be appealing to more mature students. For example, a fourth grader might read at a second grade level but might not be interested by texts written for second graders. High-low materials would be written at a second grade level but focus on topics of interest to a fourth grader. Spadorcia (2005) analyzed 180 high-low materials and found a large cluster of literature-based books that conformed to high-low standards. Graves & Liang (2004), and Worthy (1996) also have lists of high–low literature that are especially motivating to struggling readers. High-interest–low-readability materials fill a gap for struggling readers in the intermediate grades.

The difficulty of high-low materials is estimated using readability formulas. Readability formulas estimate the difficulty of books by assigning grade levels and months (Klare, 1974). The formulas are mathematical equations that use two text features to predict text difficulty. Most readability formulas rely on word-level estimates like word difficulty (based on a list of easy words) or word length (Chall & Dale, 1995). Formulas also take into account sentence length. There are many readability formulas, including the most recent iterations such as Lexiles, but they are all based on similar text features.

Readers

Often struggling readers are delayed in their development, but they nonetheless will progress through research-based developmental continua. A strong text–reader match depends upon pinpointing the reader's development, understanding the next steps for that reader, and knowing how texts will move the reader developmentally. We ground our discussions of development in the research-based theory of word recognition because struggling readers overwhelmingly falter at the word level (Ehri & McCormick, 1998; Stanovich, 1985). Readers progress through five phases of word recognition differentiated primarily by the application of various types of orthographic knowledge (Chall, 1983; Ehri, 2005; Juel & Minden-Cupp, 2000; Samuels, 1994). Ultimately, readers must become fluent and automatic in their word reading so that the majority of their cognitive focus is on comprehension (Samuels, 1994).

In the first phase, *prealphabetic*, readers do not use letter–sounds to identify words. Instead, they use paired associations to predict words (Ehri & McCormick, 1998; Juel, Griffith, & Gough, 1986). At this stage, readers may use cues such as the two os in the word *look* or a picture on the page. Although prealphabetic strategies are typical of normal development, they pose problems. Many words, for example, have double os. Prealphabetic readers must acquire concept of word, the alphabetic principle, and letter–sound knowledge. In the *partial-alphabetic* phase, readers use letter–sound knowledge to identify words (Bryne & Fielding-Barnsley, 1989, 1991; Morris, Bloodgood, Lomax, & Perney, 2005). However, partial alphabetic readers rely mostly on beginning sounds and consonant knowledge. They must learn how to decode vowels and fully blend sounds together. At the third phase, *full-alphabetic* reading, readers use all letters, including the vowels, and blend phonemes to identify words (Ehri, 1991, 1995; Ehri & McCormick, 1998; Gough & Hillinger, 1980; Gough & Juel, 1991; Juel, 1994). Readers at this phase must learn strategies to fully analyze words, and learn multiletter units. In the fourth phase, called *consolidated alphabetic*, readers move away from linear, left-to-right decoding and blending to recognizing and consolidating multiletter units in words (e.g., morphemes, syllables, rimes). In this phase readers are decoding hierarchically, searching for known units to recognize words more quickly. At this phase, readers must learn to decode multisyllable words using morphemes, practicing full decoding, and increasing automatically accessed sight words (Ehri, 2005; Ehri & McCormick, 1998). In the final automatic phase of word recognition, readers are fluent and immediate in recognizing words. They have highly developed strategies and large stores of words that they access by sight. They can recognize words both in and out of context, and the bulk of their mental energy is directed toward comprehension. In each phase, readers are acquiring a new layer of orthographic information to existing knowledge and testing their new knowledge within texts.

Text–Reader Matching

Having briefly addressed both texts and readers, we turn now toward defining a *good match*. The literature suggests that a strong text–reader match can be defined operationally, developmentally, and dispositionally. Operationally, on-level reading has been defined by noting either the percentage of words accurately read by the reader and/or the percentage of comprehension questions answered correctly (Betts, 1946; Chall & Dale, 1995; Gambrell, Wilson, & Gantt, 1981; Harrison, 1980; Klare, 1963; 1974; Lennon & Burdick, 2004; Zakuluk & Samuels, 1988). Contrary to policies in some schools, a student's reading level is not synonymous with a student's grade level. Students in a given grade may read materials of different difficulties with various levels of success. Typically, reader performance has been associated with an independent reading level and an instructional reading level. When readers can accurately recognize about 98 to 100% of the words in a text and comprehend about 90% of the text, then the material is at an independent level (Gambrell, Wilson, & Gantt, 1981; Silvaroli & Wheelock, 2004). Recreational reading, or reading at home, should be at this level. When readers can accurately recognize 90 to 95% of the words in a text and comprehend 75% of the material, then the material is at an instructional level (Chall & Dale, 1995; Harrison, 1980; Lennon & Burdick, 2004). Materials used in educational settings, or supported by teachers, are typically at an instructional level. From the perspective of word accuracy and comprehension level, an appropriate match occurs when a reader can accurately decode a certain percentage of words and understand a certain percentage of the comprehension questions. When a reader's word accuracy falls below 90%, then materials are called *frustrational*, and an appropriate match between text and reader does not exist.

Simply securing the requisite word accuracy and comprehension levels is not sufficient to make an appropriate text–reader match. We have often observed situations in which struggling readers meet the operational parameters of a match (at least 90% word accuracy and 75% comprehension) but are not moving ahead developmentally. For example, a reader might be quite accurate but using a partial-alphabetic strategy to identify words. Developmentally, the reader needs to move on to full decoding words and may require the consistency of a decodable text to do so. Other times, a reader has become fluid in decoding simple words but is ready to cope with the diversity in a more challenging text. Sometimes a reader needs to focus on fluency—accurate, swift, and expressive reading—and needs some repetition of key vocabulary. The point is that teachers must understand the development of readers and know where they need to go next.

Last, when a good text–reader match occurs, the reader is engaged, positive, and interested (Guthrie et al., 2006). We believe that the very first step in promoting a positive attitude is building aptitude. Very few people can be happy about doing something that they do poorly. Struggling readers are usually quite perceptive about their abilities, and they know when they are making legitimate progress in reading. As we are helping readers to learn how to accurately and fluently decode and comprehend a text, we give attention to their engagement. We ask them about the books that they are reading. We offer choices amongst appropriate texts. We read aloud materials that interest them. We inquire about their personal interests. We seize upon opportunities that provide authentic purposes for reading. In making a text–reader match, we must pay attention to engagement because this is the essential, personal connection that helps struggling readers use their literacy skills to meet personal goals.

We know that a reader is matched to appropriate material when he or she can identify at least 90% of the words and comprehend 75% of ideas in text. However, operational definitions are not sufficient to make a good text–reader match. A good match also must address readers' developmental needs, be they decoding competencies, fluency, transition into content-area materials, or comprehension. Finally, when readers are matched to appropriate text, they are engaged and motivated. They see literacy as meeting their personal needs, desires, and goals.

A TEXT INTERVENTION FOR A STRUGGLING READER AT THE BEGINNING STAGES OF READING

Jared was a second-grade student who had been identified by school-wide screenings as being at risk of failing to make adequate reading progress. His classroom teacher confirmed this noting that Jared was struggling to read the required materials in her class. Specifically, she indicated that Jared took an extremely long time to read assigned grade-level texts and that he frequently could recall little about what he had read once he read it. She was concerned that Jared might have a specific learning disability in reading and that he might be better served in special education. Before making a special education referral and testing, we relied on an RTI paradigm to test Jared's response to a carefully designed intervention.

Based on teacher reports, we decided that we first needed to evaluate Jared's in-class reading. We reviewed both the texts that Jared was expected to read and his accuracy in reading them. In class, the teacher primarily used three sources of reading materials: a basal reader, trade books, and a decodable reader (for the struggling readers). In the basal reader, running records indicated that Jared was reading with approximately 75% word-recognition accuracy and 70% comprehension. Jared's word-recognition accuracy increased to 80% in the decodable text, but comprehension remained at 70%. These data indicated that Jared was functioning within the frustrational range with this material. We would expect at least 90% word accuracy for instructional materials with beginning readers and closer to 75% comprehension (Betts, 1946; Chall & Dale, 1995; Harrison, 1980; Lennon & Burdick, 2004). Figure 8.1 shows the types of materials that Jared was being asked to read in his classroom and samples of the materials that we used for the intervention. The words that he struggled with are shown with strikethroughs. The classroom text samples show multiple errors, especially with multi-syllabic words containing long vowels, and with some high-frequency sight words.

We also used an informal reading inventory (Silvaroli & Wheelock, 2004) to determine Jared's instructional level in terms of different materials. Jared's instructional level was at the preprimer level and he quickly reached his frustrational level with primer materials. Comprehension was a relative strength for Jared in this assessment and he was eager and cooperative. As he was reading the passages, Jared failed to identify, or misidentified, numerous sight words. For example, he could not identify the word *were,* he substituted *when* for *would,* and he substituted *then* for *than.* Jared also struggled to decode words. He would use initial and final letters (e.g., reading *training* for *talking*), or he would try unsuccessfully to sound out words with his limited decoding knowledge. Jared correctly identified 80% of words on the Preprimer and Primer word lists and 65% of words on the first-grade list. Word-recognition errors included words such as *about, could,* and *came,* for which he read *a boat, colored,* and *come* respectively.

Classroom Materials

Passage 1

It was midnight. The light of the full moon followed the tired old car. Tomas was tired too. Hot and tired. He missed his own bed, in his own house in Texas. Tomas was on his way to Iowa again with his family. His mother and father were farm workers. [50 words]

15 errors = 70% accuracy

Passage 2

The big wagons traveled slowly. They were loaded down with picks and axes and plows, kettles and pans. The travelers had to bring most of what they would need. When they got into the West, there would be no shops where they could get things. After the wagons passed a . . . [50 words]

10 errors = 80% accuracy

Intervention Materials

Passage 1

What is a skit?
You act in a skit.
Who acts in skits?
The cast acts in skits.
The cast has a script.
The cast plans the skit.
The cast is in a craft class.
The kids snip bits of scraps.
The cast can color the cats.
You plan your cat. [51 words]

1 error = 98% accuracy

Passage 2

This is Slam. This is Dunk. Slam and Dunk are pals. Slam and Dunk like to play basketball.
It's the big game with the Bobcats.
"Hi, kids!" yell Slam's mom and dad and Dunk's mom and dad.
Then the Bobcats come in.
The Bobcats are BIG! "The Bobcats will win," says Dunk. [52 words]

1 error = 98% accuracy

FIGURE 8.1. Sample classroom and intervention passages. Errors are shown by strikethrough. Classroom materials: Passage 1 is from Mora (2002); passage 2 is from Rasmussen and Goldberg (2000). *Intervention materials:* Passage 1 is from Donovan (1998); passage 2 is from Sawyer (1998).

Jared was reading at the partial-alphabetic phase, using initial letter clues and context to predict words (Ehri & McCormick, 1998). The many word errors with similar beginning sounds confirmed this. In grade-level materials, the strategy was resulting in high rates of inaccuracy, as many words, especially content words, cannot be guessed accurately. Based on this assessment data we developed an intervention with several components. Our goal was to identify materials that (1) would build his knowledge of high-frequency words, (2) would assist Jared in developing full alphabetic skills, and (3) could be read with at least 90% accuracy.

Our first text choice was designed to build Jared's fluency with high-frequency words. We identified materials with vocabulary control, introducing and repeating high-frequency words. As described earlier, these materials present to the reader many words that he or she has already seen and systematically present only a few new words. Like many struggling readers, Jared needed repeated exposure to and practice with high-frequency words to build his competency. The sight word readers that we used allowed him to practice these words in context without being overwhelmed. We also practiced the words in isolation for 1 minute either before or after the readings. Although, there was not always a complete match between the words practiced in isolation and those in connected text, an attempt was made to be as consistent as possible.

The second component of Jared's intervention was focused on building proficiency with blending words with short vowels. To address this need, we identified decodable readers with a high concentration of short-vowel words. The consistency in vowel patterns would assist Jared in practicing blending without begin overwhelmed by many different patterns. The books selected at the beginning of the intervention tended to focus on one or two short vowels at a time (e.g., short /a/ and /i/) in combination with consonant blends (e.g., *What is a Skit*, see Figure 8.1 for a brief section of the text). As Jared continued to progress, books were selected in which multiple short vowels were presented and practiced (e.g., *Slam and Dunk: The Big Game*, see Figure 8.1). Efforts were also made to find books that included consonant blends (e.g., *sk, scr, sn,* and *st* in *What is a Skit,* see Figure 8.1). The goal was to find and use books in which a high concentration of short-vowel words were presented.

Jared was asked to reread all materials numerous times throughout our sessions. Typically, a lesson would begin with a cold (unpracticed) and hot (practiced) rereading of the books that we had read in the previous lesson. Then, each book that was introduced in the lesson was read at least three times during the session. While one might think that this would be a taxing process for Jared, we actually found that he liked the rereadings as he could see how he was getting better with each subsequent rereading. Jared's word-recognition accuracy data for four decodable and four vocabulary-controlled books over four rereading are presented in Figure 8.2. The data show that Jared's accuracy in both decodable and vocabulary-controlled texts improved in each book from the first to the fourth cold reading. Furthermore, Jared's accuracy on each first reading of a book increased across both the decodable and vocabulary-controlled books.

In terms of RTI, we had identified Jared as at risk for failing to meet reading goals. After interviews with his teacher and a review of the materials that he was reading, we came up with a simple intervention focused on making a text–reader match that met operational and developmental definitions. The intervention was implemented, and progress-monitoring data for 8 weeks indicated that Jared was making sufficient growth with the intervention. In fact, he met the reading goals that we had established. Thus, it was determined that as long as Jared continued to "respond" to the intervention, formal assessment and placement in special education (Tier 3) was unnecessary.

A TEXT INTERVENTION FOR AN
INTERMEDIATE STRUGGLING READER

Tamara was a fourth grader, who was identified by the schoolwide literacy screening, Dynamic Indicators of Basic Early Literacy Skills (DIBELS) as requiring Tier 2 instructional support (Good & Kaminski, 2002). Within the first month of school, Tamara read three passages with read-

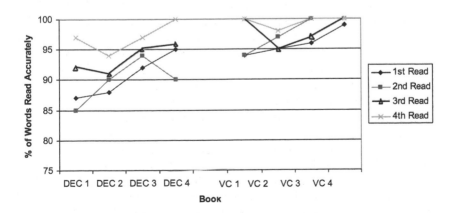

FIGURE 8.2. Jared's reading accuracy data.

ing rates of 80, 75, and 74 words correct per minute (wcpm), respectively. Her median score, 75, was significantly below the expectation of 93 wcpm at the beginning of fourth grade. Initially, Tamara's teacher did not believe that a targeted intervention was appropriate and stated that Tamara was slow in her reading but accurate. At the beginning of November, however, Tamara's teacher approached us with a seemingly different problem. Tamara was not completing her work on time, had troubles with comprehension, was not doing well in science, and was beginning to be rebellious and uncooperative.

We began by readministering a DIBELS fluency measure and found that Tamara read about 74 wcpm, a score that had remained stagnant since September and one that would compare even less favorably to the mid-year expectation of 105 wcpm. We agreed with the teacher that the fluency score, itself, was only one piece of data and limited at best. We administered the Analytical Reading Inventory, 8th Edition (ARI-8; Woods & Moe, 2007), including both narrative and expository texts and an attitude inventory (McKenna & Kear, 1999). Figure 8.3 shows the summary of these data. Both her readings of narrative and expository texts showed no more than four errors, yet her comprehension was not adequate and was worse in expository texts like the science books that she was required to read. For narrative passages, Tamara's comprehension placed her in third-grade-level materials instructionally and second grade or lower materials for independent reading. We found no patterns in the types of comprehension errors that Tamara made; she missed both text-explicit and text-implicit questions. In expository science texts, Tamara's performance was worse. She read independently at the first- to second-grade level and frustrated at third-grade level. Anecdotally, we observed that she had difficulty making sense of the science concepts described in the passages. Even when she did get questions right, it seemed that she was relying on basic recall and would have had difficulty discussing the concepts in her own words. In addition, listening to her read orally confirmed that the prosodic elements of fluency including expression, appropriate pausing, and automaticity were missing. She read without expression, was somewhat choppy and halting, and would often pause for 5 seconds or more before pronouncing some words. When we analyzed the word list reading that she did as part of the ARI-8, we noticed that she struggled with words like *scientific, nervous,* and *sparrow* that possessed multiple syllables and fell in the scientific domain. Last, when we looked at Tamara's attitude inventory, we found that her scores were 27 for recreational reading and 25 for academic reading, and both were below the 50th percentile for fourth grade. Her recreational score was at the 35th percentile, and her academic score was at the 40th percentile. Tamara was not at all happy about reading and did not see her-

Measure	Results	Comments
DIBELS Fluency Measure	September 80 Words correct/minute (wcpm) 75 wcpm 74 wcpm November 74 wcpm	
Analytical Reading Inventory Word List	Level Words correct Primer 20/20 1 20/20 2 19/20 3 16/20 4 15/20	*ever* for *everything* *patent* for *patient* *mainly* for *manage* no response for *arithmetic* *science* for *scientific* *fiesta* for *festival* *nerves* for *nervous* *after* for *afford* *spa* for *sparrow*
Analytical Reading Inventory Narrative passages	Level Word errors ?s correct 1 0 6/6 2 2 5/6 3 2 6/8 4 4 4/8 Independent Reading Level 1-2 Instructional Reading Level 3 Frustrational Reading Level 4	 Missed one explicit and one inferential question Missed two explicit and two inferential questions *Note*: Reading very choppy and stilted. Many pauses. No expression.
Analytical Reading Inventory Expository Science passages	Level Word errors ?s correct 1 0 5/6 2 3 4/6 3 5 3/8 4 8 3/8 Independent Reading Level 1-2 Instructional Reading Level Frustrational Reading Level 3-4	Missed one explicit question Missed one inferential and one explicit question Missed three inferential and two explicit questions Missed two inferential and two explicit questions *Note*: Had difficulty understanding the communication of science concepts like matter and sound waves. Could not smoothly give answers to questions from these texts.

FIGURE 8.3. Tamara's diagnostic information.

self as a capable reader. When we inquired further with Tamara's teacher about her recreational reading during the school day, we learned that Tamara typically chose very simple books and was often bored.

Tamara was transitioning to automatic reading. Although she was accurate, she was not automatic and was likely investing a great deal of energy in decoding. As Rasinski (2000) asserted in an article titled "Speed does matter in reading," for many students like Tamara, lack of fluency deteriorates motivation, decreases the amount of reading that students do, and compromises comprehension. Rasinski's statement is backed by a robust line of research verifying that fluency and comprehension are strongly related (Fuchs, Fuchs, Hosp, & Jenkins, 2001; Jenkins, Fuchs, van den Broek, Espin, & Deno, 2003; Kuhn & Stahl, 2003). In fact, researchers have attributed "the fourth-grade slump," a decline in reading performance beginning in fourth grade, to a lack of fluency and automaticity (Chall & Jacobs, 2003).

Like the other readers in this chapter, Tamara needed specific instruction that related to text–reader matching. Our Tier 2 intervention goals included: (1) increasing Tamara's fluency in expository science texts by two words correct per week, (2) increasing her comprehension of expository science texts, and (3) engaging her in more on-level recreational reading. Our intervention included repeated reading of science texts, answering questions about scientific concepts, and keeping a recreational reading log. Given Tamara's fluency problem, we began by identifying easy science passages, no harder than third grade, for Tamara to read and reread. We found a number of materials related to science topics including, Delta Science Readers, FOSS Science Stories, and STC Readers, but we liked Quick Reads the best because the set of science-related passages employed vocabulary control. As discussed earlier, vocabulary-controlled materials introduce new words and repeat familiar words systematically, keeping type/token ratios stable. The Quick Reads systematically introduced and repeated difficult science words over thematically unified sets of three passages. For instance, in a set that we used on simple machines, key vocabulary such as *force, lever, wedge,* and *inclined plane,* were not all introduced within the first passage. Instead, only a few new science words were introduced in the first passage, and then a few more in the second, and so on. In addition, when a new word was introduced, it was repeated several times throughout the passage so that the reader would have many exposures to it. This text feature provided Tamara with more support in reading and learning science words and provided her the opportunity to become confident with one new science word before another one was introduced. In addition, the Quick Reads, focused on keeping nonscience words within the most frequently occurring in English, and thereby easier.

Each section of Quick Reads contained a set of five thematically related passages with controlled vocabulary. Drawing on the research about the effectiveness of repeated readings, we formulated a four-step intervention. Every week, Tamara worked on a set of five Quick Reads passages. Each day, she listened as an adult or peer read one of the passages. Then, she practiced rereading the passage herself at least three times during the day. For each of the three readings, she timed herself for 1 minute, recorded the number of wcpm, and graphed the number of wcpm on a bar graph. At the end of the day, Tamara also reread the passage a fourth time for her reading teacher and discussed the concepts in the passage.

In addition to rereading science texts, we asked Tamara to complete the Quick Reads questions at the end of the section of passages and to discuss the content again with her classroom teacher. For the other materials that we used, we asked her to explain concepts that she learned orally, and we showed her how to go back to the text to clarify her understanding. The strategy of looking back was useful for Tamara because she was familiar with the passages through rereading. She became more fluid with the science concepts and engaged in explaining them. We also wanted to increase her on-level recreational reading because she had been floundering in that area. Fortunately, Tamara's independent level was at the second-grade level, so we could locate materials for her. We discovered that part of her problem with finding materials was that the books on her reading level all looked "babyish." She wanted chapter books that resembled the chapter books that others in her class were reading. We accessed some high-interest–low-readability materials with preteen themes (Spadorcia, 2005).

Figure 8.4 shows Tamara's fluency graph. Visually charting and demonstrating progress was intrinsically motivating for Tamara because she could see that she was getting better. The figure shows that Tamara's reading fluency increased with each unpracticed reading. In the first passage, *What is a simple machine?* Tamara read about 70 wcpm, and by the final passage, *Playing on a simple machine,* she was reading 79 wcpm.

Like many intermediate readers transitioning to reading more demanding content materials, Tamara needed practice with expository science text. She was not comfortable with the patterns and words found in these types of materials. Over the course of 5 weeks, Tamara responded to the intervention by becoming more fluent, comprehending better, and improving her attitude toward reading. Her fluency increased over nine wcpm, nearly meeting the goal we had set of two words correct per week. These results contrasted with the September-to-November progress showing no gains in fluency. The repetition and pacing of difficult, multisyllable words in the Quick Reads allowed

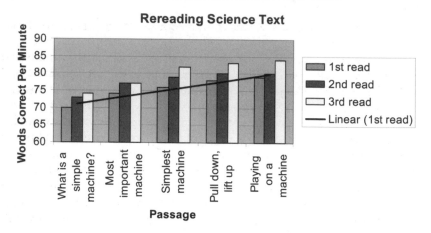

FIGURE 8.4. Tamara's fluency in science text.

Tamara to become more fluent with unfamiliar words. The increased fluency was enabling Tamara to become automatic in her word recognition and therefore to focus more on comprehension (Samuels, 1994). Anecdotally, we learned that Tamara was happier in class and more confident. By asking Tamara to keep a reading log on her recreational reading, we emphasized the importance of personal choices and engagement.

A SMALL-GROUP TEXT INTERVENTION

Although individual interventions are ideal, they are often not possible for logistical reasons. Teachers may not have the time to work with individual readers or to create specific interventions. We found that some struggling readers could be served in small-group text interventions. This final case illustrates how three struggling third graders responded to a text intervention using high–low materials. Nicole, Darren, and Chad were identified in September as not meeting the benchmark score on their state's literacy screening assessment. Subsequently, they were each then given an online reading assessment, the STAR reading test (Renaissance Learning, 2006). This modified cloze test, requires students to identify the correct answer choice that would fill in the blank for a paragraph or sentence. The test then reports an Instructional Reading Level (IRL) and a Grade Equivalent (GE). Although not a comprehensive test of reading comprehension, this assessment provides teachers with an estimate of the student's reading level. From the perspective of RTI, it is useful in that it is one of the few tests of comprehension that can be frequently administered and is approved by the National Center for Progress Monitoring (www.studentprogress.org).

We learned from the assessment that Nicole had an instructional reading level of 2.1; Darren had an instructional level of 2.3; and Chad 2.4. The goal of our intervention was simply to increase their instructional reading levels. Along with their teachers, we decided to meet with them three times per week in a book club to read and discuss books. Given their reading levels, we knew that they would need additional reading experience with materials closer to a second-grade as opposed to a third-grade level. We also noted that the most of the third grade was tackling chapter books, and these students would not be happy reading babyish pictures books. Last, we realized that meeting with the students three times per week would require them to read the books independently.

We decided that high-low materials would meet the needs of these students. We located three different products: (1) Modern Curriculum Press' MCP Early Chapter books, (2) Modern Curriculum Press' MC Comics: The Action Files, written on a 1.5 to 3.5 reading level, and (3) Wright Group's X-Zone materials (e.g., *BMX Racing*, *Autos with Attitude*, *Mini Creatures*). The text features of these materials included captivating, age-appropriate content and controlled difficulty. We chose high–low materials because these students needed to increase their reading in order to become more proficient and to experience reading as an engaging endeavor.

We met with the students from September to December. Each week, we offered the group two to three choices of books at a 2.0 reading level. We used a reading level below the students' instructional levels because we wanted them to read the material independently. As the intervention continued, we increased the reading level of the book choices. We set the page or chapter assignments for each meeting, and the students came to the book club ready to discuss the material. (When the students had not done the reading, we asked them to skip the meeting and read the assignment in a special area of the classroom. Because we knew that the materials matched their reading levels, we knew that our request was appropriate.) During the book club, we each posed questions about the book, replied to each other's questions, made predictions for the next section, and set page assignments. Every 2 weeks, each of the readers took the STAR test. Again, this was a simple, reliable assessment for progress monitoring as opposed to a full-fledged comprehensive assessment. Figure 8.5 shows the STAR results from September through December. The data indicate that Darren and Chad made significant improvement, advancing their estimated instructional reading levels by about 7 months in only 4 month's time. Nicole, on the other hand, did not. From an RTI standpoint, these data indicate that Nicole did not make the same im-

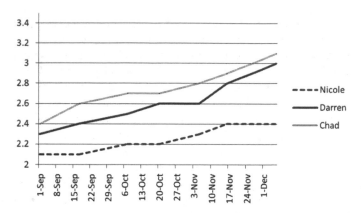

FIGURE 8.5. Nicole, Darren, and Chad's instructional reading estimates (STAR) September through December.

provement. She would require a more powerful intervention perhaps at a different Tier.

CONCLUSIONS

The results that we obtained through each of these text-based interventions substantiated the premise of this chapter; materials appropriately matched to meet students' developmental needs constitute an important intervention for struggling readers. We believe that this message is particularly significant in light of current RTI initiatives. We remind teachers, administrators, reading specialists, and literacy coaches that text–reader matching is a strong instructional intervention and should not get lost in efforts to teach specific skills. Without reading, and lots of it, learners are unlikely to apply the skills that they are learning to connected text. The benefit of applying textual interventions within an RTI framework is that as they are helping students, teachers are acquiring reliable information about a student's response to intervention. Armed with data, teachers can then position themselves to actively participate in discussions of specific learning disabilities, rather than depend on others for testing and evaluation.

We believe that the text interventions we used had four important features. First, they were all tied to development. We were careful to understand each reader's stage of development and to select texts with features matching development. Importantly, we went beyond operational definitions, knowing that struggling readers could sometimes meet requisite word-accuracy levels and not be appropriately matched. Some readers needed materials with pacing, other readers needed materials with decodability, and other readers required certain genres. Second, the progress that readers made within these text interventions was documented. In each case, we were able to document progress, using a reliable and sensitive outcome. This element of our interventions, while different from more naturalistic, observational methods, is required by RTI regulations. Third, all of the text interventions increased the amount of reading that the struggling readers did. In sheer numbers of words, readers were encountering much more text. We implore schools working with struggling readers not to forget the forest for the trees. Reading and comprehending many different types of materials is the ultimate goal that we have for struggling readers, and appropriate text–reader matching is the vehicle for making it happen.

REFERENCES

Aaron, P. G. (1997). The impending demise of the discrepancy formula. *Review of Educational Research, 67*, 461–502.

Allington, R. L. (2001). You can't learn much from books you can't read. *Educational Leadership, 60*(3), 16–19

Atkinson, T. S., Wilhite, K. L., Frey, L. M., & Williams, S. C. (2002). Reading instruction for the struggling reader: Implications for teachers of students with learning disabilities or emotional/behavioral disorders. *Preventing School Failure, 46*, 158–166.

Betts, E. A. (1946). Foundations of reading instruction. New York: American Book.

Biancarosa, G., & Snow, C. (2004). *Reading next: A vision for action and research in middle and high school literacy—A report to Carnegie Corporation of New York*. Washington, DC: Alliance for Excellent Education.

Brown, K. (1999). What kind of text—For whom and when? Textual scaffolding for beginning readers. *The Reading Teacher, 53*, 292–307.

Bryne, B., & Fielding-Barnsley, R. (1989). Phonemic awareness and letter knowledge in the child's acquisition of the alphabetic principle. *Journal of Educational Psychology, 81*, 313–321.

Bryne, B., & Fielding-Barnsley, R. (1991). Evaluation of a program to teach phonemic awareness to young children. *Journal of Educational Psychology,83*, 43–55.

Cassidy, J., & Cassidy, D. (2007). What's hot, what's not for 2007. *Reading Today, 24*(4), 1.

Chall, J. S. (1983). *Stages of reading development*. New York: McGraw-Hill.

Chall, J. S., & Dale, E. (1995). *Readability revisited: The new Dale–Chall readability formula*. Cambridge, MA: Brookline Books.

Chall, J. S., & Jacobs, V. A. (2003). Poor children's fourth-grade slump. *American Educator, 27*(1), 14–15.

Clay, M. M. (1985). *The early detection of reading difficulties*. Portsmouth, NH: Heinemann.

172 INSTRUCTIONAL STRATEGIES FOR ADAPTING TEXTS

Cole, A. (1998). Beginner-oriented texts in literature-based classrooms: The segue for a few struggling readers. *The Reading Teacher, 51*, 488–501.

Cunningham, A. E., & Stanovich, K. E. (1997). Early reading acquisition and its relation to reading experience and ability 10 years later. *Developmental Psychology, 33*(6), 934–945.

Cunningham, J. W., Spadorcia, S. A., Erickson, K., Koppenhaver, D. A., Sturm, J. M., & Yoder, D. E. (2005). Investigating the instructional supportiveness of leveled texts. *Reading Research Quarterly, 40*, 410–427.

Donovan, B. (1998). *What is a skit?* San Francisco: Gateway Learning.

Ehri, L. C. (1991). Learning to read and spell words. In L. Rieben & C. A. Perfetti (Eds.), *Learning to read: Basic research and its implications* (pp. 57–74). Hillsdale, NJ: Erlbaum.

Ehri, L. C. (1995). Phases of development in learning to read words by sight. *Journal of Research in Reading, 18*, 116–125.

Ehri, L. C. (2005). Learning to read words: Theory, findings, and issues. *Scientific Studies of Reading, 9*(2), 167–197.

Ehri, L. C., & McCormick, S. (1998). Phases of word learning: Implications for instruction with delayed and disabled readers. *Reading and Writing Quarterly: Overcoming Learning Difficulties, 14*, 135–163.

Fletcher, J. M., Francis, D. J., Shaywitz, S. E., Lyon, G. R., Foorman, B. R., Stuebing, K. K., et al. (1998). Intelligent testing and the discrepancy model for children with learning disabilities. *Learning Disabilities Research and Practice, 13*, 186–203.

Foorman, B. R., Francis, D. J., Davidson, K. C., Harm, M. W., & Griffin, J. (2004). Variability in text feature in six grade 1 basal reading programs. *Scientific Studies of Reading, 8*, 167–197.

Francis, D. J., Fletcher, J. M., Stuebing, K. K., Lyon, G. R., Shaywitz, B. A., & Shaywitz, S. E. (2005). Psychometric approaches to the identification of LD: IQ and achievement scores are not sufficient. *Journal of Learning Disabilities, 38*, 98–108.

Fuchs, D., & Fuchs, L. S. (2006). Introduction to response to intervention: What, why, and how valid is it? *Reading Research Quarterly, 41*(1), 93–99.

Fuchs, D., Mock, D., Morgan, P. L., & Young, C. L. (2003). Responsivness-to-intervention: Definitions, evidence, and implications for the learning disabilities construct. *Learning Disabilities Research and Practice, 18*, 151–171.

Fuchs, L. S., Fuchs, D., Hamlett, C. L., Walz, L., & Germann, G. (1993). Formative evaluation of academic progress: How much growth can we expect? *School Psychology Review, 22*, 27–48.

Fuchs, L. S., Fuchs, D., Hosp, M. K., & Jenkins, J. R. (2001). Oral reading fluency as an indicator of reading competence: A theoretical empirical, and historical analysis. *Scientific Studies of Reading, 5*(3), 239–256.

Fuchs, L. S., Fuchs, D., & Speece, D. L. (2002). Treatment validity as a unifying construct for identifying learning disabilities. *Learning Disabilities Quarterly, 25*, 33–46.

Gambrell, L. B., Wilson, R. M., & Gantt, W. (1981). Classroom observations of task-attending behaviors of good and poor readers. *Journal of Educational Research, 74*(6), 400–404.

Gersten, R., & Dimino, J. (2006). Rethinking special education for students with reading difficulties (yet again). *Reading Research Quarterly, 41*(1), 99–108.

Good, R. H., & Kaminski, R. A. (Eds.). (2002). *Dynamic indicators of basic early literacy skills* (6th ed.). Eugene, OR: Institute for the Development of Educational Achievement. Available *dibels.uoregon.edu*.

Gough, P. B., & Hillinger, M. L. (1980). Learning to read: An unnatural act. *Bulletin of the Orton Society, 30*, 179–196.

Gough, P. B., & Juel, C. (1991). The first stages of word recognition. In L. Rieben & C. A. Perfetti (Eds.), *Learning to read: Basic research and its implications* (pp. 47–56). Hillsdale, NJ: Erlbaum.

Graves, B., & Liang, L. A. (2004). Transitional chapter books. *Book Links, 13*(5), 12–13.

Gresham, F. M. (2002). Responsiveness to intervention: An alternative approach to the identification of learning disabilities. In R. Bradley, L. Danielson, & D. P. Hallahan (Eds.), *Identification of learning disabilities: Research to practice* (pp. 467–519). Mahwah, NJ: Erlbaum.

Gough, P. B., & Juel, C. (1991). The first stages of word recognition. In L. Rieben & C. A. Perfetti (Eds.), *Learning to read: Basic research and its implications* (pp. 47–56). Hillsdale, NJ: Erlbaum.

Guthrie, J., Wighfield, A., Humenick, N. M., Preencevich, K. C., Taboada, A., & Barbarosa, P. (2006). Influences of stimulating tasks on reading motivation and comprehension. *Journal of Educational Research, 99*(3), 232–245.

Harris, T. L., & Hodges, R. E. (Eds.). (1995). *The literacy dictionary: The vocabulary of reading and writing*. Newark, DE: International Reading Association.

Harrison, C. (1980). *Readability in the classroom*. Cambridge, UK: Cambridge University Press.

Hicks, C. P., & Villaume, S. K. (2000). Finding our own way: Critical reflections of literacy development of two reading recovery children. *The Reading Teacher, 54*, 398–412.

Hiebert, E. (1998). *Text matters in learning to read* (CIERA Report #1-001). Ann Arbor, MI: Center for the Improvement of Early Reading Achievement.

Hiebert, E. (2005). *Word zones for 5,586 most frequent words*. Retrieved June 1, 2006, from *textproject.org/resources/word-zones-list*.

Hiebert, E., & Fisher, C. W. (2002, April). *Text matters in developing fluent reading*. Paper presented at the annual meeting of the American Educational Research Association, New Orleans, LA.

Hiebert, E., & Mesmer, H. A. (2005). Perspectives on the difficulty of beginning reading. In D. Dickinson & S. Neuman (Eds.), *Handbook of early literacy* (2nd ed., pp. 395–409). New York: Guilford Press.

Hoffman, J. V. (2002). WORDs (on words in leveled texts for beginning readers). In D. Schallert, C. M. Fairbanks, J. Worthy, B. Maloch, & J. V. Hoffman (Eds.), *51st Yearbook of the National Reading Conference* (pp. 59–81). Oak Creek, WI: National Reading Conference.

Hoffman, J. V., Roser, N. L., Salas, R., Patterson, E., & Pennington, J. (2001). Text leveling and little books in first grade. *Journal of Literacy Research, 33*, 507–528.

Houghton Mifflin. (2006). *The American Heritage dictionary of the English language* (4th ed.). New York: Author.

International Reading Association. (2006). The role of reading specialist in the RTI process. In *New roles in response to intervention: Creating success for schools and children*. Retrieved March 9, 2007, from *www.reading.org/downloads/resources/rti_role_definitions.pdf*.

International Reading Association. (2007). *Implications for reading teachers in response to intervention (RTI)*. Retrieved June 25, 2007, from *www.reading.org/downloads/resources/rti0707_implications.pdf*.

Invernizzi, M., Juel, C., Swank, L., & Meier, J (2005). Phonological awareness literacy screening (PALS). Charlottesville: Rector and The Board of Visitors of the University of Virginia.

Jenkins, J. R., Fuchs, L. S., van den Broek, P., Espin, C. L., & Deno, S. L. (2003). Sources of individual differences in reading comprehension and reading fluency. *Journal of Educational Psychology, 95,* 719–729.

Juel, C. (1994). *Learning to read and write in one elementary school*. New York: Springer-Verlag.

Juel, C., Griffith, P. L., & Gough, P. B. (1986). Reading and spelling strategies of first grade children. In J. A. Niles & R. V. Lalik (Eds.), *Issues in literacy: A research perspective* (pp. 307–309). Oak Creek, WI: National Reading Conference.

Juel, C., & Minden-Cupp, C. (2000). Learning to read words: Linguistic units and instructional practices. *Reading Research Quarterly, 35,* 458–492.

Juel, C., & Roper/Schneider, D. (1985). The influence of basal readers on first grade reading. *Reading Research Quarterly, 20,* 134–152.

Klare, G. (1963). *The measurement of readability*. Ames: University of Iowa Press.

Kuhn, M. R., & Stahl, S. A. (2003). Fluency: A review of developmental and remedial practices. *Journal of Educational Psychology, 95,* 3–21.

Lennon, & Burdick. (2004). *The Lexile Framework as an approach for reading measurement and success*. Retrieved June, 2, 2006, from *www.lexile.com/PDF/Lexile-Reading-Measurement-and-Success-0504.pdf*.

Lyon, G. R. (1995a). Research initiatives in learning disabilities: Contributions from scientists supported by the National Institute of Child Health and Human Development. *Journal of Child Neurology, 10*(Suppl. 1), S120–S126.

Lyon, G. R. (1995b). Toward a definition of Dyslexia. *Annals of Dyslexia, 45,* 3–27.

Marston, D. (2005). Tiers of intervention in responsiveness to intervention: Prevention outcomes and learning disabilities identification patterns. *Journal of Learning Disabilities, 38*(6), 539–544.

McKenna, M. C., & Kear, D. J. (1999) Measuring attitude toward reading: A new tool for teachers. In S. J. Barrentine (Ed.), *Reading assessment principles and practices for elementary teachers* (pp. 1999–214). Newark, DE: International Reading Association.

Menon, S., & Hiebert, E. (2005). A comparison of first graders reading with little books or literature-based anthologies. *Reading Research Quarterly, 40*(1), 12–38.

Mesmer, H. A. E. (1999). Scaffolding a crucial transition using text with some decodability. *The Reading Teacher, 53,* 130–142.

Mesmer, H. A. E. (2001a). Examining the theoretical claims about decodable text: Does text decodability lead to greater application of letter–sound knowledge in first grade readers? In J. Hoffman, D. Schalbert, C. Fairbanks, J. Worthy, & B. Maloch (Eds.), *Fiftieth Yearbook of the National Reading Conference, 50,* 444–459.

Mesmer, H. A. E. (2001b). Decodable text: A review of what we know. *Reading Research and Instruction, 40,* 462–483.

Mesmer, H. A. E. (2004). The art of balancing instructional materials for beginning readers: Becoming a wise consumer. *Balanced Reading Instruction, 10,* 1–11.

Mesmer, H. A. E. (2006). Beginning reading materials: A national survey of primary teachers' reported uses and beliefs. *Journal of Literacy Research, 38*(4), 389–425.

Mesmer, H. A. E. (2008). *Tools for matching readers to texts: Research-based practices.* New York: Guilford Press.

Mora, P. (2002). Tomas and the library lady. In C. Bereiter, A. Brown, J. Campione, I. Carruthers, R. Case, J. Hirshberg, et al. *Open Court Reading* (Level 2, Unit 1, pp. 84–85). Columbus, OH: SRA/McGraw-Hill.

Morris, D. (2006). *The Howard Street tutoring manual.* New York: Guilford Press.

Morris, D., Bloodgood, J. W., Lomax, R. G., Perney, J. (2005). Developmental steps in learning to read: A longitudinal study in kindergarten and first grade. *Reading Research Quarterly, 38*(3), 302–328.

National Institutes of Child Health and Human Development. (2000). *National Reading Panel Report. Teaching children to read: An evidence-based assessment of the scientific research literature on reading and its implications for reading instruction* (NIH Publication No. 00-4769). Washington, DC: U.S. Government Printing Office.

O'Connor, R. E., Bell, K. M., Harty, K. R., Larkin, L. K., Sackor, S. M., & Zigmond, N. (2002). Teaching reading to poor readers in the intermediate grades: A comparison of text difficulty. *Journal of Educational Psychology, 94,* 474–485.

O'Malley, K., Francis, D. J., Foorman, B. R., Fletcher, J. M., & Swank, P. R. (2002). Growth in precursor and reading-related skills: Do low-achieving and IQ-discrepant readers develop differently? *Learning Disabilities Research and Practice, 17,* 19–34.

Rashotte, C., & Torgeson, J. K. (1985). Repeated reading and reading fluency in learning disabled children. *Reading Research Quarterly, 20,* 180–188.

Rasinski, T. V. (2000). Speed does matter in reading. *The Reading Teacher, 54*(2), 146–151.

Rasmussen, D., & Goldberg, L. (2000). The wagon master. In *Kittens and children* (Level E, pp. 243–247). Columbus, OH: SRA/McGraw-Hill.

Renaissance Learning. (2006). *Matching students to books: How to use readability formulas and continuous monitoring to ensure reading success.* Wisconsin Rapids, WI: Author.

Roller, C. (1998). *So . . . What's a tutor to do?* Newark, DE: International Reading Association.

Samuels, S. J. (1994). Toward a theory of automatic information processing in reading, revisited. In R. B. Ruddell, M. R. Ruddell, & H. Singer (Eds.), *Theoretical models and processes of reading* (4th ed.). Newark, DE: International Reading Association.

Sawyer, C. (1998). *Slam and Dunk and the big game.* San Francisco: Gateway Learning.

Silvarolli, N. J., & Wheelock, W. H. (2004). *The classroom reading inventory* (10th ed.). New York: McGraw-Hill.

Spadorcia, S. (2005). Examining high-interest, low-level books. *Reading and Writing Quarterly, 21*(1), 33–59.

Spadorcia, S. A. (2005). Examining the text demands of high-interest, low-level books. *Reading and Writing Quarterly, 21,* 33–59.

Stanovich, K. E. (1985). Explaining the variance in reading ability in terms of psychological processes: What we learned? *Annals of Dyslexia, 35,* 67–96.

Stein, M., Johnson, B., & Gutlohn, L. (1999). Analyzing beginning reading programs: The relationship between decoding instruction and text. *Remedial and Special Education, 20,* 257–287.

Texas Education Agency & University of Texas System. (2006). *Texas Primary Reading Inventory.* Austin, TX: Author.

Vaughn, S., & Fuchs, L. S. (2003). Redefining learning disabilities as inadequate response to instruction: The promise and potential problems. *Learning Disabilities Research and Practice, 18,* 137–146.

Vadasy, P. F., Sanders, E. A., & Peyton, J. A. (2005). Relative effectiveness of reading practice or word-level instruction in supplemental tutoring: How text matters. *Journal of Learning Disabilities, 38,* 364–382.

Vellutino, F. R., & Scanlon, D. M. (1987). Phonological coding, phonological awareness, and reading ability: Evidence from a longitudinal and experimental study. *Merrill–Palmer Quarterly, 33,* 321–363.

Vellutino, F. R., Scanlon, D. M., & Lyon, G. R. (2000). Differentiating between difficult-to-remediate and readily remediated poor readers: More evidence against the IQ-discrepancy definition of reading disability. *Journal of Learning Disabilities, 33,* 223–238.

Vellutino, F. R., Scanlon, D. M., & Sipay, E. R. (1996). Cognitive profiles of difficult-to-remediate and readily remediated poor readers, early intervention as a vehicle for distinguishing between cognitive and experential deficits as basic causes for specific reading disabilities. *Journal of Educational Psychology, 88*(4), 601–638.

Woods, M. L., & Moe, A. J. (2007). *Analytical Reading Inventory* (8th ed.). Upper Saddle River, NJ: Merrill Prentice Hall.

Worthy, J. (1996). A matter of interest: Literature that hooks reluctant readers and keeps them reading. *Reading Teacher, 50*(3), 204–212.

Zakaluk, B. L., & Samuels, S. J. (1988). *Readability: Its past, present, and future* (pp. 14–34). Newark, DE: International Reading Association.

Zipf, G. K. (1935). *The psycho-theory of language.* Boston: Houghton Mifflin.

9

Placing and Pacing Beginning Readers in Texts

The Match between Texts and Children's Knowledge of Words

KATHLEEN J. BROWN

One of beginning readers' most important tasks is building word-recognition automaticity: the ability to identify words on the page—accurately, quickly, and effortlessly (Adams, 1990; Rayner, Foorman, Perfetti, Pesetsky, & Seidenberg, 2002). Children who develop this ability easily are more likely to be successful readers and more likely to find reading rewarding than their peers who do not develop this ability easily. Why? Automatic word recognition allows readers to spend most of their cognitive resources on understanding text, rather than on decoding individual words (LaBerge & Samuels, 1974; Perfetti, 1991, 1992). Expending diminishing effort translates into achievement and motivation for reading more. For many children, this synergy generates a practice effect that cannot be underestimated. Good readers can consume copious quantities of text, which, in turn, fuels an upward spiral of general academic achievement that has significant long-term benefits (Cunningham & Stanovich, 1998; Share & Stanovich, 1995).

Conversely, beginning readers who struggle with word recognition and do not receive adequate intervention often slip into a "negative spiral" of achievement and motivation that ensures an ever-widening gap between them and their more successful peers (Juel, 1988; Share & Stanovich, 1995; Stanovich, 1986; Tunmer, Chapman, & Prochnow, 2003). Research suggests that children who fall behind as early as kindergarten are at risk for reading problems (Good, Simmons, & Kame'enui, 2001;Velluntino et al., 1996), and most of those children who continue struggling as they progress through the grades show clear evidence of word-recognition difficulties (Ehri, 1997; Shankweiler et al., 1999).

Given the importance of word-recognition automaticity in successful reading, how can educators be most effective at helping beginners establish this ability? This chapter is based on the premise that educators need to understand word-recognition development and be able to use that knowledge in making instructional decisions about their students (Brady & Moats, 1997). By recognizing what beginning readers know about words, educators can use this knowledge to select optimal texts and instructional routines.

To support the goal of developing understanding about word recognition and its translation to instruction, this chapter is organized into four sections. The first provides a research-based theoretical framework on how beginning readers acquire the ability to recognize words and uses a fictional example to demonstrate the framework in practice. The second section describes three areas of instructional decision making that relate to choosing text for beginning readers: text type, text difficulty, and prompts for unfamiliar words. The third section returns to the fictional characters from the first section and uses a case study to illustrate how educators can place and pace beginners in text to maximize what they know and what they are learning about words. The chapter closes with a discussion of some long-standing gaps in our knowledge about the relationships between texts and word-recognition development, and the impact these gaps may have on classroom practice.

A THEORETICAL FRAMEWORK
ON WORD RECOGNITION DEVELOPMENT

Current views on word-recognition automaticity are grounded in cognitive theories that seek to explain how expert reading occurs and how novice readers become experts. These theories point to the importance of interactive connections between different types of information that are developed and stored in readers' long-term memories (Adams, 2001;

Perfetti, 1991, 1992; Rayner et al., 2002). Cognitive theorists often use the term *representation* to describe an individual unit of information in memory. This heuristic suggests that individuals mentally "represent" that which they perceive about the world. Representations can, and certainly do, vary among individuals who differ in myriad ways—from background knowledge on a topic to quality of phonological perception (Brady, 1997; Bransford, Nitsch, & Franks, 1977; Kintsch, 1974).

With regard to the cognitive act of reading, representations include, but are not limited to: information about letter features (e.g., circles, lines), letter names (e.g., *t*, *f*, *d*), word meanings (e.g., mean, vituperative), conceptual knowledge (e.g., *Voldemort* personifies *evil*), speech sounds (e.g., /t/, /ch/, /ug/, /den/), syntactic knowledge (e.g., It is better to say "Harry *is* the hero" than "Harry *are* the hero"), and so on. For word-recognition development in particular, three types of cognitive representations have special importance: semantic (meaning-based) representations, phonological (speech sound-based) representations, and orthographic (spelling-based) representations (Perfetti, 1991; 1992).

How do cognitive representations for printed words develop? From birth, children with language-processing abilities in the normal range experience the world around them while interacting with language users. Through those interactions, children develop understandings (i.e., semantic representations) for that which they encounter (Bloom, 1994; Nelson, 1973). As children hear language used, they gradually develop phonological representations that bond to their understandings, and then draw on those representations as they begin to use language themselves (Liberman, 1999; Metsala, 1999; Walley, 1993). It is important to note that children (and most adults) are wholly unconscious of these cognitive structures, yet they use them effortlessly in the pursuit of communicating and constructing meaning (Liberman, 1999; Savin & Bever, 1970; Warren, 1971).

Consider how young children develop fundamental concepts. As young children interact with others, they develop understandings and language for concepts such as *chair* and *sit*. When someone invites a child to sit, the child's semantic and phonological representations for that concept are activated. The child understands and/or communicates, as inclined. With more experiences and language interactions, the child adds related semantic and phonological representations such as *sofa, relax, scoot over, bench, sit still,* and so on. Over time, connections among these and other related representations strengthen, extend, or atrophy, depending on use and experience.

Just as semantic and phonological representations are built from experience and interaction, orthographic representations (i.e., spellings) are built as well. Before children receive print-related instruction at home or school, they have no orthographic representations in memory. Current theory suggests that the first orthographic representations typically are established when children develop grapheme–letter name correspondences. For example, they associate the grapheme *m* with a name: /em/ (Adams, 1990; Ehri & Wilce, 1979). At this time, larger orthographic representations for blends, digraphs, syllables, and words are likely not to exist in children's memories (Ehri, 1998; Gough, Juel, & Griffith, 1992).

What about toddlers and preschoolers who can identify commercial products, their names, and perhaps even several words (e.g., *mom, love*) in print, before they can identify individual letters reliably? Typically, these children are using strategies such as configuration (letter and/or word shape) and environmental cues (e.g., the salient aspects of logos) as a means of identification (Gough et al., 1992). These strategies do not rely on the alphabetic principle of matching speech sounds to print (Chall, 1983; Ehri, 2005; Seymour & Elder, 1986) and, as such, these strategies are prealphabetic. Moreover, research suggests that prealphabetic strategies do not build orthographic representations effectively, and, as children encounter other words with similar shapes or logo features, these strategies quickly lose their utility (Libscomb & Gough, 1990; Masonheimer, Drum, & Ehri, 1984).

This is the point where children develop metalinguistic awareness and the alphabetic principle. Once children understand that letters represent speech sounds, and know how to apply this knowledge successfully in the service of blending small, phonetically regular words, they are ready to begin building orthographic representations beyond the grapheme–phoneme level (Goswami, 2001; Watson, 2001).

The following fictional example illustrates this transition in early word-reading development. Five-year-old Ian is midway through kindergarten. He has mastered almost all grapheme–phoneme correspondences, with the exception of *y*, *w*, and some confusion with *j* and *g*. He can identify both his first and last names. However, if incorrect, yet similar-looking letters are substituted within either name, Ian fails to notice (Masonheimer et al., 1984).

Ian's kindergarten teacher, Mrs. Buhrmaster, is aware of his abilities and provides instruction designed to help Ian use what he knows about letters and sounds to learn to read words. She directly teaches a few, simple high-frequency words such as *the* and *is*. She begins teaching lax (short) vowel sounds and provides modeling and practice in how to blend simple, phonetically regular words (Ehri, Satlow, & Gaskins, 2006). Finally, Mrs. Buhrmaster provides students with text that allows for opportunities for skill practice and transfer (Juel & Roper/Schneider, 1985; Wise & Olson, 1995). These texts are not great literature, but neither are they strangled nonsense: They include a controlled mix of phonetically regular and high-frequency words (Anderson, Hiebert, Scott, & Wilkinson, 1985; Beck & Juel, 1995).

Through phonics instruction and practice in text, the process of building orthographic representations for words begins in earnest for Ian. One day, he encounters the word *sad* in text. His memory already holds robust semantic and phonological representations for this word. That is, he understands the concepts involved and uses the word adeptly in oral language. But he cannot identify the word at sight because an orthographic representation for the full word does not yet exist in memory. Ian uses the strategy he learned from Mrs. Buhrmaster and phonologically recodes (i.e., blends) each sound (i.e., /s/-/a/-/d/). He is able to hold those sounds in phonological working memory long enough to activate his existing phonological representation, which speeds the correct, coarticulated pronunciation of the word: /sad/ (Brady, 1997; Liberman, 1999). Simultaneously, Ian's semantic representations for this word are activated, and the various meanings he holds for it are available (Adams, 2001; Rayner et al., 2002). Exercising this strategy and identifying words correctly, or at least "coming close" in matching letters and sounds is beneficial for beginning readers (Christensen & Bowey, 2005; Stuart, 1990; Stuart & Coltheart, 1988).

For beginning readers, a single success may not be sufficient to produce a full, orthographic representation of a word. When subsequently encountering the word *sad*, Ian may need to re-employ his blending strategy. With more phonics instruction and practice in appropriate text, Ian will have many opportunities to phonologically recode across this and other similar words (e.g., *mad, dad, bad, had*). As he does, he "fully analyzes the word" (Gaskins, Ehri, Cress, O'Hara, & Donnelly, 1996; Share, 1995). That is, he repeatedly matches graphemes to corresponding phonemes. Share and his colleagues (Share, 1995; Share & Jorm, 1983) suggest that this process of phonological recoding forms the basis for a "self-teaching mechanism" by which readers learn new words and bring them to an automatic level.

After a sufficient number of trials, Ian will look at the word *sad*, and instead of blending all three letter–sounds serially, he may blend the onset (i.e., *s-*) with the rime unit (i.e., *-ad*) and then say, /s-ad/, or he may simply say the word in its entirety. The former achievement suggests that the orthographic unit *-ad* has been acquired and is available for use (Bowey & Hansen, 1994; Goswami, 1986; Treiman, Goswami, & Bruck, 1990). The latter achievement suggests that the full word has a consolidated orthographic representation in memory that allows all of its letters to be processed "in parallel," rather than serially (Adams, 1990, 2001; Ehri & Wilce, 1983; Rayner et al., 2002). More specifically, the letters have bonded together as a single spelling unit, and blending the constituent parts is no longer necessary. As a result, when Ian sees the word in its printed form, his visual perception encodes a single unit (Ehri & Wilce, 1983). That visual information activates the matching orthographic representation, which in turn, simultaneously activates its bonded phonological and semantic representations. Ian now identifies and understands the word in approximately one-quarter of a second (Rayner, 1997). In sum, the word *sad* has become part of Ian's sight vocabulary. Upon seeing it in print, he is able to recognize it accurately, quickly, and without conscious attention (Adams, 1990).

Over time, Ian will acquire more and more word-level orthographic representations. Many of those representations share spelling patterns (Wylie & Durrell, 1970). Overlapping orthography at the syllable and intra-syllable levels plays a synergistic role for representational development. As Ian repeatedly encounters spelling patterns that are used across many words (e.g., *spr, ee, ur, ight*), and phonologically recodes them, this helpful redundancy speeds the development of representations for single-syllable words that share orthography (e.g., *seed, breed*) (Adams, 2001; Ehri, 1998; Share, 1995).

Once in place, these syllable-level representations become extremely important. They make it possible for Ian to use orthographic units larger than letter–sounds. This ability is a prerequisite for bringing polysyllabic words to an automatic level (Templeton, 1992; Treiman et al, 1990). For example, to identify the word *transportation* and eventually build a complete orthographic representation that allows automatic recognition, Ian must be able to decode at the syllable level (i.e., *trans- -por- -ta- -tion*) and hold those units in phonological memory long enough to pronounce the word (Scarborough & Brady, 2002). Blending serially—letter–sound by letter–sound—would not be effective, nor would sampling initial phonemes and guessing from context. With enough successful trials, made possible by existing syllable-level orthographic representations, *transportation* will become part of Ian's sight vocabulary (Treiman, Mullennix, Bijeljac-Babic, & Richmond-Welty, 1995).

Knowledge of syllable-level orthographic units aids not only the development of automaticity but also forms the basis for a highly effective strategy for identifying unfamiliar words. That is, expert readers use their knowledge of spelling patterns and syllable types to quickly "chunk" parts of an unfamiliar word and generate a pronunciation that, if not accurate, is close enough to adjust with the help of context and word-meaning knowledge (Ehri, 2005; Lukatela & Turvey, 1994). For example, when a novice reader encounters the word *locate*, and initially recodes it as /lŏk/ - /āt/, that pronunciation may fail to activate an existing phonological representation. However, it may be close enough to trigger the correct word that the reader has heard but never seen in print. As a result, the reader quickly adjusts pronunciation by opening the first syllable to give it a tense vowel sound and producing a word for which semantic and phonological representations do exist.

Of course, the rate at which children acquire orthographic knowledge varies considerably. For some children, the ready availability of a precise, stable orthographic representation may require no more than a few, or perhaps a single, successful phonological recoding encounter(s) with a word (Share, 2004). For other children, many more successful recoding encounters may be necessary (Ehri & Saltmarsh, 1995; Reitsma, 1983). The ease (or lack thereof) with which children acquire orthographic knowledge directly impacts the development of word-recognition automaticity, and, ultimately, their overall reading fluency (Samuels, Schermer, & Reinking, 1992; Stanovich, 1986).

THREE AREAS OF INSTRUCTIONAL DECISION MAKING RELATED TO TEXTS: TEXT TYPE, TEXT DIFFICULTY, AND PROMPTS FOR UNFAMILIAR WORDS

To greater or lesser degrees, text can provide opportunities to reinforce and extend what beginners are learning about words and the reading process (Brown, 1999/2000). Thus, educators who possess a solid understanding of how beginning readers develop orthographic representations, and who have knowledge about the types and difficulty levels of available text, can use that understanding and knowledge to place and pace students in texts that maximize opportunities to practice what they already know and what they are currently learning about recognizing words (Brown, 1999/2000, 2003). Text, then, becomes a form of instructional scaffolding that educators maintain, extend, or diminish in response to student performance.

Over the last quarter century, researchers, educators, policymakers, and publishers have paid increasing attention to text for beginning readers (Hiebert, 2005; Hoffman, Roser, Salas, Patterson, & Pennington, 2001; Mesmer, 2006). The result has been an enormous surge in the number of texts published, as well as some drastic pendulum swings in text content and government policy regulating the kinds of texts used in primary-grade classrooms (for a review, see Hiebert, 2005). These changes have impacted educators in diverse ways (Mesmer, 2006). In some schools, educators have free rein to choose texts for beginning readers. In other schools, educators are required to use materials from a core program for all or most of the allotted instructional time. In some primary-grade classrooms, texts are plentiful and of high quality. In others, quantity and/or quality remain sparse. However, as diverse as these environments may be, most primary-grade teachers are faced with making ongoing decisions about the texts they use with their beginning readers. This section of the chapter provides a description of text types, text difficulty, and instructional prompts: information that may help educators scaffold text for beginners in ways that have the potential to contribute to word-recognition development (Brown, 1999/2000, 2003).

Text Type

To select text effectively and efficiently for beginning readers, educators need to be able to identify the types of text available and the difficulty levels of those texts. Text type and difficulty are shaped by the control an author exerts in word choice, sentence structure, and even the amount of text placed on a single page. With varying degrees of success, authors who write text for beginning readers use this control to make what they write accessible to beginning readers (Anderson et al., 1985; Beck & McCaslin, 1978).

Textual control has an inverse relationship with literary complexity (Brown, 1999/2000). That is, the *most controlled* texts also are those with the *least complexity*. This relationship is illustrated in Figure 9.1 by excerpts from a simple, predictable text, a decodable text, a high-frequency text, two mixed texts at different levels of difficulty, and an easy-reader text. All exert extensive control over written language to provide access for readers whose sight vocabularies and decoding strategies are not yet equal to the demands of literature. This control necessarily reduces the texts' potential for literary complexity.

It is important to note that different types of texts exert different *types* of control. Authors of *predictable texts* (see Figure 9.1) use refrains that range from very simple (e.g., one line with one new word per page) to complex (e.g., three lines with several new words). Within those refrains, readers may encounter words with a wide range of orthographic complexity (e.g., *it*, *on*, *lettuce*, *cheese*, *pickles*). In isolation, or even just apart from the refrain, most of the words in these texts are beyond their readers' sight vocabularies and decoding strategies (Leu, DeGroff, & Simons, 1986). Nevertheless, once a sufficient portion of the refrain in a simple, predictable text has been modeled aloud, many children can use memory for the refrain, context, illustrations, and the beginning sounds of words to complete the text on their own and reread it later (Leu et al., 1986). Predictable texts are especially suited for children at the very beginning of reading development who need to develop general, foundational knowledge about text, such as directionality and concept of word (Clay, 2005; Morris, 1992).

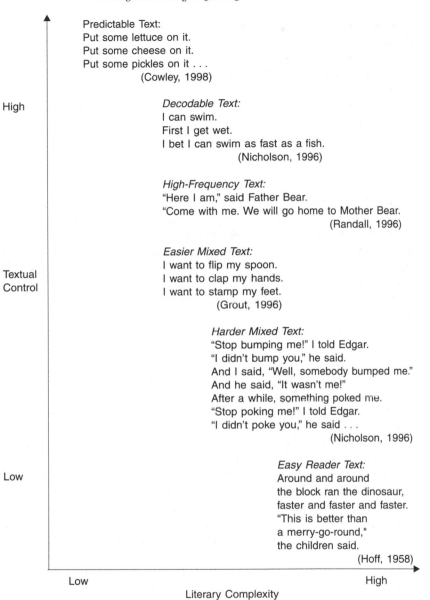

High

Textual
Control

Low

Predictable Text:
Put some lettuce on it.
Put some cheese on it.
Put some pickles on it . . .
          (Cowley, 1998)

Decodable Text:
I can swim.
First I get wet.
I bet I can swim as fast as a fish.
          (Nicholson, 1996)

High-Frequency Text:
"Here I am," said Father Bear.
"Come with me. We will go home to Mother Bear.
          (Randall, 1996)

Easier Mixed Text:
I want to flip my spoon.
I want to clap my hands.
I want to stamp my feet.
          (Grout, 1996)

Harder Mixed Text:
"Stop bumping me!" I told Edgar.
"I didn't bump you," he said.
And I said, "Well, somebody bumped me."
And he said, "It wasn't me!"
After a while, something poked me.
"Stop poking me!" I told Edgar.
"I didn't poke you," he said . . .
          (Nicholson, 1996)

Easy Reader Text:
Around and around
the block ran the dinosaur,
faster and faster and faster.
"This is better than
a merry-go-round,"
the children said.
          (Hoff, 1958)

Low   High
          Literary Complexity

FIGURE 9.1. Relationship between textual control and literary complexity.

Authors of *decodable* and *high-frequency texts* have a different audience: beginning readers who are breaking the alphabetic code. As such, these authors use a different kind of control to make their writing accessible. In decodable text (see Figure 9.1), authors emphasize particular orthographic elements, ranging from simple to more difficult (e.g., *ap*, *ike*, *oi*). To avoid the strangled prose of the "Nan can fan Dan" linguistic readers of the 1970s (Anderson et al., 1985), authors of more current decodable texts include high-frequency words of comparable difficulty in syntactic structures that approximate children's speech patterns (Beck & Juel, 1995; Tatham, 1970). The result is more natural sounding, yet still controlled text.

Authors of *high-frequency text* also control orthography but deliberately slant the mix toward the most frequent words in written English (see Figure 9.1). These words may or may not be phonetically regular (e.g., *here*, *said*, *come*, *too*). The remaining words in these texts usually include less frequent, but decodable words (e.g., *lost*) and a smattering of more difficult words included for reader interest (e.g., *honey*). These authors repeat high-frequency words many times within and across texts, moving from simple (e.g., *me*) to more complex (e.g., *about*). These texts are reminiscent of the whole-word, look–say basal readers that held sway in classrooms from the 1950s until the late 1980s (Hiebert, 2005; Hiebert & Martin, 2001; Hoffman et al., 2001).

Authors of *mixed text* use three types of control: predictability, decodability, and high-frequency words to compose text for beginning readers at a wide range of levels (see Figure 9.1). Similar to decodable and high-frequency texts, mixed texts usually follow a scope and sequence to control orthographic difficulty, yet mixed texts also employ refrain as support (Englebretson, Hiebert, & Juel, 1998; Hiebert, 1998). To increase difficulty, authors include increasing amounts of "cold text" before refrains become apparent, and the refrain themselves become more challenging (see Figure 9.1). Thus, depending on level of difficulty, mixed text may be effective for beginning readers across a wide range of development (i.e., partial to early consolidated phases).

Authors of *easy reader text* can compose well-written, engaging prose more readily than those who write more controlled text, because their audience requires less support (see Figure 9.1). Easy-reader authors can assume their readers have established a basic sight vocabulary and possess fairly sophisticated decoding skills. These abilities sharply reduce the need for text control. As a result, authors of easy readers have considerable latitude with regard to word choice and syntactic structure, and easy readers tend to be more complex and "literary" than predictable, decodable, or high-frequency text. However, easy readers still exert more control than authentic literature (see Figure 9.1).

Text Difficulty

In many primary-grade classrooms, texts for beginning readers are arranged in levels of difficulty that are represented alphabetically or numerically (e.g., Fountas & Pinnell, 1999; Morris, 2005). Each level requires multiple titles to provide sufficient opportunities for practice.

Given the individual reading differences in any primary-grade classroom, conducting valid, reliable assessment is a necessary first step for placing students in appropriate text—that is, text they can read with satisfactory accuracy, speed, and comprehension (Morris, 2005). Conventional wisdom in the field tells us that an appropriate level of text difficulty allows practice for that which students already know, and a small amount of challenge in wielding new learning (i.e., instructional level). When students demonstrate satisfactory performance within a level, they can move to the next slightly more-difficult level comprised of text with slightly less control.

Prompts for Unfamiliar Words

Most beginners make errors and "get stuck" on words even when reading in controlled text. These situations are "teachable moments" that educators can use to reinforce word knowledge (Brown, 2003). Choosing the right prompt for the right word at the right time sends an important message to beginning readers about how to identify unfamiliar words. The message is, "What you have learned about decoding words can help you. It's much better than guessing." Moreover, carefully chosen prompts can encourage students to parse through words thoroughly. In turn, the process of fully analyzing words (i.e., phonologically recoding) may help students refine and stabilize imprecise orthographic representations, which will hasten word-recognition automaticity (Ehri et al., 2006; Share, 1995).

USING TEXT TO SUPPORT AND EXTEND BEGINNERS' KNOWLEDGE ABOUT WORDS: A CASE STUDY

The third section of this chapter uses a fictional case study to illustrate how a solid understanding of word-recognition development can help educators make effective decisions about placing and pacing beginning readers in text. The case study relies on a description of two teachers (Mrs. Buhrmaster, who we met earlier, and Mrs. Holstrom) who interact with a beginning reader (Ian) over the course of kindergarten and the beginning of first grade. The characters and the classrooms in this case study are composites—drawn from my interactions with hundreds of beginning readers and primary-grade teachers in diverse settings, via my experience as a classroom teacher, methods professor, researcher, lead trainer for intervention practica in Title I schools, and intervention tutor.

The case study is not intended to represent primary-grade educators, students, and classrooms in general (many face more significant challenges than the fictional characters presented here). Nevertheless, it may be helpful in demonstrating that knowledge of how beginners acquire the ability to read words can inform educators' decisions regarding the use of instructional text with their students.

Ian in Early Kindergarten

Many children develop print awareness through interactions with caregivers before they ever enter elementary school. These children come to school knowing how books work—an important prerequisite for learning how to read (Adams, 1990). But, for children who lack these experiences, print awareness must be built at school. Beyond "print has meaning" and directionality basics, beginning readers need to develop a "concept of word"—that is, how spoken words match written words in connected text. Beginning readers demonstrate this knowledge in the act of finger pointing through simple texts (Morris, Bloodgood, Lomax, & Perney, 2003).

Easy, predictable text is helpful for developing concept of word (Clay, 2005; Morris, 2005). At the beginning of kindergarten, whenever Mrs. Buhrmaster was ready to start a new book with Ian's reading group, she "echo-read" this type of text. That is, she pointed word-by-word under the print with her finger as she read aloud a line of text—slowly, but with appropriate prosody. In response, Ian and the others in his group echoed her language and finger-pointed the same line in their own copies. After this scaffolded first pass, the students were able to re-read the text with partners and then on their own.

There is no doubt that Ian lacked orthographic representations for most words in these texts. In fact, in early kindergarten, he relied primarily on memory for the refrain, context, pictures, and the first letter–sound in words to "recite-read" his way through text (Savage, Stuart, & Hill, 2001; Tunmer & Chapman, 1998). So, if he did not look carefully at words, how could this type of text help Ian begin to develop orthographic representations?

Remember, during early kindergarten, Ian had no word-level orthographic representations. At that point in his reading development, he was still building single grapheme–phoneme representations (e.g., $s = /s/$), and he was not yet blending across words. Nevertheless, Ian could point accurately in many predictable texts, and he knew exactly where he was on the page. Then, if he encountered an unfamiliar word, he was ready to use the first letter–sound in combination with the picture and memory to trigger the correct word. These behaviors are consistent with what

Ehri (1998) calls *partial-alphabetic reading* and what Morris and his colleagues (2003) postulate as a precursor to more sophisticated forms of word identification.

Mrs. Buhrmaster deliberately reinforced this strategy with specific prompts. For example, during a reread of *Little Things* (Randell, Giles, & Smith, 1996), an easy, predictable text, Ian stalled out on the word *crane* in the sentence "My crane is little." Mrs. Buhrmaster gently tapped her pencil under the first letter in that word and prompted, "Sound?" When Ian responded "/k/," she gestured to the picture. When Ian failed to remember the word—it was not part of his oral language—Mrs. Buhrmaster said, "Crane," and directed Ian to reread the sentence on his own. Mindful of Ian's level of reading development and the status of his orthographic representations, Mrs. Buhrmaster knew that providing prompts for *-ane* and *cr-* would be neither effective nor efficient uses of time (Ehri & Robbins, 1992). She also knew that simply cueing the picture would miss an important opportunity to reinforce the use of letter–sound knowledge in identifying unfamiliar words. The prompts she chose reminded the kindergartener to look at the word and to use what he knew about letters before resorting to the picture or asking for help.

In contrast, beginning readers who fail to point accurately are less likely to be successful with unfamiliar words (Morris et al., 2005). They are unable to locate within the sentence and have no recourse but to guess—without *any* orthographic clues. When this happens, valuable opportunities to reinforce letter–sound knowledge in the act of reading go by the wayside.

Ian in Late Kindergarten

With print awareness in place, Mrs. Buhrmaster endeavored to help Ian and his peers "break the alphabetic code," and progress from partial- to full-alphabetic readers. Full-alphabetic readers utilize *all* of the letter-sounds in a simple, phonetically regular word—even the vowel (Ehri, 1998, 2005; Ehri & Robbins, 1992).

The term "breaking the code" references a well-documented transition in a beginning reader's development (Ehri, 1998, 2005; Gough & Hillinger, 1980). Chall (1983) described this transition as "glued to print," an apt metaphor for the choppy, word-by-word manner with which code-breaking readers tend to move through text. Some parents and educators become concerned when they witness this phenomenon because these readers often make nonsensical errors and sound less fluent than they did weeks earlier—even when rereading familiar text!

However, remember where these readers are with regard to development. They have not consolidated enough word-level orthographic representations to allow automatic word recognition to any noticeable degree (Ehri, 1998, 2005). So, until a sufficient number of representations for entire words are established in memory, they have no recourse but to move through nonpredictable text in this halting manner—decoding a vast majority of the words they encounter.

Eventually, as partial-alphabetic readers scrutinize and blend simple words during systematic, explicit, isolated phonics instruction, and while reading appropriate text (Wise & Olson, 1995), important changes occur: Individual letter–sound connections (e.g., b = /b/, i = /i/, g = /g/) start to bond, or amalgamate, into larger orthographic units (Share, 1995; Share & Jorm, 1983). These orthographic units bond with larger (and eventually word-level) phonological and semantic representations (e.g., *big* = /big/). Over time, beginners' sight vocabularies grow, and they begin to operate as consolidated readers for some words, while remaining full- or partial-alphabetic readers for others (Ehri, 2005; Rayner et al., 2002). Commensurately, they make fewer nonsense errors, and a semblance of fluency emerges (Chall, 1983).

If "breaking the code" sounds like work, it can be—more so for some children than for others. Blending and coarticulating words in text requires attention, skill execution, and persistence (Adams, 1990). When educators and parents observe readers in this phase of development they may witness body language and comments that express cognitive exertion—from fatigued sighs to outright resistance, "I can't read *that*!" And, individual children vary in their thresholds for this kind of exertion, as well as in their cognitive abilities for handling more challenging text.

For all of these reasons, it is important for educators to match code-breaking readers with texts of appropriate type and difficulty. A steady diet of text that is too difficult or too easy may sap motivation and/or may not provide sufficient practice. For example, a text like *Danny and the Dinosaur* (Hoff, 1958), which includes complex syntax and polysyllabic words with challenging vowel patterns (see Figure 9.1) likely does not provide enough control for early-alphabetic beginners who have only a few consolidated orthographic representations and who lack strategies for decoding unfamiliar words with complex vowel patterns. On the other hand, a predictable text like *A Monster Sandwich* (Cowley, 1998), may provide too much support for readers at this level of development (see Figure 9.1). Strong refrain can make text so predictable and memorable that readers need only glance at the words. They may sound fluent, but their performance in this text may be more of an exercise in recitation than in reading.

Three types of text merit consideration for beginners who are learning to appreciate the alphabetic nature of written English and who need to build word-level orthographic representations in memory: decodable text, high-frequency text, and mixed text. All three text types use a specific corpus of words multiple times within and across texts, but without a dominating refrain (Brown, 1999/2000). As such, beginning readers are less able to rely on context, memory, and illustrations when they read these texts. Rather, the demands of the text require readers to phonologically recode words (Share, 1995), a process that current theory would suggest is more likely to facilitate the development of word-level representations than working in text for which there is no need or no possibility of doing so.

To set the stage for breading the code, Mrs. Buhrmaster pushed for mastery of troublesome letter–sound correspondences, taught lax vowel sounds, and provided modeling and feedback for a blending strategy (Christensen & Bowey, 2005). By February, Ian's reading group was ready: They could blend across simple, phonetically regular words, and they knew several high-frequency words at sight.

Mrs. Buhrmaster then decreased her use of predictable text and increased her use of decodable, high-frequency text and mixed text for their reading group. In particular, she combed her core program and classroom bookshelves for texts that paralleled the scope and sequence of her word-study instruction, aiming for a "two-for-one" return: success in reading those specific texts and valuable reinforcement of specific phonic elements and high-frequency words (Juel & Roper/Schneider, 1985; Mesmer, 1999). Both types of success increase the likelihood of building orthographic representations and eventual automaticity for the included words (Beck & McCaslin, 1978; Juel & Roper/Schneider, 1985; Stein, Johnson, & Gutlohn, 1999).

Whenever she previewed a new text with the group, Mrs Buhrmaster frontloaded words that might present orthographic challenge. She did so by pointing to particular words in the text she showed to the group, and asking students to find those words in their own texts (Brown, Fields, & Morris, 2007a). Once positioned on a particular word, Mrs. Buhrmaster then walked her students through the tricky words by asking them to blend the letter–sounds. She always finished up with, "So, what's the word?" so that each student in the group had an opportunity to verbally (and hopefully, visually) consolidate the entire word. In addition, Mrs. Buhrmaster continued to provide echo-reading support for the first portion of the text (Brown et al, 2007a). Once she was convinced that the group was ready to go solo, she moved the group members into partner reading, while she coached and provided feedback.

This instructional protocol worked well for decodable texts like *My Lost Top* (Engles. 1996) that targets words with lax vowels (e.g., *did*, *it*, *fast, best*) and easy high-frequency words (e.g., *my, was*) in a story about a top that goes so fast, its owner can't keep up. Mrs. Buhrmaster chose this text because most members of the group were showing proficiency with lax vowels, both in word study and in assisted reading texts. She knew that Ian might have some trouble, so she volunteered to be his partner for the first reading. When he struggled with four-letter, decodable words like *snap*, she encouraged him to finger-tap each sound (Wilson, 1996) and then "say the word fast." This strategy was effective at helping Ian hang onto the sounds and coarticulate the word before the sounds degraded from phonological memory (Scarborough & Brady, 2002). Once he identified the word successfully, she directed him to back up to the beginning of the phrase or sentence and "try it again." She hoped that these two successful phonological recodings of the words, along with successive rereads of the text, would move Ian closer to full representation and automaticity for these words (Christensen & Bowey, 2005; Ehri & Robbins, 1992; Share, 1995).

In addition to choosing texts that targeted specific orthographic patterns, Mrs. Buhrmaster also chose texts of equivalent difficulty that emphasized easy, high-frequency words like *come, said,* and *here.* Since high-frequency words comprise a hefty percentage of any text (Nagy & Anderson, 1984), she knew that it was important for Ian and the others to build precise representations for these words. Once they did, these words could function as islands of safety in a sea of what otherwise might be unfamiliar print.

Ian and his reading group peers finished their kindergarten year successfully, reading decodable and high-frequency text of gradually increasing difficulty. This textual scaffolding and Mrs. Buhrmaster's systematic, explicit, isolated word-study instruction helped them to enter first grade with word-level orthographic representations (i.e., sight vocabulary) as demonstrated by passing scores in the preprimer-level "flash" word list (Morris, 2005) and performances on DIBELS indicators in the benchmark ranges—achievements that boded well for future success (Good et al., 2001).

Ian in Grade 1

When Ian's first-grade teacher, Mrs. Holstrom, looked over his cumulative folder in early September, she smiled with relief. Here was another student whose end-of-kindergarten assessments suggested that he had already developed print awareness and had broken the code. When she modeled the first two pages of a mid-first-grade text, and Ian read the next three pages on his own, she knew that he was on his way to developing fluency.

In choosing text to support Ian's development, Mrs. Holstom knew that more advanced beginners could do without the kind of control that some of her other first graders needed from predictable, decodable, and high-frequency text. On the other hand, Ian definitely wasn't ready to read authentic literature on his own. Mrs. Holstrom assessed Ian's oral-reading accuracy and rate using an informal reading inventory and determined from his scores (94% accurate with 25 words per minute) that Ian was reading on a late preprimer level—equivalent to what a normally achieving first grader would read in November or so (Morris, 2005; Morris, Tyner, & Perney, 2000). With this in mind, she looked to mixed texts and easy readers to give Ian appropriate textual scaffolding (Juel & Minden-Cupp, 2000).

Mixed texts and easy readers may provide significant motivational and cognitive benefits for advanced beginners. The diminished control that characterizes these texts makes the task of locating books that interest a particular child easier than during earlier stages of development because a wider range of topics and storylines are available. Children interested in specific topics (e.g., bats) or who get hooked on a series (e.g., Little Bear) may have access to mixed texts and easy readers in classrooms, schools, and public libraries. In addition, these texts use common, single and multisyllabic words in simple, syntactic patterns. This kind of textual control provides repetition that may help advanced beginners refine and extend their corpus of orthographic representations. As a result, students' sight vocabularies grow, and they recognize more and more words automatically. Increased automaticity, in turn, improves prosody (Schwanenflugel, Hamilton, Kuhn, Wisenbaker, & Stahl, 2004). The confluence of these abilities allows advanced beginners to spend more of their cognitive resources on constructing meaning (Perfetti, 1991; Stanovich, 1991).

Mrs. Holstrom did her best to choose text that matched her word-study instruction for this stage of reading development. In particular, she looked for interesting mixed texts and easy readers that included the most frequent orthographic patterns for each vowel—for example, those found in closed words (e.g., *cap*), open words (e.g., *so*), and words with a consonant–vowel–consonant–final *e* pattern (CVCe) (e.g., *lake*), as well as in words with frequent rime units (e.g., *pink*). She knew that as Ian and his reading-group peers consolidated these representations, they would be able to use a more sophisticated strategy for identifying unfamiliar words: the analogous use of patterns from words and syllables they already know to decode words they do not know (Bowey & Hansen, 1994; Ehri, 2005; Gaskins et al., 1996/1997; Lukatela & Turvey, 1994). For example, a reader who knows the word *corn* at sight may be able to use the *-or* vowel pattern to read *fork* and *snort*, and the chunk *-orn* to read *horn* and *thorn*.

Mrs. Holstrom also used prompts to reinforce this strategy when

Ian and other members of his reading group encountered unfamiliar words. One day, as she observed Ian's group rereading *The Hiccups Would Not Stop* (Bloksberg, 1996), a late preprimer mixed text that emphasizes basic *o* vowel patterns, Ian stopped just before the word *hope* in "I hope so." Ian had successfully sorted and read words with this vowel pattern during word study (Bear, Invernizzi, Templeton, & Johnston, 2004), but when he saw *hope* in context, he stopped and looked up at his teacher. Mrs. Holstrom prompted, "What's the vowel pattern?" Ian looked back down at the word and said, "*o*–consonant–*e*." When Mrs. Holstrom followed up with, "What's the vowel sound?" Ian replied, "/o/," and then successfully decoded the word.

The prompts Mrs. Holstrom used in this situation took full advantage of Ian's level of word-recognition development. Note that she did not prompt for the first sound and then provide the word for the student. Nor did she prompt Ian to blend, because she recognized that the word's orthography did not lend itself to serial blending. Rather, by focusing Ian's attention on the vowel pattern, Mrs. Holstrom hoped to help him phonologically recode the word quickly and accurately—in a way that asked him to fully analyze the word (Ehri et al., 2006). Her goal in doing so was to help Ian establish a more complete representation for this word in memory.

CONCLUSIONS AND QUESTIONS FOR THE FUTURE

For children like Ian, who enter first grade meeting or exceeding grade-level expectations, and who receive quality instruction and text from exemplary educators, this kind of outcome may be expected. However, two unresolved issues impede educators from being as effective and efficient as they might be—especially for students at risk for reading difficulties. These issues include: (1) lack of consensus about the scope and sequence for orthography in beginning-reader text, and (2) lack of consensus for the optimum oral-reading accuracy and rate benchmarks used to place and pace students in text levels.

With regard to orthography, many researchers and educators would agree that text for beginning readers should exert a good measure of orthographic control so that beginning readers can access text and practice what they are learning (Beck & Juel, 1995; Foorman Francis, Fletcher, Schatschneider, & Mehta, 1998; Juel & Roper/Schneider, 1985). However, neither researchers nor educators understand exactly how this control should be implemented within and across beginning texts. Specifically, what types and difficulty levels of orthography should occur in which text levels for beginning readers? How frequently should each type occur within and across levels? What is the best pace for introducing new, unique, and/or singleton words in text for beginning readers? What measure of orthographic control is most effective for readers who seem to have difficulty establishing sight vocabulary? This issue has special relevance for at-risk readers as they move beyond developing print awareness to breaking the code, where the requirements for effort and persistence are heightened. For these more fragile readers, the type and frequency of words they encounter in text may affect their ability to build the word-level orthographic representations that they need to establish automaticity and fluency.

With these beginning readers in mind, it is important to note that the orthographic content of current texts for beginning readers places greater cognitive and linguistic demands on students than ever before (Ball & Cohen, 1996; Hiebert, 2005; Hiebert & Martin, 2001; Hoffman et al., 2001). For example, Hiebert's (2005) analysis of six widely used commercial programs demonstrated that over 40 years, texts for beginning readers have increased markedly in length, and these texts use new, unique words and singleton words at a rate that may well outstrip the capacity of many first graders. These changes in texts have not occurred as result of research findings, in fact, Hiebert and Martin (2001) cited a lack of studies that focus on orthographic content and frequency in these texts. Rather, textbook adoption trends in Texas and California, and the repercussions from these trends in other states, indicate that the dramatic changes in these texts have been wrought by pendulum shifts in teaching philosophy, governmental policy, and commercial publishing—not by empirical research.

With regard to the optimum oral reading accuracy and rate benchmarks for pacing students' progression in leveled text, the field has been, and continues to be, driven by tradition rather than research findings. For more than 60 years, educators have adhered to the notion that progress to more difficult text levels should be guided by satisfactory oral-reading accuracy and rate and comprehension scores (see, e.g., Betts, 1946). However, there has been, and continues to be, a distinct lack of consensus for specific criteria. Some assessments set the minimum criterion for instructional, oral-reading accuracy at 90% (Clay, 2005) or 95% (Ekwall & Shanker, 2000; Morris, 1999), and still others set an increasingly stringent criterion as text difficulty increases (Brown, Fields, & Morris, 2007b).

Oral-reading rate criteria are grounded in even less consensus. Some assessments do not include rate as a placement or pacing measure (Clay, 2005). Others use rate as a criterion, adopting benchmarks from norms that represent normally achieving readers at different times during the school year (Brown et al., 2007b; Morris, 1999). Although it would seem that using these norms as rate benchmarks has good content validity, there are no empirical studies to corroborate this tradition. For example, research suggests that first graders who finish the school year reading at least 40 words correct per minute have made satisfactory progress and are likely to continue to make satisfactory progress (Good et al., 2001). Does this mean that children who are reading end-of-first-grade level text should meet or exceed that rate before moving on to more difficult text? Perhaps, to achieve optimum progress, the rate criterion should be higher—or lower. What are the optimum rate benchmarks for struggling readers? Is it more effective for struggling readers to establish stronger fluency at lower levels of text difficulty—even though they may already have met the norm-driven benchmark? Or, is it more effective to move struggling readers into more difficult text and simply increase the amount of support?

With these issues in mind, educators need to use their knowledge of word recognition development to be selective and judicious in their use of texts for beginning readers. In particular, they need to be aware that their core programs and guided reading leveled libraries may not be sufficient with regard to text type, level of difficulty, or sufficient titles for independent practice. To provide sufficient textual scaffolding for all of their students, educators may need to supplement with additional texts.

Finally, educators and researchers must issue a clarion call for rigorous studies on optimum orthographic control in text for beginning readers and optimum use of those texts to place and pace readers. In the absence of sufficient evidence from empirical research, educators have been left to draw on tradition, the pendulum swings of governmental policy, commercial materials, and their own anecdotal evidence to make decisions about these important issues. The shortcomings of this situation for both educators and beginning readers merit prompt action.

REFERENCES

Adams, M. J. (1990). *Beginning to read: Thinking and learning about print*. Cambridge, MA: MIT Press.

Adams, M. J. (2001). Alphabetic anxiety and explicit, systematic phonics instruction: A cognitive science perspective. In S. B. Neuman & D. K. Dickinson (Eds.), *Handbook of early literacy research* (pp. 66–80). New York: Guilford Press.

Anderson, R. C., Hiebert, E. H., Scott, J. A., & Wilkinson, I. G. (1985). *Becoming a nation of readers: The report of the commission on reading*. Washington, DC: The National Institute of Education.

Ball, D. L., & Cohen, D. K. (1996). Reform by the book: What is—or might be—

the role of curriculum materials in teaching learning and instructional reform? *Educational Researcher, 25*, 6–8.

Bear, D. R., Invernizzi, M., Templeton, S., & Johnston, F. (2004). *Words their way: Word study for phonics, vocabulary, and spelling instruction.* Columbus, OH: Pearson

Beck, I. L., & Juel, C. (1995). The role of decoding in learning to read. *American Educator, 19*, 8–42.

Beck, I. L., & McCaslin, E. S. (1978). *An analysis of dimensions that affect the development of code-breaking ability in eight beginning-reading programs.* (LRDC Report No. 1978/6). Pittsburgh, PA: University of Pittsburgh Learning and Research Center.

Betts, E. A. (1946). *Foundations of reading instruction.* New York: American Book Company.

Bloom, P. A. (1994). Recent controversies in the study of language acquisition. In M. A. Gernsbacher (Ed.), *Handbook of psycholinguistics* (pp. 741–780). San Diego, CA: Academic Press.

Bowey, J. A., & Hansen, J. (1994). The development of orthographic rimes as units of word recognition. *Journal of Experimental Child Psychology, 58*, 465–488.

Brady, S. A. (1997). Ability to encode phonological representations: An underlying difficulty in poor readers. In B. Blachman (Ed.), *Foundations of reading acquisition and dyslexia* (pp. 21–48). Mahwah, NJ: Erlbaum.

Brady, S., & Moats, L. (1997). *Informed instruction for reading success: Foundations for teacher preparation.* Baltimore: The International Dyslexia Association.

Bransford, J. D., Nitsch, K. E., & Franks, J. J. (1977). Schooling and facilitation of knowing. In R. C. Anderson, R. J. Spiro, & W. E. Montague (Eds.), *Schooling and the acquisition of knowledge* (pp. 31–55). Hillsdale, NJ: Erlbaum.

Brown, K. J. (1999/2000). What kind of text for whom, when?: Textual scaffolding for beginning readers. *The Reading Teacher, 53*, 292–307.

Brown K. J. (2003). What do I say when they get stuck on a word?: Aligning prompts with students' development during guided reading. *The Reading Teacher, 56*, 720–733.

Brown, K. J., Fields, M. K., & Morris, D. (2007a). *Preserving the power of one-on-one intervention in a small group format.* Manuscript in preparation.

Brown, K. J., Fields, M. K., & Morris, D. (2007b). *UURC Reading Level Assessment Criteria.* Unpublished manuscript, University of Utah Reading Clinic.

Chall, J. S. (1983). *Stages of reading development* (2nd ed.). Fort Worth, TX: Harcourt-Brace.

Christensen, C. A., & Bowey, J. A. (2005). The efficacy of orthographic rime, grapheme–phoneme correspondence, and implicit phonics approaches to teaching decoding skills. *Scientific Studies of Reading, 9*, 327–350.

Clay, M. M. (2005). *Literacy lessons designed for individuals: Part two.* Portsmouth, NH: Heinemann.

Cunningham, A., & Stanovich, K. E., (1998). What reading does for the mind. *American Educator, 22*, 8–15.

Ehri, L. C. (1997). Sight word learning in normal readers and dyslexics. In B.

Blachman (Ed.), *Foundations of reading acquisition and dyslexia* (pp. 163–189). Mahwah, NJ: Erlbaum.

Ehri, L. C. (1998). Grapheme–phoneme knowledge is essential for learning to read words in English. In J. L. Metsala & L. C. Ehri (Eds.), *Word recognition in beginning literacy* (pp. 3–40). Mahwah, NJ: Erlbaum.

Ehri, L. C. (2005). Learning to read words: Theory, findings, and issues. *Scientific Studies of Reading, 9,* 167–188.

Ehri, L. C., & Robbins, C. (1992). Beginners need some decoding skill to read words by analogy. *Reading Research Quarterly, 27,* 12–26.

Ehri, L. C., & Saltmarsh, J. (1995). Beginning readers outperform older disabled readers in learning to read words by sight. *Reading and Writing: An Interdisciplinary Journal, 36,* 250–287.

Ehri, L. C., & Wilce, L. S. (1983). Development of word identification speed in skilled and less skilled beginning readers. *Journal of Educational Psychology, 75,* 3–18.

Ehri, L. C., & Wilce, L. S. (1979). The mnemonic value of orthography among beginning readers. *Journal of Educational Psychology, 71,* 26–40.

Ehri, L. C., Satlow, E., & Gaskins, I. (2006). *Word reading instruction: Graphophonemic analysis strengthens the keyword analogy method for struggling readers.* Manuscript submitted for publication.

Ekwall, E. E., & Shanker, J. L. (2000). *Ekwall/Shanker Reading Inventory* (4th ed.). Boston: Allyn & Bacon.

Englebretson, J. M., Hiebert, E. H., & Juel, C. (1998). *Ready readers.* Parsippany, NJ: Modern Curriculum Press.

Foorman, B. R., Francis, D. J., Fletcher, J. M., Schatschneider, C., & Mehta, P. (1998). The role of instruction in learning to read. *Journal of Educational Psychology, 90,* 37–55.

Fountas, I. C., & Pinnell, G. S. (1999). *Matching books to readers: Using leveled books in guided reading, K–3.* New York: Heinemann.

Gaskins, I., Ehri, L., Cress, C., O'Hara, C., & Donnelly, K. (1996/1997). Procedures for word learning: Making discoveries about words. *The Reading Teacher, 50,* 312–327.

Good, R. H., Simmons, D. C., & Kame'enui, E. J. (2001). The importance and decision-making utility of a continuum of fluency-based indicators of foundational reading skills for third-grade high-stakes outcomes. *Scientific Studies of Reading, 5,* 257–288.

Goswami, U. (1986). Orthographic analogies and reading development. *Quarterly Journal of Experimental Psychology, 42,* 73–83.

Goswami, U. (2001). Early phonological development and the acquisition of literacy. In S. B. Neuman & D. K. Dickinson (Eds.), *Handbook of early literacy research* (pp. 111–125). New York: Guilford Press.

Gough, P. B., & Hillinger, M. L. (1980). Learning to read: An unnatural act. *Bulletin of the Orton Society, 30,* 171–176.

Gough, P. B., Juel, C., & Griffith, P. L. (1992). Reading, spelling, and the orthographic cipher. In P. B. Gough, L. C. Ehri, & R. Treiman (Eds.), *Reading acquisition* (pp. 35–48). Hillsdale, NJ: Erlbaum.

Hiebert, E. H. (1998). *Early literacy instruction.* Fort Worth, TX: Harcourt Brace.

Hiebert, E. H. (2005). State reform policies and the task textbooks pose for first-grade readers. *Elementary School Journal, 105,* 245–266.

Hiebert, E. H., & Martin, L. A. (2001). The texts of beginning reading instruction. In S. B. Neuman & D. K. Dickinson (Eds.), *Handbook of early literacy research* (pp. 361–376). New York: Guilford Press.

Hoffman, J., Roser, N., Salas, R., Patterson, E., & Pennington, J. (2001). Text leveling and little books in first-grade reading. *Journal of Literacy Research, 33,* 507–528.

Juel, C. (1988). Learning to read and write: A longitudinal study of fifty-four children from first through fourth grades. *Journal of Educational Psychology, 80,* 437–447.

Juel, C., & Minden-Cupp, C. (2000). Learning to read words: Linguistic units and instructional strategies. *Reading Research Quarterly, 35,* 458–492.

Juel, C., & Roper/Schneider, D. (1985). The influence of basal readers on first-grade reading. *Reading Research Quarterly, 20,* 134–152.

Kinstch, W. (1974). *The representation of meaning in memory.* Hillsdale, NJ: Erlbaum.

LaBerge, D., & Samuels, S. J. (1974). Toward a theory of automatic information processing in reading. *Cognitive Psychology, 6,* 293–323.

Leu, D. J. Jr., DeGroff, L. J. C., & Simons, H. D. (1986). Predictable texts and inter-active-compensatory hypotheses: Evaluating individual differences in reading ability, context use, and comprehension. *Journal of Educational Psychology, 78,* 347–352.

Liberman, A. M. (1999). The reading researcher and the reading teacher need the right theory of speech. *Scientific Studies of Reading, 3,* 95–112.

Libscomb, L., & Gough, P. B. (1990). Word length and first word recognition. In J. Zutell & S. McCormick (Eds.), *Thirty-ninth yearbook of the national reading conference* (pp. 217–222). Chicago: National Reading Conference.

Lukatela, G., & Turvey, M. T. (1994). Visual lexical access is initially phonological: Evidence from phonological priming by homophones and psuedohomophones. *Journal of Experimental Psychology, 123,* 331–353.

Masonheimer, P. E., Drum, P. A., & Ehri, L. C. (1984). Does environmental print identification lead children into word reading? *Journal of Reading Behavior, 16,* 257–271.

Mesmer, H. A. (1999). Scaffolding a crucial transition using texts with some decodability. *The Reading Teacher, 53,* 130–142.

Mesmer, H. A. (2006). Beginning reading materials: A national survey of primary teachers' reported uses and beliefs. *Journal of Literacy Research, 38,* 389–425.

Metsala, J. L. (1999). Young children's phonological awareness and nonword repetition as a function of vocabulary development. *Journal of Educational Psychology, 91,* 3–19.

Morris, D. (1992). Concept of word: A pivotal understanding in the learning-to-read process. In S. Templeton & D. R. Bear (Eds.), *Development of orthographic knowledge and the foundations of literacy: A memorial festschrift for Edmund H. Henderson* (pp. 53–77). Hillsdale, NJ: Erlbaum.

Morris, D. (1999). The role of clinical training in the teaching of reading. In D.

Evensen & P. Mosenthal (Eds.), *Advances in reading/language research: Vol. 6. Rethinking the role of the reading clinic in a new age of literacy* (pp. 69–100). Stamford, CT: JAI Press.

Morris, D. (2005). *The Howard Street tutoring manual: Teaching at-risk readers in the primary grades* (2nd ed.). New York: Guilford Press.

Morris, D., Bloodgood, J. W., Lomax, R. G., & Perney, J. (2003). Developmental steps in learning to read: A longitudinal study in kindergarten and first grade. *Reading Research Quarterly, 38,* 302–328.

Morris, D., Tyner, B., & Perney, J. (2000). Early steps: Replicating the effects of a first-grade reading intervention program. *Journal of Educational Psychology, 92,* 681–693.

Nagy, W. E., & Anderson, R. C. (1984). How many words are there in printed school English? *Reading Research Quarterly, 19,* 304–330.

Nelson, K. (1973). Structure and strategy in learning to talk. *Monographs of the Society for Research in Child Development, 381–382*(Serial no. 149).

Perfetti, C. A. (1991). Representations and awareness in the acquisition of reading competence. In L. Rieben & C. Perfetti (Eds.), *Learning to read: Basic research and its implications* (pp. 33–44). Hillsdale, NJ: Erlbaum.

Perfetti, C. A. (1992). The representation problem in reading acquisition. In P. Gough, L. C. Ehri, & R. Trieman, (Eds.), *Reading acquisition* (pp. 145–174). Hillsdale, NJ: Erlbaum.

Rayner, K. (1997). Understanding eye movements in reading. *Scientific Studies of Reading, 1,* 317–341.

Rayner, K., Foorman, B. F., Perfetti, C. A., Pesetsky, D., & Seidenberg, M. S. (2002). How psychological science informs the teaching of reading. *Psychological Science in the Public Interest, 2*(2), 31–74.

Reitsma, P. (1983). Printed word learning in beginning readers. *Journal of Experimental Child Psychology, 75,* 321–339.

Samuels, S. J., Schermer, N., & Reinking, D. (1992). Reading fluency: Techniques for making decoding automatic. In S. J. Samuels & A. E. Farstrup (Eds.), *What research says about reading instruction* (2nd ed., pp. 142–144). Newark, DE: International Reading Association.

Savage, R., Stuart, M., & Hill, V. (2001). The role of scaffolding errors in reading development: Evidence from a longitudinal and a correlational study. *British Journal of Educational Psychology, 71,* 1–13.

Savin, H. B., & Bever, T. G. (1970). The nonperceptual reality of the phoneme. *Journal of Verbal Learning and Verbal Behavior, 9,* 295–302.

Scarborough, H. S., & Brady, S. A. (2002). Toward a common terminology for talking about speech and reading: A glossary of the "phon" words and some related terms. *Journal of Literacy Research, 34,* 299–336.

Schwanenflugel, P. J., Hamilton, A. M., Kuhn, M. R., Wisenbaker, J., & Stahl, S. A. (2004). Becoming a fluent reader: Reading skill and prosodic features in the oral reading of young readers. *Journal of Educational Psychology, 96,* 119–129.

Seymour, P. H. K., & Elder, L. (1986). Beginning reading without phonology. *Cognitive Neuropsychology, 3,* 1–36.

Shankweiler, D., Lundquist, E., Katz, L., Stuebing, K. K., Fletcher, J. M., Brady, S., et al. (1999). Comprehension and decoding: Patterns of association in children with reading difficulties. *Scientific Studies of Reading, 3,* 69–94.

Share, D. L. (1995). Phonological recoding and self-teaching: Sine qua non of reading acquisition. *Cognition, 55,* 151–218.

Share, D. L. (2004). Orthographic learning at a glance: On the time course and developmental onset of self-teaching. *Journal of Experimental Child Psychology, 87,* 267–298.

Share, D. L., & Jorm, A. J. (1983). Phonological recoding and reading acquisition. *Applied Psycholinguistics, 4,* 103–147.

Share, D. L., & Stanovich, K. E. (1995). Cognitive processes in early reading development: Accommodating individual differences into a mode of acquisition. *Issues in Education: Contributions from Educational Psychology, 1,* 1–57.

Stanovich, K. E. (1986). Matthew effects in reading: Some consequences of individual differences in the acquisition of literacy. *Reading Research Quarterly, 21,* 360–406.

Stanovich, K. E. (1991). Word recognition: Changing perspectives. In R. Barr, M. L. Kamil, P. Mosenthal, & P. D. Pearson (Eds.), *Handbook of reading research* (Vol. 2, pp. 418–452). New York: Longman.

Stein, M., Johnson, B., & Gutlohn, L. (1999). Analyzing beginning reading programs: The relationship between decoding instruction and text. *Journal of Remedial and Special Education, 20,* 275–287.

Stuart, M. (1990). Factors influencing word recognition in pre-reading children. *British Journal of Psychology, 81,* 135–146.

Stuart, M., & Coltheart, M. (1988). Does reading develop in a sequence of stages? *Cognition, 30,* 139–181.

Tatham, S. M. (1970). Reading comprehension of materials written with select oral language patterns: A study of grades two and four. *Reading Research Quarterly, 3,* 402–426.

Templeton, S. (1992). Theory, nature and pedagogy of higher-order orthographic development in older students. In S. Templeton & D. R. Bear (Eds.), *Development of orthographic knowledge and the foundations of literacy: A memorial festschrift for Edmund H. Henderson* (pp. 253–278). Hillsdale, NJ: Erlbaum.

Treiman, R., Goswami, U., & Bruck, M. (1990). Not all nonwords are alike: Implications for reading development and theory. *Memory and Cognition, 18,* 559–567.

Treiman, R., Mullennix, J., Bijeljac-Babic, R., & Richmond-Welty, E. D. (1995). The special role of rimes in the description, use, and acquisition of English orthography. *Journal of Experimental Psychology: General, 124,* 107–136.

Tunmer, W. E., & Chapman, J. W. (1998). Language prediction skill, phonological recoding ability, and beginning reading. In C. Hulme & R. Joshi (Eds.), *Reading and spelling: Development and disorders* (pp. 33–67). Mahwah, NJ: Erlbaum.

Tunmer, W. E., Chapman, J. W., & Prochnow, J. E. (2003). Preventing Matthews effects in at-risk readers: A retrospective study. In B. R. Foorman (Ed.), *Preventing and remediating reading difficulties: Bringing science to scale* (pp. 121–164). Baltimore: York Press.

Vellutino, F. R., Scanlon, D. M., Sipay, E. R., Small, S. G., Pratt, A., Chen, R., et al.

(1996). Cognitive profiles of difficult-to-remediate and readily remediated poor readers: Early intervention as a vehicle for distinguishing between cognitive and experiential deficits as basic causes of specific reading disability. *Journal of Educational Psychology, 88,* 601–638.

Walley, A. (1993). The role of vocabulary development in children's spoken word recognition and segmentation ability. *Developmental Review, 13,* 286–350.

Warren, R. M. (1971). Identification times for phonemic components of graded complexity and for spelling of speech. *Perception and Psychophysics, 9,* 345–349.

Watson, R. (2001). Literacy and oral language: Implications for early literacy acquisition. In S. B. Neuman & D. K. Dickinson (Eds.), *Handbook of early literacy research* (pp. 43–53). New York: Guilford Press.

Wilson, B. A. (1996). *Wilson reading system.* Millbury, MA: Wilson Language Training.

Wise, B., & Olson, R. (1995). Computer-based phonological awareness and reading instruction. *Annals of Dyslexia, 45,* 99–122.

Wylie, R. E., & Durrell, D. D. (1970). Teaching vowels through phonograms. *Elementary English, 47,* 787–791.

CHILDREN'S BOOKS

Bloksberg, R. (1996). *The hiccups would not stop.* Parsippany, NJ: Modern Curriculum Press.

Cowley, J. (1998). *A monster sandwich.* Bothell, WA: Wright Group.

Engles, D. (1996). *My lost top.* Parsippany, NJ: Modern Curriculum Press.

Grout, B. J. (1996). *A fun place to eat.* Parsippany, NJ: Modern Curriculum Press.

Hoff, S. (1958). *Danny and the dinosaur.* New York: Scholastic.

Minarik, E. (1968). *A kiss for Little Bear.* New York: HarperCollins.

Nicholson, C. (1996). *Bedtime at Aunt Carmen's.* Parsippany, NJ: Modern Curriculum Press.

Nicholson, C. (1996). *I can swim.* Parsippany, NJ: Modern Curriculum Press.

Randell, B. (1996). *Honey for Baby Bear.* Crystal Lake, IL: Rigby.

Randell, B., Giles, J., & Smith, A. (1996). *Little things.* Crystal Lake, IL: Rigby.

✺ 10 ✺

When the "Right Texts"
Are Difficult for Struggling Readers

ALISON K. BILLMAN
KATHERINE HILDEN
JULIET L. HALLADAY

The question of what texts are appropriate to use with beginning and struggling readers is an issue of great interest to researchers, teachers, clinicians, and parents alike. Since Betts (1946) first drew attention to the need to have appropriate texts in order for students to read accurately and meaningfully, scholars have affirmed the importance of providing students with texts they can read with a high degree of accuracy. In this chapter, we consider research-based solutions for students who, for a variety of reasons, are not highly proficient with texts that they need or want to read. These texts may be a part of the typical curriculum of the school—the content-area texts with which many students struggle— or even the literature selections in student anthologies that often contain numerous rare and multisyllabic words (Hiebert, Chapter 1, this volume). Other difficult texts may be ones that students are eager to read because of an interest or expertise but are texts written beyond their reading ability.

Proficient reading development for elementary students depends upon opportunities to engage with appropriate texts, since the characteristics of a text appear to mediate students' gains in areas such as fluency (e.g., Hiebert, 2005) and vocabulary (e.g., Sternberg, 1987). At the same time, focusing solely on students' developing reading skill is not enough. Instructional texts must also provide students with content that engages them, motivates them, and helps them build the background knowledge that is required for being good readers and thinkers. Engagement with texts that offer the right amount of challenge and are not too easy can also motivate students to engage in additional reading (e.g., Miller & Meece, 1999; Turner & Paris, 1995). In other words, texts must not be simply *readable*; they must contain information and ideas worth reading.

Providing students with texts they can read and understand while simultaneously furthering their reading abilities is more difficult than it might seem. The appropriateness of a reader–text match is complicated by numerous student and text variables. While much of the research on text difficulty focuses on matching texts to students' decoding and fluency abilities, some students may struggle with texts for other reasons, such as lack of background knowledge and experience or limitations in receptive vocabulary (e.g., Whitehurst & Lonigan, 1998). Not every struggling reader has the same set of issues, and not all issues involve decoding and fluency (e.g., Cain & Oakhill, 2006; Riddle-Buly & Valencia, 2002).

While reader–text match may be considered during reading instruction, there are situations across the school day where students may be expected to read texts that do not match their decoding and fluency abilities. For example, in elementary classrooms, students are often expected to read and learn from the same text or texts, regardless of the diversity in their reading abilities (Hiebert, Chapter 1, this volume). In an examination of elementary science and social studies textbooks, Chall and Conard (1991) found that most of the textbooks were written at least one or two grade levels above the grade level at which they were being used. Not surprisingly, they also found that many students struggled to comprehend these texts. Students may also encounter difficult texts when their interest in a topic or their need for particular content information is not available in texts written at their appropriate reading level (Duke, 2000; Duke & Billman, Chapter 6, this volume). For instance, struggling first- or second-grade readers interested in learning more about tornadoes may struggle to find a text that they can read successfully and that contains the precise terminology that will enable them to learn some of the essential science vocabulary relevant to the topic.

READERS STRUGGLE WITH TEXT
FOR DIFFERENT REASONS IN DIFFERENT WAYS

There are numerous characteristics of readers that may make specific texts difficult (Riddle-Buly & Valencia, 2002). In their analysis of a group of struggling fourth-grade readers, Riddle-Buly and Valencia (2002) found that similar scores on a state reading assessment masked a range of differences in individual reading skills. While the identified reading difficulties fit into three general categories—word identification, fluency, and meaning—a detailed analysis of individual student's performance revealed ten different profiles of struggling readers. For example, some struggling readers read quickly and accurately with poor comprehension, while others read slowly and haltingly with good comprehension. Riddle-Buly and Valencia's analysis demonstrated that struggling readers are not all alike and that not all reading problems are decoding problems.

Reasons Students Might Struggle with Texts

Students may struggle because they bring different skill levels of fluency and word recognition to a text; however, they also bring specific sets of background knowledge about the topic along with varying levels of strategies for gaining meaning from text. As an example, while educators reading this chapter will be fluent decoders of this text as well as an advanced biology text, they may have difficulties comprehending an article from a scientific journal on neurology due to limited background and experiences with neurology. While educators may be able to pronounce the words in the neurology journal, they may not know the precise meaning of those words. Overall, they likely do not have the background knowledge to gain more than a superficial understanding of the articles in the neurology journal.

A student's limited background experiences may also be related to limitations in vocabulary, genre, or topical knowledge. While research has shown that the richness of experiences with language and the world in general contribute to a student's overall success (Hart & Risley, 1995; Whitehurst & Lonigan, 1998), the exact dimensions of a particular student's background may mediate or impede the reading of a particular text. Anderson and Pearson (1984) concluded that readers' prior knowledge is a strong influence on their comprehension of texts. That is, the ways readers interact with texts, including the predictions and inferences they make, are influenced by their prior knowledge. For instance, Hansen (1981) found that instruction which encouraged second graders to connect prior knowledge to the texts they were reading significantly improved their ability to answer inferential questions about those stories. Bos and Anders (1990) have also noted that incomplete or weak schema for the topics covered in text can negatively impact the comprehension of middle school students with learning disabilities. In an intervention study focusing on vocabulary instruction, they found that students' prior knowledge of science topics, such as fossils, was a significant covariate in predicting vocabulary knowledge and reading comprehension of science content passages.

A student's ability to make relevant connections to prior knowledge is as critical as the nature or extent of a student's prior knowledge. Williams (1993, 1998) demonstrated that adolescent readers with learning disabilities had great difficulty identifying themes of stories and subsequently making accurate predictions. She concluded that this difficulty may be partially due to these students' idiosyncratic connections to background knowledge. For example, students with learning disabilities often have cognitive inhibition, or the inability to suppress inaccurate or irrelevant connections to the text. While less attention has focused on irrelevant prior knowledge connections made by elementary students, it is reasonable to think that similar trends would hold for younger, struggling readers, too. According to Miller (2002), instruction focused on distinguishing between irrelevant and helpful connections needs to begin early, even as early as first grade.

Students' prior experiences with print and the world also include exposure to vocabulary. The idea that vocabulary knowledge is related to reading comprehension makes intuitive sense, but there is also a substantial research base to support this (Anderson & Freebody, 1981; Cain, Oakhill, & Bryant, 2004; Davis, 1944; National Reading Panel, 2000; Stahl & Fairbanks, 1986). In a recent study, the vocabulary knowledge of third graders who performed similarly on a word recognition measure but differently on a comprehension measure was compared (Cain & Oakhill, 2006). The students with low comprehension scores performed significantly worse than students with high comprehension scores on a measure of receptive vocabulary. This pattern is similar to that reported by Riddle-Buly and Valencia (2002). In that study of fourth-grade struggling readers, the average score on a receptive vocabulary measure was nearly two-thirds of a standard deviation lower than the mean normative score. While knowledge of relevant vocabulary enables readers to recognize words in text, facility with the vocabulary of a text means that readers can also integrate their semantic knowledge to give richer and more extensive meaning to the text.

A characteristic that is often neglected in discussions of poor comprehension has to do with task persistence. Many students with learning disabilities appear to have little persistence in reading texts, and this lack of task persistence contributes to poor attention and, subsequently, poor comprehension (McKinney, Osborne, & Schulte, 1993). Gersten, Fuchs, Williams, and Baker (2001) note that learning and applying comprehension strategies can be a daunting task for younger readers and those with learning disabilities. Therefore, these students, "must be taught, coaxed, and encouraged to use strategies that they are only beginning to master" (p. 286). Paris and Oka (1989) recommend that issues around task persistence be considered in the design of instruction. They explain that successful comprehension instruction for students with learning disabilities should include teaching students how to set goals and make positive attributions about their strategy use.

Ways Struggling Students Differ

Leach, Scarborough, and Rescola (2003) found that 41% of fourth- and fifth-grade students identified with a reading disability in their study had not been identified as having a reading disability in the third grade or before. This finding suggests that this group of students may not have been remarkably different from their peers in decoding and fluency prior to fourth and fifth grade. Catts, Hogan, and Fey (2003) classified struggling readers in second and fourth grade as having one of four diagnoses: (1) dyslexia (word-recognition problems and good listening comprehension), (2) hyperlexia (listening comprehension problems and good word recognition), (3) learning disabled (problems with both word recognition and listening comprehension), and (4) nonspecified reading disorder (poor comprehension despite word recognition and listening comprehension scores within an acceptable range). In fourth grade, 13.2% of their sample fell into this final category. The researchers concluded that other variables beyond word recognition and listening comprehension likely contributed to their reading comprehension deficits.

While Catts and his colleagues do not hypothesize about the variables that may be at the root of these nonspecified reading problems, Leach et al. (2003) suggest that difficulties in reading comprehension are often related to deficiencies in oral language, background knowledge, metacognitive awareness, strategy use, and memory capacity. They underscore the importance of matching instructional interventions to individual students' deficiencies, rather than to overall grade level. Given the variety of potential factors contributing to any one reader's ability to successfully read a particular text, we believe that matching texts *and* instructional interventions to students offers increased opportunities for their ultimate success as readers.

INSTRUCTIONAL STRATEGIES FOR SUPPORTING STRUGGLING READERS WITH CHALLENGING TEXTS

We have organized our review of research for supporting struggling readers into three areas: (1) instructional activities that mediate reader factors such as fluency and decoding difficulties or limited background; (2) instruction that prepares struggling readers to read more difficult texts; and (3) researched models that combine strategy instruction with scaffolded support for reading difficult texts.

Instructional Activities That Mediate Reader Factors

Reading Aloud

A common technique for providing struggling and beginning readers with opportunities to engage with challenging texts is the read-aloud event (Morrow & Brittain, 2003). The read-aloud is a context where students can be introduced to new vocabulary and genres, while building the background knowledge that undergirds proficient reading and developing content-area knowledge (e.g., Pappas, Varelas, Barry, & Rife, 2004; Smolkin & Donovan, 2003; Whitehurst & Lonigan, 1998). Much of the research around the value of reading aloud to children has focused on preschool and primary-grade children. These studies have shown that high-quality, interactive read-alouds have a significant impact on the language competency and vocabulary of children (e.g., Dickenson & Tabors, 2001; Duke & Kays, 1998; McGee & Schickedanz, 2007; Rosenhouse, Feitelson, & Kita, 1997; Whitehurst et al., 1988). High-quality read-alouds are characterized by verbal interactions between the reader and the listeners, with these interactions including elaborations of vocabulary and content (e.g., Oyler & Barry, 1996; Whitehurst & Lonigan, 1998).

Morrow (1988) noted that repeated interactive read-alouds seem to be most effective for children of low ability. Morrow (1988) found that 4-year-olds who experienced interactive read-alouds asked more questions and made more comments during the posttest read-aloud. This finding could be interpreted as evidence that the 4-year-olds were more actively processing the text. Secondly, the children that experienced repeated read-alouds (as opposed to only hearing a text one time) made more interpretive responses and more responses that focused on print and story structure.

Drawing on work in second-grade classrooms, Pappas and her colleagues (2004) argue that high-quality read-alouds of informational texts are especially critical for student learning. Many second graders, especially struggling readers, have difficulty accessing the content of informational texts without these teacher-led experiences. These interactive sessions—described as dialogic inquiry—become the venue for clarifying and elaborating scientific content in ways that support students coming to deeper scientific understanding.

Similarly, Smolkin and Donovan (2003) propose that information book read-alouds can make a difference for emerging and struggling readers. Smolkin and Donovan (2001) compared story book and informational book read-alouds. They note that students who experienced interactive read-alouds with informational books were more likely to initiate comprehension-related or meaning-seeking responses when compared to student responses during interactive story book read-alouds. While student content learning is not measured in this study, they do suggest that information read-alouds may support comprehension-related reasoning.

There is little research that examines student content learning during informational read-alouds. However, in one study that examined students' understanding of informational texts, Moss (1997) assessed the oral retellings of 20 first graders after one-on-one read-alouds. Moss found that most students scored well on the retelling, suggesting that even young students are able to understand expository text that they encounter through read-alouds. Unfortunately, Moss does not mention the readability level of the text read to the students (only one text was used), so we do not know for sure if the read-aloud was a difficult text or one that the students could have read on their own.

While studies of read-alouds with older students is limited, Allington and Johnston (2002), in their study of exemplary fourth-grade literacy teachers, highlight one teacher whose instructional routines included read-alouds. In this teacher's classroom, texts for read-alouds were chosen deliberately to support content. Further, the teacher used these texts as a context for teaching new vocabulary as well as for teaching and modeling comprehension strategies. Although the report does not articulate the teacher's interactions with struggling readers, Allington and Johnston (2002) do note that the read-aloud event was a venue in which all students had access to specific content.

More research using reading aloud to support struggling readers, particularly those who are in the middle grades and beyond, would be beneficial. Based on existing evidence, however, it seems reasonable to view read-alouds as a means of meditating access to the content of a difficult text in upper- as well as primary-grade classrooms. Recommendations for structuring a high-quality read-aloud include steps that introduce and elaborate on the content of the text prior to reading. The purpose of such foundational activities is to build students' background knowledge on the topic and to activate relevant background knowledge that is useful for comprehension during the read-aloud (e.g., McGee & Schickedanz, 2007; van Kleeck, Stahl, & Bauer, 2003). During reading, teachers can lead students in activities that support understanding of complex or new vocabulary (e.g., Beck & McKeown, 2001) and give students opportunities to question and respond (Barrantine, 1996; Pappas et al., 2003). Finally, teachers can support comprehension and analytical thinking by engaging students in discussions about the text that include follow-up questioning and summarizing (McGee & Schickedanz, 2007).

Partner Reading and Peer Coaching

Another commonly used strategy to support reading of difficult texts is peer-assisted instruction. This strategy pairs students of similar or different abilities in structured routines around reading. Some pairings—in which students with similar reading profiles are assigned similar responsibilities—are designed to be collaborative (e.g., Fuchs, Fuchs, Mathes, & Simmons, 1997), while other models position older or more advanced students as tutors for younger or less able students (Fuchs, Fuchs, Kazdan, & Allen, 1999; Labbo & Teale, 1990; Van Keer & Verhaeghe, 2005). These models are characterized by engaging students in partner reading and practice of strategies related to word identification, comprehension, rereading, and explanations or feedback (Fuchs et al., 1999; Labbo & Teale, 1990; Mathes, Howard, Allen, & Fuchs, 1998; Van Keer & Verhaeghe, 2005). Benefits to students tend to vary based on the responsibilities within the dyads and the ages of the students (Fuchs et al., 1999). Student tutoring roles tend to have a greater impact on the reading achievement of students in upper-elementary grades, but even younger students have shown benefits from participating as either tutees or tutors (Mathes et al., 1998; Van Keer & Verhaeghe, 2005). In particular, this model of structuring interactions with texts has proven to be effective with lower-achieving students (Fuchs et al., 1997, 1999; Mathes et al., 1998; Mathes, Torgeson, Clancy-Manchetti, Nicholas, Robinson, et al., 2003; Van Keer & Verhaeghe, 2005).

Successful frameworks for structuring peer interactions include teacher-directed preparation for reading that models routines and targeted activities or strategies for engaging with text. An example of a tested model is Peer-Assisted Learning Strategies, or PALS (Fuchs et al., 1997). PALS takes place in classrooms and is characterized by one-to-one peer tutoring where student partners read and practice the strategies of summarizing and predicting. Studies of PALS in primary and upper-elementary classrooms have shown to benefit all students, with low achieving students making more gains across time (Fuchs et al., 1997; Mathes, Grek, Howard, Babyak, & Allen, 1999; Mathes et al., 1998).

A modified version of PALS has even proven effective with first graders (Mathes et al., 1998, 1999). The first-grade PALS is structured around two strategic reading routines based on effective early-literacy instruction: (1) a sounds and words routine that focuses on code-based language practice and (2) a partner-read-aloud routine that attends to comprehension strategies like predicting and summarizing. Observations during PALS showed that first graders were highly engaged in reading and consistently followed routines. While all students benefited from PALS, the lowest-achieving students showed the greatest gains (Mathes et al., 1998). A part of the study that may have contributed to the efficacy of the intervention was the attention that teachers paid to book selection. This component of teachers' careful choice of texts for the reading events may have meant that the texts were less difficult than is the case with typical first-grade texts such as those that Hiebert (Chapter 1, this volume) describes.

Cross-Age Reading and Tutoring

Programs that have structured peer interactions where older or more-skilled readers are paired with younger or less-skilled readers have proven to benefit the student tutor nearly as much as the student tutee (Labbo & Teale, 1990; Van Keer & Verhaeghe, 2005). As tutors learn specific routines for interacting with their tutees around text—providing help, elaborating, and reading aloud—they are put in the position to practice essential skills that support their own reading development. In a study that paired struggling fifth-grade readers with kindergartners as read-aloud partners, Labbo and Teale (1990) found that the older struggling readers scored significantly higher on standardized reading-achievement measures than control and alternative treatment groups. Additionally, the attitudes of these students toward reading improved and the amount of time they spent reading increased. Similarly, Van Keer and Verhaeghe (2005) report that cross-age tutoring along with same-age tutoring significantly improved reading comprehension of fifth graders. This same study paired second graders in same-age tutoring dyads. The second graders were less able to carry out the responsibilities of tutoring and benefited less in these situations. However, second graders made comparable gains when working with the teacher or the fifth-grade tutor. In each of these studies, the tutors or older readers participated in training, spent time practicing, and then were coached. This body of research suggests that pairing students in these ways provides support for the tutee with texts that are difficult; at the same time, the preparation engages the tutor in reading activities that support fluency, regulated use of comprehension strategies, and motivation for engaging with texts. While the tutors may not be reading difficult texts themselves, they are preparing for reading and practicing reading in ways that support their personal reading development.

Using Easier Texts to Build Background and Vocabulary

We are hesitant to suggest strategies that are not research based. However, priming students with easier texts that have content similar to that of more difficult texts is a recommendation that makes intuitive sense and has been proposed by scholars (Fielding & Roller, 1992; Duke & Billman, Chapter 6, this volume). These simpler texts are easier to decode and can expose challenged readers to new vocabulary and build related background knowledge. By introducing students to topic-related terminology and content, reading these simpler texts may support students in their future interactions with more difficult texts about related topics. While this practice may be an effective method for mediating readers' limited content and background knowledge, the efficacy of this strategy requires additional empirical validation.

Instruction That Prepares Struggling Readers to Read More Difficult Texts

A focus of researchers has been on identifying instruction that gives students, especially those who are initially less proficient readers, the strategies and knowledge they need to comprehend challenging texts. The forms of instruction found to be especially effective in developing proficiencies among struggling readers include: (1) vocabulary, (2) text structure, and (3) comprehension strategies (specifically summarizing and questioning). We note, while many of the following studies do not focus specifically on "difficult" texts, struggling readers have been shown to improve their reading comprehension. A likely assumption is that, prior to the instruction, these texts were difficult for struggling readers.

Vocabulary Instruction

Limitations in vocabulary knowledge are a significant source of reading difficulties for many struggling readers, because vocabulary knowledge and reading comprehension are highly correlated (e.g., Anderson & Freebody, 1981). When struggling readers are presented with challenging texts, they frequently face a significant number of unknown vocabulary words. Targeted instruction can assist struggling readers to build vocabulary and subsequently to comprehend difficult texts.

There are two key points to consider when planning vocabulary instruction to support struggling readers with difficult texts. First, words are learned both through direct teaching and through incidental exposure (Pressley, 2006; Sternberg, 1987). Teachers need to teach some words directly, but they must also teach students strategies that maximize their ability to learn vocabulary from context. Second, the incremental nature of word learning means that there are often many small steps between a first exposure to a word and complete mastery of the word's usage (Nagy & Scott, 2000; Schwanenflugel, Stahl, & McFalls, 1997). Therefore, effective instruction must involve direct instruction of essential words, repeated exposure to new words in context, and opportunities to increase depth of word knowledge (National Reading Panel, 2000; Stahl & Fairbanks, 1986). To this end, Stahl and Nagy (2006) advocate for a comprehensive approach to vocabulary instruction that includes three main components: teaching specific words, immersing students in a rich language environment, and developing generative vocabulary knowledge in the form of transferable strategies for learning additional words.

To help students deal with challenging texts, teachers can teach key words and terms directly, either during teacher-led read-alouds or during separate lessons. Providing word meanings and practicing them through use in sample sentences and work with synonyms appears to have a positive effect on word knowledge beyond what is gained simply from learning words in context (Pany, Jenkins, & Schreck, 1982). Once words have been introduced, teachers can provide students with repeated exposure to these new words through language experiences such as read-alouds, class discussion, and a range of texts.

In addition to teaching individual words and providing rich exposure to words in context, teachers can also assist struggling readers by teaching them to use vocabulary strategies that draw on contextual clues and morphological characteristics of individual words. For example, an unfamiliar word may have morphemes (i.e., root, prefix, or suffix) that readers can use as aids in inferring its meaning. As an example, words such as *moveable* and *removable* can be inferred from students' knowledge of the word *move*. Nagy and Anderson (1984) have estimated that as many as 60% of the unknown words that students encounter in texts from the middle grades and beyond are words with morphological roots and affixes. When students are taught to use knowledge of morphemes in decoding new words, rather than relying simply on letter–sound correspondences, the number of unfamiliar words they can understand increases substantially.

Text-Structure Instruction

Knowledge of text structure supports a reader's comprehension and memory of text. In fact, effective readers process different genres differently (Goldman & Rakestraw, 2000). This has several implications for teachers. First, it suggests that students should be exposed to a variety of genres in order to develop understanding of different text structures (Duke, 2000; Duke & Bennett-Armistead, 2003). Second, it suggests that teachers should support students' development of this understanding through instruction. Text-structure instruction can take a variety of forms; for example, the direct teaching of text structures, the direct teaching of language that is common to the genre, the use of visual representations of text structure to support interactions with text, to name a few (Goldman & Rakestraw, 2000).

When considering struggling students, research on teaching the structure of stories has focused on the primary grades. This work has shown that elementary students with learning disabilities benefit from learning to apply knowledge of structure when reading narrative texts (Carnine & Kinder, 1985; Idol, 1987; Idol & Croll, 1987; Newby, Caldwell, & Recht, 1989; Williams, Brown, Silverstein, & deCani, 1994). Armed with knowledge of story structure and the ability to identify story elements, struggling readers are more able to tackle the reading of texts that are difficult for them.

Learning about the structures of informational texts, not simply those of stories, has also proven useful to struggling readers, as illustrated by a program of research led by Williams (Williams, Hall, & Lauer, 2004; Williams, Hall, deCani, Lauer, Stafford, et al., 2005; Williams, Nubla-Kung, Pollini, & Stafford, 2007). One focus of this program of research has been to investigate the effects of explicitly teaching cause and effect text structure to at-risk second graders during science and social studies instruction. This intervention specifically combines vocabulary instruction with text-structure instruction. Content-area vocabulary as well as vocabulary that signals text structure is explicitly explained and modeled through examples. In addition, students are taught to use generic cause–effect questions and graphic organizers to help identify and analyze cause–effect paragraphs. This program of research has included attention to the difficulty of text, with Williams et al. (2007) giving at-risk second graders texts with an average readability of second to third grade—texts that are likely at the instructional or even frustration level for these particular students. Despite the difficulty of the texts, students who received the intervention were able to comprehend and learn significantly more content than students in the control condition. Since effects of the vocabulary instruction and the text-structure instruction were not separated out in this study, we cannot know whether vocabulary instruction and text-structure instruction work synergistically or separately to support comprehension. However, we do know this type of instruction appears to facilitate struggling readers' comprehension of difficult texts.

Comprehension Strategies: Summarizing and Questioning

A particular focus of researchers over the past 25 years has been the comprehension benefits of teaching individual strategies to developing readers (e.g., National Reading Panel, 2000; Pressley, 2006; RAND Reading Study Group, 2001). In this review, we discuss two of many strategies that have proven to foster comprehension for students with reading disabilities—questioning and summarizing. We recognize that these strategies are not the only ones these students benefit from. Rather, we include them as illustrative examples.

First, special-education students seem to benefit from learning to ask questions when reading expository texts. Simmonds (1992) examined the impact of the question–answer–relationships (QARs) strategy. QARs consist of teaching students to distinguish between three types of questions: questions that are text explicit and *right there,* questions that are text explicit and require the reader to *think and search,* and questions that are script implicit and require the reader to synthesize information across the text *on my own* (Raphael & Pearson, 1985). While Simmonds focused on special-education students, the QARs strategy is one that is tested and recommended for all students (Raphael & Au, 2005; Raphael & Pearson, 1985; Raphael & Wonnacott, 1985). The concrete language of QARs seems to scaffold students' developing abilities to construct meaning from difficult texts.

Students also seem to benefit from learning to ask questions across various genres. In that respect, the QARs heuristic can be used for thinking about and planning for comprehension instruction in the context of content-area learning (Raphael & Au, 2005). Teaching students to ask *why* questions can also lead to improvements in comprehension of narrative texts (Pressley, Wood, Woloshyn, Martin, King, et al., 1992). Asking *why* questions seems to encourage students to relate what they already know to the content they are reading. However, the questioning strategy only appears to be effective when students possess relevant prior knowledge about the topic of the text (Woloshyn, Paivio, & Pressley, 1994; Woloshyn, Pressley, & Schneider, 1992).

Summarizing is also an effective strategy for mediating struggling readers' access to difficult texts. Chan (1991) found that fifth- and sixth-grade students with reading disabilities benefited from learning how to summarize expository texts. In Chan's project, the effective instruction involved learning to delete redundant information, delete trivial information, locate topic sentences, and identify main ideas. Other researchers have also found that students benefit from instruction that teaches them how to summarize the texts they are reading (e.g., Gajria & Salvia, 1992; Nelson, Smith, & Dodd, 1992; Winograd, 1984).

Comprehension Instruction

When it comes to comprehension instruction for struggling readers, it appears that *how* one teaches is as important as *what* one teaches (Duffy, 1993; Mariage, 1995). There are several characteristics of effective comprehension instruction that studies reviewed in this chapter have in common. First, effective instruction, of either individual or multiple comprehension strategies, is characterized by teacher modeling. This modeling appears to foster greater gains when it occurs across a variety of materials. That is, a diverse set of texts seems to increase the likelihood that students can transfer the taught strategies to novel texts. Think-alouds are especially effective for modeling reading strategies for all readers (see Kucan & Beck, 1997, for a review). During think-alouds, teachers talk about what they do when they confront confusing parts of texts—for example, when they encounter unknown words. They predict what the text might be about, and summarize what they believe is important to remember from the text. Think-alouds are not only beneficial when teachers model their thinking, but also when students think aloud as well (e.g., Bereiter & Bird, 1985; Pressley et al., 1992).

Second, students seem to benefit from direct, explicit instruction (see Pressley, 2006, for a discussion). In direct instruction, the teacher explains how, when, and where to use various comprehension strategies. For example, teachers explain that it is important to make predictions when first starting to read a story and that summarizing monitors what is being learned. Direct, explicit instruction has long been supported by comprehension strategies research (e.g., Brown, Pressley, Van Meter, & Schuder, 1996; Duffy, Roehler, & Hermann, 1988; Duffy et al., 1987).

Finally, effective comprehension strategies instruction also involves rich and varied opportunities for guided student practice. Over time, as students become more proficient, teachers can gradually release responsibility for using the strategy to the students (Pearson & Gallagher, 1983). This "gradual release" happens during guided practice, in which students practice the strategy across a variety of texts and situations. Key to guided practice is feedback, which is provided not only by the teacher but also by other students. Learning about comprehension is not quiet work, but rather involves rich opportunities to discuss the texts as well as the strategies the students are learning. However, we note that despite the best comprehension instruction, struggling readers will not improve their comprehension overnight. Rather, this type of instruction needs to occur over the course of months, and perhaps even years. (Pressley et al., 1992)

Models That Combine Strategy Instruction with Scaffolded Support for Reading

Researchers have developed and tested a variety of frameworks that combine strategy instruction with routines designed to support struggling readers as they read texts that are difficult. These frameworks support teachers in implementing effective routines for teaching comprehension strategies. Common across these models is explicit instruction in a set of strategies, along with training in a particular structure for reading and discussion around the texts. A number of these models have proven to increase struggling readers' comprehension and use of reading comprehension strategies.

Reciprocal Teaching

One of the most noted of these frameworks is reciprocal teaching (Palincsar & Brown, 1984). In this model, students are taught four comprehension strategies: summarizing, questioning, clarifying, and predicting. Students are trained to use these strategies through modeling and scaffolding that is gradually removed as students become competent. In the original study, seventh-grade students who were good decoders but poor comprehenders made measurable gains in comprehension and particularly in the use of the four target strategies (Palincsar & Brown, 1984). The original study primarily used experimenter-developed comprehension measures to monitor student gains in comprehension. However, 3 months after the intervention, a follow-up administration of the Gates–MacGinitie Standardized Reading test showed that four of six RT students made gains in comprehension. In a follow-up study with similar ability students from fourth and seventh grades, Lysynchuk, Pressley, and Vye (1990) used standardized reading comprehension assessments to measure differences in treatment and control groups. Students in the treatment group performed significantly better than those who did not receive RT training.

It is important to note that the criteria for identifying participants in both the Palincsar and Brown (1984) and Lysynchuk, Pressley, and Vye (1990) studies required that students have adequate decoding skills but poor comprehension, characteristics of one of the groups of struggling readers identified by Riddle-Buly and Valencia (2002). That is, the original intervention studies focused on a select group of struggling readers. On the other hand, in a review of the research using RT as an intervention, Rosenshine and Meister (1994) report that studies involving heterogeneous groups found that RT results in similar gains in comprehension for most students. It is important to note that comprehension gains differed within and across the reviewed studies depending on the type of measure used, with gains on experimenter-developed measures greater than gains on standardized measures.

Collaborative Strategic Reading

In the tradition of RT, Klingner, Vaughn, and Schumm (1998) developed a model called collaborative strategic reading (CSR). This model is similar to RT in that it provides comprehension strategy instruction. However, in the case of CSR, students practice the comprehension strategies in cooperative groups. Within these cooperative groups, students are assigned specific jobs for monitoring reading and using strategies for comprehending the text before, during, and after reading. Studies of CSR have focused on struggling readers in fourth and fifth grades, as well as English language learners (ELLs) in culturally diverse classrooms. In all cases, use of the CSR model has resulted in improved reading comprehension scores on standardized tests, improved content learning, and has supported vocabulary acquisition for students with learning disabilities and for ELLs (Klingner & Vaughn, 1999). We note that these studies did not identify specific subtypes of struggling readers (e.g., good decoders but poor comprehenders), and participants were included, in general, if they had learning disabilities or if they were learning English as a second language.

POSSE

Englert and Mariage (1991) developed a framework for supporting readers with learning disabilities. POSSE, an acronym for the comprehension strategies of predicting, organizing, searching, summarizing, and evaluating, is a program that uses graphic organizers to support students' reading and recall of information. As with RT and CSR, POSSE is characterized by peer-mediated instruction with teacher modeling and gradual release of responsibility. Over the course of a 2-month treatment, students with learning disabilities in fourth, fifth, and sixth grade became increasingly strategic and demonstrated improved reading comprehension and recall of information, although they did not completely internalize the reading strategies. Englert and Mariage suggest that adding the graphic organizer helps to make comprehension processes visible and scaffolds the use of associated strategies.

Concept-Oriented Reading Instruction

While all of the models presented to this point have included reading of informational text, the focus of concept-oriented reading instruction (CORI) is on integrating literacy and content-area instruction. CORI consists of specific science and social studies units. Strategy instruction that supports specific learning tasks is combined with the content instruction (Guthrie, Wigfield, & Perencevich, 2004; Swan, 2003). Another component of this model is the inclusion of activities that are designed to motivate struggling students to learn. Through the use of hands-on materials, students are provided opportunities to personalize the content by asking their own questions about the topic being studied. The CORI model has resulted in gains in content learning, as well as improvements in students' motivation, comprehension, and use of strategies for deriving meaning from text. This model holds promise for struggling readers who often are less motivated to engage in reading texts that are difficult. Additionally, CORI includes special supports for struggling readers; for example, scaffolded instruction with graphic organizers like concept maps and charts that are used for writing final projects.

SUMMARY AND CONCLUSIONS

While we have chosen to highlight certain comprehension processes, instructional practices, and routines that support struggling readers as they engage with difficult texts, we want to underscore our recognition that reading and comprehension are complex. Developing successful readers involves more than one way of structuring interactions with students. Notably missing from this set of suggestions and models are instructional practices that support decoding and fluency. While this list presents suggestions for supporting struggling readers with the demands of difficult texts, we by no means consider any of them a complete reading program. That said, including some of these practices in a balanced reading program can make measurable differences for struggling readers.

As previously explained, research has indicated that it is important wherever and whenever possible to provide students with texts that are appropriately matched to their reading abilities. However, providing appropriately matched texts is not always possible in the realities of classrooms. For example, appropriately leveled-texts may not be available on every topic covered in the curriculum. Instructional resources may not be available for all proficiency levels to be accommodated for every topic. In instances such as these, schools and teachers need to be equipped with strategies for supporting students, especially those who struggle with reading.

While there are research-based strategies that teachers can draw on for designing instruction, there are still questions that need to be addressed about students and their achievement when reading difficult books. While models that combine comprehension strategy instruction and routines such as CORI, RT, and CSR have been tested, the target group has often been elementary students. We wonder about the viability of instruction plus strategy routines such as these for younger, primary-grade students. First graders participating in the PALS program were able to follow routines that supported story reading and word recognition (Mathes et al., 1998, 1998). Given that success, we wonder what kind of model might structure younger students' participation in collaborative discussions in situations where they are reading to learn. In contrast to this under-researched area for younger students, there is a plethora of research that reports the positive impact on the language and literacy development of preschool and primary-grade children, when teachers read aloud to them, and there is little that examines this strategy for older students. We do not know of any research that articulates a tested model or set of strategies for using reading aloud to support older, struggling readers or students with learning disabilities. Research that examines the impact of interactive read-alouds with older students is important for understanding the potential of this strategy for supporting older, struggling students.

While we have explored ways to mediate students' engagement with difficult texts, we feel there are also unanswered questions about the possible role or impact of difficult books when reading or learning to read. For one, are books that do not match students' decoding and fluency levels ever appropriate? Is there an influence when students' interest in a difficult book mediates their persistence for reading the book? If so, how does that affect reading development? Other questions might consider features of the difficult text. Some types of text, particularly informational texts, use visual features besides words to convey information. What is learned from these aspects of an informational text when the student cannot decode the words in the text? And, as previously stated, does priming students with an easier text improve comprehension of a related, more difficult text. We need empirical studies to provide answers to these questions.

As we have explored this topic in preparation of this chapter, we feel fortunate to draw on the work of so many colleagues who are passionate about the needs of struggling readers. That said, we feel there are still many opportunities for researchers to build programs of research that will provide new and important information about how to support struggling readers and their interactions with texts that are difficult.

REFERENCES

Allington, R. L., & Johnston, P. H. (2002). *Reading to learn: Lessons from exemplary fourth-grade classrooms.* New York: Guilford Press.

Anderson, R. C., & Freebody, P. (1981). Vocabulary knowledge. In J. Guthrie (Ed.), *Comprehension and teaching: Research reviews* (pp. 77–117). Newark, DE: International Reading Association.

Anderson, R. C., & Pearson, P. D. (1984). A schema-theoretic view of basic processes in reading. In P. D. Pearson (Ed.), *Handbook of reading research* (Vol. 1, pp. 255–291). White Plains, NY: Longman.

Barrantine, S. (1996). Engaging with reading through interactive read-alouds. *Reading Teacher, 50,* 36–43.

Beck, I. L., & McKeown, M. G. (2001). Text talk: Capturing the benefits of read-aloud experiences for young children. *Reading Teacher, 55,* 10–20.

Bereiter, C., & Bird, M. (1985). Use of thinking aloud in identification and teaching of reading comprehension strategies. *Cognition and Instruction, 2,* 131–156.

Betts, E. A. (1946). *Foundations of reading instruction.* New York: American Book.

Bos, C. S., & Anders, P. L. (1990). Effects of interactive vocabulary instruction on the vocabulary learning and reading comprehension of junior-high learning disabled students. *Learning School Journal, 96,* 385–414.

Brown, R., Pressley, M., Van Meter, P., & Schuder, T. (1996). A quasi-experimental validation of transactional strategies instruction with low-achieving second grade readers. *Journal of Educational Psychology, 88,* 18–37.

Cain, K., Oakhill, J., & Bryant, P. (2004). Children's reading comprehension ability: Concurrent prediction by working memory, verbal ability, and component skills. *Journal of Educational Psychology, 96,* 31–42.

Cain, K., & Oakhill, J. (2006). Profiles of children with specific reading comprehension difficulties. *British Journal of Educational Psychology, 76,* 683–696.

Carnine, D., & Kinder, B. D. (1985). Teaching low-performing students to apply generative and schema strategies to narrative and expository material. *Remedial and Special Education, 6,* 20–30.

Catts, H. W., Hogan, T. P., & Fey, M. E. (2003). Subgrouping poor readers on the basis of individual differences in reading-related abilities. *Journal of Learning Disabilities, 36,* 151–164.

Chall, J. S., & Conard, S. S. (1991). *Should textbooks challenge students?* New York: Teachers College Press.

Chan, L. K. S. (1991). Promoting strategy generalization through self-instructional training in students with reading disabilities. *Journal of Learning Disabilities, 24,* 427–433.

Davis, F. B. (1944). Fundamental factors of comprehension in reading. *Psychometrika, 9,* 185–197.

Dickinson, D. K., & Tabors, P. O. (2001). *Beginning literacy and language.* Baltimore: Brookes.

Duffy, G. D. (1993). Rethinking strategy instruction: Four teachers development and their low achievers' understandings. *Elementary School Journal, 93,* 231–247.

Duffy, G. D., Roehler, L. R., & Hermann, G. (1988). Modeling mental processes helps poor readers become strategic readers. *Reading Teacher, 41,* 762–767.

Duffy, G. D., Roehler, L. R., Sivan, E., Rackliffe, G., Book, C., Meloth, M., et al. (1987). Effects of explaining the reasoning associated with using reading strategies. *Reading Research Quarterly, 22,* 347–368.

Duke, N. K. (2000). 3.6 minutes per day: The scarcity of informational texts in first grade. *Reading Research Quarterly, 35,* 202–224.

Duke, N. K., & Bennett-Armistead, S. (2003). *Reading and writing informational text in the primary grades: Research-based practices.* New York: Scholastic.

Duke, N. K., & Kays, J. (1998). "Can I say 'Once upon a time?' ": Kindergarten children developing knowledge of information book language. *Early Childhood Quarterly, 13,* 285–318.

Englert, C. S., & Mariage, T. V. (1991). Making students partners in the comprehension process: Organizing the reading "POSSE." *Learning Disability Quarterly, 14,* 123–138.

Fielding, L., & Roller, C. (1992). Making difficult books accessible and easy books acceptable. *Reading Teacher, 45,* 678–685.

Fuchs, D., Fuchs, L. S., Mathes, P. G., & Simmons, D. C. (1997). Peer-assisted learning strategies: Making classrooms more responsible to diversity. *American Educational Research Journal, 34,* 174–206.

Fuchs, L. S., Fuchs, D., Kazdan, S., & Allen, S. (1999). Effects of peer-assisted learning strategies in reading with and without training in elaborated help. *Elementary School Journal, 99,* 201–219.

Gajria, M., & Salvia, J. (1992). The effects of summarization instruction on text comprehension of students with learning disabilities. *Exceptional Children, 58,* 508–516.

Gersten, R., Fuchs, L., Williams, J. P., & Baker, S. (2001). Teaching reading comprehension strategies to students with learning disabilities: A review of research. *Review of Educational Research, 71,* 279–320.

Goldman, S. R., & Rakestraw, J. A. (2000). Structural aspects of constructing meaning from text. In M. L. Kamil, P. B. Mosenthal, P. D. Pearson, & R. Barr (Eds.), *Handbook of reading research* (Vol. 3, pp. 545–561). Mahwah, NJ: Erlbaum.

Guthrie, J. T., Wigfield, A., & Perencevich, K. C. (Eds.). (2004). *Motivating reading comprehension: Concept-oriented reading instruction.* Mahwah, NJ: Erlbaum.

Hansen, J. (1981). The effects of inference training and practice on young children's reading comprehension. *Reading Research Quarterly, 16,* 391–417.

Hart, B., & Risley, T. R. (1995). *Meaningful differences in the everyday experience of young American children*. Baltimore: Brookes.

Hiebert, E. H. (2005). The effects of text difficulty on second graders' fluency development. *Reading Psychology, 26*, 183–209.

Idol, L. (1987). Group story mapping: A comprehension strategy for both skilled and unskilled readers. *Journal of Learning Disabilities, 20*, 196–205.

Idol, L., & Croll, V. J. (1987). Story-mapping training as a means of improving reading comprehension. *Learning Disability Quarterly, 10*, 214–229.

Klingner, J. K., & Vaughn, S. (1999). Promoting reading comprehension, content learning, and English acquisition through collaborative strategic reading (CSR). *Reading Teacher, 52*, 738–747.

Klingner, J. K., Vaughn, S., & Schumm, J. S. (1998). Collaborative strategic reading during social studies in heterogeneous fourth-grade classrooms. *Elementary School Journal, 99*, 3–21.

Kucan, L., & Beck, I. L. (1997). Thinking aloud and reading comprehension research: Inquiry instruction and social interaction. *Review of Educational Research, 67*, 271–299.

Labbo, L. D., & Teale, W. H. (1990). Cross-age reading: A strategy for helping poor readers. *Reading Teacher, 43*, 362–369.

Leach, J. M., Scarborough, H. S., & Rescola, L. (2003). Late-emerging reading disabilities. *Journal of Educational Psychology, 95*, 211–224.

Lysynchuk, L. M., Pressley, M., & Vye, N. J. (1990). Reciprocal teaching improves standardized reading comprehension performance in poor comprehenders. *Elementary School Journal, 90*, 469–484.

Mariage, T. (1995). Why students learn: The nature of teacher talk during reading. *Learning Disability Quarterly, 18*, 214–234.

Mathes, P. G., Grek, J. K., Babyak, A. E., & Allen, S. (1999). Peer-assisted learning strategies for first-grade readers: A tool for preventing early reading difficulties. *Learning Disabilities Research and Practice, 14*, 50–60.

Mathes, P. G., Howard, J. K., Allen, S., & Fuchs, D. (1998). Peer-assisted learning strategies for first-grade readers: Responding to the needs of diverse learners. *Reading Research Quarterly, 33*, 62–94.

Mathes, P. G., Torgeson, J. K., Clancy-Manchetti, J., Nicholas, K., Robinson, C., & Grek, M. (2003). A comparison of teacher-directed versus peer-assisted instruction to struggling first-grade readers. *Elementary School Journal, 103*, 459–479.

McGee, L. M., & Schickedanz, J. A. (2007). Repeated interactive read-alouds in preschool and kindergarten. *Reading Teacher, 60*, 752–760.

McKinney, J. D., Osborne, S. S., & Schulte, A. C. (1993). Academic consequences of learning disability: Longitudinal prediction of outcomes at 11 years of age. *Learning Disabilities Research and Practice, 8*, 19–27.

Miller, D. (2002). *Reading with meaning: Teaching comprehension in the primary grades*. Portsmouth, NH: Stenhouse.

Miller, S. D., & Meece, J. L. (1999). Third graders' motivational preferences for reading and writing tasks. *Elementary School Journal, 100*, 19–35.

Morrow, L. M. (1988). Young children's responses to one-to-one story readings in school settings. *Reading Research Quarterly, 23*, 89–107.

Morrow, L. M., & Brittain, R. (2003). The nature of storybook reading in the elementary school: Current practices. In A. van Kleeck & S. A. Stahl (Eds.), *On reading books to children: Parents and teachers* (pp. 140–158). Mahwah, NJ: Erlbaum.

Moss, B. (1997). A qualitative assessment of first grader's retelling of expository text. *Reading Research and Instruction, 37,* 1–13.

Nagy, W. E., & Anderson, R. C. (1984). How many words are there in printed school English? *Reading Research Quarterly, 19*(3), 304–330.

Nagy, W. E., & Scott, J. A. (2000). Vocabulary processes. In M. L. Kamil, P. Mosenthal, P. D. Pearson, & R. Barr (Eds.), *Handbook of reading research* (Vol. 3, pp. 269–284). Mahwah, NJ: Erlbaum.

National Reading Panel. (2000). *Teaching children to read: An evidence-based assessment of the scientific research literature on reading and its implications for reading instruction.* Washington, DC: National Institute of Child Health and Human Development.

Nelson, J. R., Smith, D. J., & Dodd, J. M. (1992). The effects of a summary skills strategy to students identified as learning disabled on their comprehension of science text. *Education and Treatment of Children, 15,* 228–243.

Newby, R. F., Caldwell, J., & Recht, D. R. (1989). Improving the reading comprehension of children with dysphonetic and dyseidetic dyslexia using story grammar. *Journal of Learning Disabilities, 22,* 373–380.

Oyler, C., & Barry, A. (1996). Sharing authority: Student initiations during teacher-led read-alouds of information books. *Teaching and Teacher Education, 12,* 149–160.

Palincsar, A. S., & Brown, A. L. (1984). Reciprocal teaching of comprehension-fostering and comprehension monitoring activities. *Cognition and Instruction, 1,* 117–175.

Pany, D., Jenkins, J. R., & Schreck, J. (1982). Vocabulary instruction: Effects in word knowledge and reading comprehension. *Learning Disability Quarterly, 5*(3), 202–215.

Pappas, C., Varelas, M., Barry, A., & Rife, A. (2004). Promoting dialogic inquiry in information books read-alouds: Young urban children's ways of making sense in science. In E. W. Saul (Ed.), *Crossing borders in literacy and science instruction: Perspectives on theory and practice* (pp. 161–189). Newark, DE: International Reading Association.

Paris, S. G., & Oka, E. R. (1989). Strategies for comprehending text and coping with reading difficulties. *Learning Disability Quarterly, 12,* 32–42.

Pearson, P. D., & Gallagher, M. C. (1983). The instruction of reading comprehension. *Contemporary Educational Psychology, 8,* 317–334.

Pressley, M. (2006). *Reading instruction that works: The case for balanced teaching.* New York: Guilford Press.

Pressley, M., Wood, E., Woloshyn, V. E., Martin, V., King, A., et al. (1992). Encouraging mindful use of prior knowledge: Attempting to construct explanatory answers facilitates learning. *Educational Psychologist, 27,* 91–110.

RAND Reading Study Group. (2001). *Reading for understanding: Towards an R&D program in reading comprehension.* Santa Monica, CA: RAND Education.

Raphael, T. E., & Au, K. H. (2005). QAR: Enhancing comprehension and test taking across the grades and content areas. *Reading Teacher, 59*, 206–221.

Raphael, T. E., & Pearson, P. D. (1985). Increasing awareness of sources of information for answering questions. *American Educational Research Journal, 22*, 217–235.

Raphael, T. E., & Wonnacott, C. A. (1985). Heightening fourth-grade students' sensitivity to sources of information for answering comprehension questions. *Reading Research Quarterly, 20*, 282–296.

Riddle-Buly, M., & Valencia, S. W. (2002). Below the bar: Profiles of students who fail state reading assessments. *Educational Evaluation and Policy Analysis, 24*, 219–239.

Rosenshine, B., & Meister, C. (1994). Reciprocal teaching. *Review of Educational Research, 64*, 479–530.

Rosenhouse, J., Feitelson, D., & Kita, B. (1997). Interactive reading aloud to Israeli first graders: Its contribution to literacy development. *Reading Research Quarterly, 32*, 168–183.

Schwanenflugel, P. J., Stahl, S. A., & McFalls, E. L. (1997). Partial word knowledge and vocabulary growth during reading comprehension. *Journal of Literacy Research, 29*(4), 531–553.

Simmonds, E. P. M. (1992). The effects of teacher training and implementation of two methods of improving the comprehension skills of students with learning disabilities. *Learning Disabilities Research and Practice, 7*, 194–198.

Smolkin, L. B., & Donovan, C. A. (2001). The contexts of comprehension: The information book read aloud, comprehension acquisition, and comprehension instruction in a first grade classroom. *Elementary School Journal, 102*, 97–122.

Smolkin, L. B., & Donovan, C. A. (2003). Supporting comprehension acquisition for emerging and struggling readers: The interactive information book read-aloud. *Exceptionality, 11*, 25–38.

Stahl, S. A., & Fairbanks, M. M. (1986). The effects of vocabulary instruction: A model-based meta-analysis. *Review of Educational Research, 56*, 72–110.

Stahl, S. A., & Nagy, W. E. (2006). *Teaching word meanings*. Mahwah, NJ: Erlbaum.

Sternberg, R. J. (1987). Most vocabulary is learned from context. In M. G. McKeown & M. E. Curtis (Eds.), *The nature of vocabulary acquisition*. Hillsdale, NJ: Erlbaum.

Swan, E. (2003). *Concept-oriented reading instruction: Engaging classrooms, life-long learners*. New York: Guilford Press.

Turner, J. C., & Paris, S. G. (1995). How literacy tasks influence students' motivation for literacy. *Reading Teacher, 30*, 410–441.

Van Keer, H., & Verhaeghe, J. P. (2005). Effects of explicit reading strategies instruction and peer tutoring on second and fifth graders' reading comprehension and self-efficacy perceptions. *Journal of Experimental Education, 73*, 291–329.

van Kleeck, A., Stahl, S. A., & Bauer, E. B. (Eds.). (2003). *On reading books to children: Parents and teachers*. Mahwah, NJ: Erlbaum.

Whitehurst, G. J., Falco, F. L., Lonigan, C. J., Fischel, J. E., DeBaryshe, B. D., Valdez-Manchaca, M. C., et al. (1988). Accelerating language development through picturebook reading. *Developmental Psychology, 24,* 552–559.

Whitehurst, G. J., & Lonigan, C. J. (1998). Child development and emergent literacy. *Child Development, 69,* 848–872.

Williams, J. P. (1993). Comprehension of students with and without learning disabilities: Identification of narrative themes and idiosyncratic text representations. *Journal of Educational Psychology, 85,* 631–641.

Williams, J. P. (1998). Improving the comprehension of disabled readers. *Annals of Dyslexia, 48,* 213–238.

Williams, J. P., Brown, L. G., Silverstein, A. K., & deCani, J. S. (1994). An instructional program in comprehension of narrative themes for adolescents with learning disabilities. *Learning Disability Quarterly, 17,* 205–221.

Williams, J. P., Hall, K. M., deCani, J. S., Lauer, K. D., Stafford, K. B., & DeSisto, L. A. (2005). Expository text comprehension in the primary grade classroom. *Journal of Educational Psychology, 97,* 538–550.

Williams, J. P., Hall, K. M., & Lauer, K. D. (2004). Teaching expository text structure to young at-risk learners: Building the basics of comprehension instruction. *Exceptionality, 12*(3), 129–144.

Williams, J. P., Nubla-Kung, A. M., Pollini, S., & Stafford, K. B. (2007). Teaching cause-effect text structure through social studies content to at-risk second graders. *Journal of Learning Disabilities, 40,* 111–120.

Winograd, P. (1984). Strategic difficulties in summarizing texts. *Reading Research Quarterly, 19,* 404–425.

Woloshyn, V. E., Paivio, A., & Pressley, M. (1994). Using elaborative interrogation to help students acquire information consistent with prior knowledge and information inconsistent with prior knowledge. *Journal of Educational Psychology, 86,* 79–89.

Woloshyn, V. E., Pressley, M., & Schneider, W. (1992). Elaborative interrogation and prior knowledge effects on learning of facts. *Journal of Educational Psychology, 84,* 115–124.

❦ 11 ❧

Teaching Adolescents
Who Struggle with Text
Research and Practice

MARY E. CURTIS

Some adolescents embrace reading. They engage in it willingly, readily citing favorite authors and works. Other teens seem to find little value in reading. Although they appear to encounter few difficulties when asked to do so, they rarely choose to read on a voluntary basis. For others still, reading is an obvious and constant struggle. Their inability to deal with text in their everyday lives frustrates them, and they see little hope in their ability to ever gain much facility to do so.

This third group of readers is the focus of this chapter. My hope is to convince those who work with older struggling students that the key to finding the appropriate texts for helping them is recognition of the sources of their reading difficulties. In making my case, I draw from the research literature as well as my 10 years of experience working at the Reading Center at Girls and Boys Town, a laboratory for older at-risk adolescents with reading problems. Among the 300 or so youth who arrive at Boys Town's home campus in Omaha, Nebraska, each year, reading achievement typically lags 2 to 3 years behind their grade placement in school.

I begin the chapter with a brief overview of reading development, to provide a context for understanding adolescents' reading difficulties. Profiles of adolescent learners with different reading difficulties follow, with emphasis placed on their strengths and needs in terms of various aspects of reading (print, meaning vocabulary, and comprehension). Research relevant to each learner is reviewed, and examples of instructional techniques found to be effective with the learners are described. Central to the review of the research literature and the discussion of instructional techniques is a focus on the features of appropriate texts for helping them to improve.

A DEVELOPMENTAL APPROACH

Much of the conversation about adolescent literacy over the past several years has been focused on comprehension, in particular, on the reading habits, strategies, and dispositions of teens identified as not comprehending as well as we might like. Such concerns are understandable. Based on the latest results from the National Assessment of Education (NAEP), as many as 65% of 12th graders seem unable to demonstrate mastery of the prerequisite knowledge and skills fundamental for proficient reading comprehension at their grade level (Grigg, Donahue, & Dion, 2007).

Viewing adolescent literacy primarily through comprehension can be problematic, however. As observed by Knott more than 20 years ago:

> The task facing those who want to improve instruction in literacy in secondary schools is complex. It is not simply one of changing tasks in which students engage (e.g., write more, read more) or in changing instructional strategies (e.g., ask higher-level questions; write more complex answers). The change must also include a change in the way in which literacy and instruction are viewed and delivered. What is needed is a framework that can be used to guide the development of a new direction. (1986, p. 80)

A possible framework for adolescent literacy is to view it within the context of overall reading development. To illustrate, consider the value of thinking about adolescent reading in terms of Chall's theory of stages of reading development (see Chall, Jacobs, & Baldwin, 1990). According to Chall, readers go through a series of six stages, marked by differing challenges presented to them via the medium (the printed words and sounds) as well as the message (the meanings, concepts, information, and ideas represented). Table 11.1 presents a summary of Chall's stages of reading development.

TABLE 11.1. Chall's Stages of Reading Development

Stage	Major qualitative characteristics
Stage 0: Prereading	Readers are able to "say back" materials that have been read to them repeatedly. Although they are not really reading yet—in the sense of identifying the words on a page—they understand that books have meaning and that letters written on a page stand for words.
Stage 1: Initial reading and decoding	Readers associate letters with sounds and spoken words with printed ones. Only a fraction of words whose meanings are known can be read, however.
Stage 2: Confirmation and fluency	Readers are "ungluing" from print—becoming less dependent on having to sound out each word, allowing more attention to be focused on the meaning. Listening comprehension is still better than reading, however.
Stage 3: Reading for learning the new	Readers are able to decode in a more or less automatic way, and reading is used to learn new ideas and to gain new knowledge. Reading and listening comprehension are about equal. However, readers are able to read words they do not know the meanings of, and they can encounter words that, although not totally new, are not totally known. Without instruction, confusion and frustration can result, and interest and motivation can fade away.
Stage 4: Multiple viewpoints	Readers are able to understand a broad range of materials. Still developing is the ability to integrate the different viewpoints and perspectives experienced through reading.
Stage 5: Construction and reconstruction	Readers use reading for their personal and professional needs in such a way that prior knowledge gets synthesized and analyzed by what they read. Reaching this stage depends on broad knowledge of the content being read, high degree of efficiency in reading it, and the ability to form an opinion that can be supported.

Note. Based on Chall (1983, pp. 85–87) and Curtis and Longo (1999, pp. 8–10).

According to Chall, students begin by acquiring knowledge about how spoken language works, and how print represents spoken language (Stage 0). Once they learn to associate letters with sounds and spoken words with printed ones (Stage 1), they start recognizing words with enough ease to allow them to focus their attention on the text's meaning (Stage 2). This focus on meaning, in turn, allows them to use their reading skills to acquire new information and ideas from a broad range of materials (Stage 3). As they become more proficient, they learn to recognize the different viewpoints and perspectives that they encounter (Stage 4). And through reading, they learn to synthesize and analyze their prior knowledge and beliefs, often reconstructing what they know and believe based on their understanding of a text (Stage 5).

For some teens, reading and understanding a broad range of materials poses little difficulty. Still developing for them, however, is the ability to organize, assess, and integrate the variety of viewpoints and perspectives encountered in reading materials at the secondary level. On a test like the NAEP, these students have difficulty when tasks require them to make a critical judgment and to explain their reasoning. In Chall's theory, these readers are at Stage 4. With regard to instruction, literacy experiences that enhance their ability to deal with more than one set of facts, more than a single theory, and more than one particular viewpoint will promote the most growth.

For other teens, words are decoded with enough ease so that they are able to focus on the author's message. But, because they know the meanings of too few of the words that they are able to recognize, their comprehension suffers. Retrieving information from a text can pose problems for them on a test like the NAEP. Difficulty in comprehending becomes a roadblock for acquiring new information and ideas (Stage 3). In terms of instruction, emphasis needs to be placed on increasing their knowledge and awareness of word meanings, along with expanding their strategies for dealing with words that they do not know.

Other students can struggle because of issues with the print aspects of reading (Stages 1 and 2). They may experience difficulties in identifying words accurately, or they may be unable to do so with enough ease to facilitate comprehension. Instruction needs to help them to recognize in print the meaning that they would be able to get if they were listening.

The focus of the remainder of this chapter is on how placing a reader's strengths and needs within a developmental perspective can help teachers in selecting texts that will promote reading improvement. Equally important to appreciate, however, is that viewing adolescent literacy within a developmental framework also helps students to understand their reading abilities and what it will take for them to continue their growth as readers. When teens have a sense of where they are in terms of a continuum of reading achievement, we have found that they will readily seek out and become engaged in the kinds of knowledge and skills that can move them along to the next stage of reading (Curtis, 1995; Curtis & Longo, 1997a, 1997b, 1999). As one of our students described her situation:

> When I first got here, it was hard for me to read. I didn't read at all. Now I can get interested in books and I know what they're talking about. I know I can read. It's not that somebody has to push me to do it. I want to read." (in Hyland, 1998, p. 26)

In what follows, I discuss research and practice in selecting texts for adolescents who have strengths and needs in three different areas of reading. The first area has to do with fluency in dealing with print, involving the processes and knowledge of word recognition. The second has to do with vocabulary, involving breadth and depth of knowledge about word meanings. The third has to do with comprehension, involving the interaction between a reader and a text that occurs as the reader constructs an understanding of the text.

PROFILE 1: PRINT FLUENCY

Skill in reading requires that words be identified accurately and with efficiency and ease. When readers can identify words accurately and automatically—without conscious attention—they are able to focus their processing on getting meaning from what they read.

John[1] is an example of an adolescent who experienced difficulties in reading because of his difficulties with print. John was 15 years old and in the 9th grade when his reading was tested. When he was asked to define words whose meanings are known by most students at his grade level, John gave clear and concise definitions. But when asked to read words aloud, he began to falter on words at a 4th-grade level, sometimes substituting real words (e.g., he said *creation* for *certain*) and sometimes nonwords (*an-a store* for *ancestor*).

When presented with text, John showed a similar pattern of strengths and needs. Asked to read silently, he gave an oral summary of a sixth-grade level passage that indicated he understood what he had read. However, when asked to read aloud a passage at the fourth-grade level, John repeated words and word phrases frequently and omitted some words. His errors were real word substitutions (*notice* for *note* and *sung* for *sang*). When given a third-grade level passage to read aloud, he made no errors at all. He read slowly, however (about 100 words correct per minute).

At present, we don't know how prevalent print-related reading problems are for older readers. In a recent study of fourth graders who had failed a statewide reading assessment, researchers found that four out of five of those students had problems dealing with some aspect of print (Valencia & Riddle Buly, 2004). Similar results have been found

---

[1]The information about students' reading abilities described in this chapter was obtained using the Diagnostic Assessments of Reading test (see Roswell, Chall, Curtis, & Kearns, 2005). All of the students' names have been changed.

with adults who are enrolled in basic education classes (see *www.nifl.gov/readingprofiles*).

In my own work with at-risk youth, we found that one out of every 10 adolescents had serious difficulties identifying words, and one out of every 8 read too slowly to remember how a sentence began by the time they reached its end (Curtis & Longo, 1999). Working with a representative sample of ninth graders from a single high school, Rasinski and his colleagues (2005) found a similar result: 36 out of the 303 students they tested (12%) read text aloud at rates below 100 words correct per minute, the cutoff they identified as indicating a significant concern for reading fluency. Torgesen and his colleagues also found that print-related skills continued to explain a substantial amount of variation in comprehension through high school (see Torgesen et al., 2007).

Regardless of exact numbers, we can assume that a sizeable group of adolescents find themselves in the same situation as John. Like him, they may have difficulty in identifying words, and to compensate, they abandon decoding and start guessing at the words. But since their guesses are often incorrect, it becomes difficult for them to understand. Even when they read accurately, they read much more slowly than younger students reading at the same grade level (Bristow & Leslie, 1988; Curtis, 1997). Pretty soon, they start looking for ways to avoid reading altogether. This last point was conveyed quite powerfully and succinctly by another teen who, when asked to finish the following sentence, *I'd rather read than . . .* , responded, "die."

What types of instructional techniques and texts are appropriate for working with teens who experience these kinds of difficulty with print? Repeated reading is one technique that has been widely recognized as having the potential to improve students' reading accuracy and rate (National Institute of Child Health and Human Development, 2000). In repeated reading, students read and reread texts while monitoring the changes that take place with each repetition. As students improve with each repetition, the gains they make on specific passages are expected to generalize to overall improvements in oral reading and comprehension.

According to Rasinski (2003), passages used for repeated readings should be short (between 50 and 500 words), and should be read initially at an 85 to 95% accuracy level. If students read exceedingly slow (less than 50 words per minute [wpm]) or make many errors, Rasinski recommends that teachers provide students with support during the initial readings. Hiebert (2007) recommends that fluency instruction follow a curriculum, starting with short texts (between 50 and 150 words) composed mostly of high-frequency words and words with simple vowel patterns, and moving toward those containing less-frequent words and more-complex vowel patterns.

Technology holds some promise for facilitating repeated reading instruction, via software that has the ability to "listen" to a reader's oral reading and to flag errors, to assist in the pronunciation of words, and to supply the meanings of words in the text (Adams, 2006). Also important is that the texts are ones that will make the effort to practice worthwhile. This seems to have been one of the criteria for a collection of passages put together by Blachowicz (2004), ones selected specifically for doing repeated reading with adolescent struggling readers. The texts are all brief (200 words long) and organized according to ten levels of difficulty. Each level contains 72 fiction and nonfiction passages, with the fiction excerpted from books by young adult authors and the nonfiction discussing people and topics of interest to young adult readers. Hiebert (2008) has also gathered sets of short texts on science, social studies, arts and culture, and literature and language, designed for repeated reading instruction with adolescents.

We know from a meta-analysis conducted on 18 studies investigating the effects of repeated reading (Therrien, 2004) that the technique seems to work best when: (1) students read aloud to adults, and (2) adults correct the errors that students make during reading. In addition, Therrien concluded that students should be encouraged to read for both speed and comprehension.

Based on the positive outcomes associated with teacher support, teacher feedback, and emphasis on comprehension, some reviewers have suggested that frequent practice in reading aloud with teacher guidance may be as effective as repeated reading in improving students' print-level skills (Kuhn & Stahl, 2003; Torgesen et al., 2007). As Kuhn and Stahl (2003) concluded, studies that compared repeated and nonrepeated reading "found no difference in effects between repeated reading of a small number of texts and nonrepetitive reading of a larger set of texts. It is not the repetition that leads to the effect but the amount of time spent reading connected text" (p. 17).

In other words, the value of repeated reading instruction may rest on how much it increases the amount of reading that students do. With older struggling readers, I have found that a technique called collaborative oral reading works very well in accomplishing this goal (Curtis, 1996, 2004; Curtis & Longo, 1999). In collaborative oral reading, a small group of students (from four to six) read aloud together with an adult. Members of the group all take turns reading short amounts of text (from three to five lines), with the reader passing the reading to anyone in the group he or she chooses, and at any point in the text that he or she wants (mid-paragraph, mid-sentence, or even mid-word). Passing the reading at unpredictable points ensures that everyone must follow along as someone reads, keeping the level of each group member's engagement high. And, since each person reads only a very short amount of text, even the least-able reader can participate comfortably.

The role of the adult is to provide students with the words they don't recognize and to correct misread words that interfere with understanding of the content. In addition, each time the adult takes a turn, students are provided with a model of fluent reading. Depending on the level of support that students need, the adult can read more frequently or larger amounts of text. During collaborative oral reading, the group stops occasionally to discuss what is being read. Discussion ensures students' comprehension, maintains their interest in what they are reading, and promotes a sense of community.

I have used mostly narrative texts with this technique, since students' familiarity with their overall structure seems to help their understanding while their attention is directed toward the print. And, by using longer narratives (between 100 to 150 pages), students begin to see the same words and language rhythms occurring over and over again, building not only accuracy and rate, but also skill in phrasing and expression involved in prosody. Informational texts might work as well, especially those in which key concepts are repeated (Hiebert, 2007).

For struggling adolescent readers, collaborative oral reading requires that they become comfortable with taking risks. Since we want them to apply what they know about decoding to identify new words, we need to praise them for making the effort, even when the result is an error. Students who receive appropriate feedback and support from an adult view collaborative oral reading as a very helpful and enjoyable activity. The technique also works best when the print-level skills of all students in the group are within one-to-two grade levels of each other. Ability grouping eliminates the discomforts that can arise when teens are asked to read aloud in a heterogeneous group (Curtis & Longo, 1999).

Working with students whose oral reading accuracy was at the second- to fourth-grade level, we found that their reading rate went from 130 wpm to 143 wpm after 14 weeks of using collaborative oral reading (Curtis, 1996). For students reading at the fourth- to sixth-grade level, rate went from 128 wpm to 140 wpm. These results compare quite favorably with those from studies of repeated reading with students of the same age. For example, after a year of using a repeated reading technique, Marchand-Martella, Martella, Orlob, and Ebey (2000) found that ninth graders reading at the fourth-grade level went from 121 wpm to 131 wpm. Valleley and Shriver (2003) found that, after 10 weeks of a repeated reading intervention, three high school students gained an average of 13 wpm on ninth-grade-level materials.

Table 11.2 contains a list of some books that have worked well for collaborative oral reading. In choosing books for adolescents to read

TABLE 11.2. Books Recommended for Collaborative Oral Reading

Fourth-grade reading level

The Crow-Girl, by Bodil Bredsdorff
Escape from Fire Mountain, by Gary Paulsen
Nightjohn, by Gary Paulsen
The Secret School, by Avi
Sing Me a Death Song, by Jay Bennett

Fifth-grade reading level

Canyons, by Gary Paulsen
Flight #116 Is Down, by Caroline Cooney
Freedom Crossing, by Margaret Clary
Holes, by Louis Sachar
Letters from Rifka, by Karen Hesse
Maniac Magee, by Jerry Spinelli
Seedfolks, by Paul Fleischman
Something Upstairs, by Avi
Whispers from the Dead, by Joan Lowery Nixon

Sixth-grade reading level

Children of the River, by Linda Crew
Dicey's Song, by Cynthia Voight
Escape from Warsaw, by Ian Serraillier
A Family Apart, by Joan Lowery Nixon
How Angel Peterson Got His Name, by Gary Paulsen
My Daniel, by Pam Conrad
The River, by Gary Paulsen
The Watsons Go to Birmingham—1963, by Christopher Paul Curtis

Seventh-grade reading level

Lyddie, by Katherine Patterson
The Road to Memphis, by Mildred Taylor
The True Confessions of Charlotte Doyle, by Avi
Two Old Women, by Velma Wallis

Eighth-grade reading level

Balzac and the Little Chinese Seamstress, by Dai Sijie
The Story of a Shipwrecked Sailor, by Gabriel Garcia Marquez
Wouldn't Take Nothing for My Journey Now, by Maya Angelou

aloud, I have met with the most success when I have followed some advice I first read about in *Voice of Youth Advocates* (*www.voya.com*), a magazine that publishes reviews of young adult books and articles about trends and themes in young adult literature. That advice was: A book is a chance to try someone else's life on for size. In other words, rather than trying to find books that feature people whose lives are similar to their own, I have found that students enjoy books whose protagonists introduce them to experiences not as familiar to them, such as civil rights (*The Watsons Go to Birmingham—1963*), immigration (*Land of Hope*), the holocaust (*Escape from Warsaw*), the underground railroad (*Freedom Crossing*), slave trading (*Something Upstairs*), and so on (Curtis & Longo, 2000).

Collaborative oral reading has the potential to help students improve in fluency, and it has the additional advantage of being something they enjoy doing. Collaborative oral reading combines two activities students value: a teacher reading aloud to them and students reading aloud to each other (Ivey & Broaddus, 2001). When a teacher and students read the same book together in a group, a community of readers soon forms. As one of our students described it: "When I hear other peers read, it makes me want to read. In my other classes, I didn't like to read. Now I participate in class because this class has helped me" (Curtis, Longo, & Chmelka, 1994).

PROFILE 2: VOCABULARY

Even taking the most conservative estimates, meaning vocabulary is an area in which adolescents experience enormous growth. By grade 6, students know the meanings of more than 7,500 root words. By grade 8, that number has grown to at least 11,000, and by grade 12, it has been estimated to be around 15,000 or more (Biemiller, 1999).

Due to the sheer number of words, teaching students how to use context to learn new meanings has, in the past, been viewed as the only reasonable route (e.g., see Sternberg, 1987). However, many adolescents who lack adequate vocabulary also have difficulty in comprehending, thereby hindering their ability to learn new vocabulary from context. More recently, the effectiveness of explicit vocabulary instruction has been recognized, particularly for adolescents. As summarized by Kamil (2003):

> The NRP review showed that while learning from context is important, direct instruction of vocabulary is effective in improving both vocabulary and comprehension. The implication is that *both* direct, explicit instruction *and* learning from context are important. A further implication is that explicit instruction *may* be useful in closing the gap between students with the highest levels of vocabulary knowledge, and those with the lowest. (p. 11)

Mark is an example of a student whose comprehension was being held back by his vocabulary. At age 15 and in the ninth grade,

Mark's print skills were quite strong. He was able to recognize many words appropriate to his grade level, and when he mispronounced words, his errors suggested that he had never before heard the words that he was trying to sound out (e.g., he said *in-it-ate* for *initiate*, and *au-then-city* for *authenticity*). His results when reading text were similar. He could read twelfth-grade-level texts with a high degree of accuracy; when he did make errors, the errors reflected more a lack of familiarity with the word itself than with the phonics underlying it (e.g., he said "in-tu-tion-i-zed" for *institutionalized*). Mark's reading rate was only fair (about 110 wcpm on twelfth-grade-level text), but again, his rate seemed more a reflection of his lack of understanding of the text than its cause.

Mark was able to provide correct answers to questions about an eighth-grade-level text that he read silently, but he had difficulty synthesizing the information enough to provide a summary. By far his area of greatest need, however, was in vocabulary. When asked to define words, he began to have problems with meanings known by most middle school students. On word meanings known by most high school students—words like *abundant* and *essential*—his knowledge was almost nonexistent.

National studies such as NAEP confirm that time spent reading is positively correlated with reading ability (Perie & Moran, 2005). However, NAEP results also indicate that adolescents spend little time reading outside of school, with only 30% of 13-year-olds and 22% of 17-year-olds reporting that they read almost every day for fun (Perie & Moran, 2005). Mark's vocabulary most likely did not grow because he did not engage in wide and varied reading. But, at this point, when faced with trying to improve his vocabulary, our best bet may be to begin by providing him with more structured opportunities, since naturally occurring contexts are frequently not explicit enough to assist him in learning all the word meanings he needs to know (Beck, McKeown, & Kucan, 2002).

In my own efforts in this area, I have found that informational texts work especially well for vocabulary instruction. I think this is true for at least two reasons. Most important, perhaps, teens who struggle with reading because of poor vocabularies often find the effort to learn new meanings worthwhile if they can also learn something new about their world. Since the main purpose of reading informational text is to obtain new information that you need or want to know (Duke & Billman, Chapter 6, this volume), informational text can serve this goal better than fiction.

Secondly, I find that informational text lends itself better than narrative does to providing experiences with the kinds of word meanings that struggling adolescent readers need to know. The notion of word tiers, described by Beck, McKeown, and Kucan (2002), is helpful here. Tier 1 consists of basic word meanings—concrete words that are part of a student's oral vocabulary, like *store* and *word* and *truck*. Tier 2 words are more abstract—words like *consequence* and *assume*—ones that occur frequently in written language across a variety of academic areas. Tier 3 consists of domain-specific words—words such as *photosynthesis* or *pentameter* that are fairly low frequency and associated with particular content areas.

Tier 2 words play an increasingly important role in the meaning of materials at the middle school level and beyond. Chall and her colleagues analyzed a variety of content-area textbooks used at different grade levels (Chall, Bissex, Conard, & Harris-Sharples, 1996). At grades 1 through 3, they found a preponderance of short, familiar words requiring knowledge of labels for concrete objects encountered in everyday experiences. By grades 4 through 6, however, the textbooks used a more varied vocabulary, one still generally familiar, but requiring an awareness of more abstract terms (e.g., *rotate, absorbs, regarded, limited*).

Tier 2 words are also the ones that many struggling adolescents do not know. For instance, Mark was unfamiliar with the meanings of words like *maintain, vague,* and *essential*—words that occur more frequently in written language than in conversation, and ones which he had missed out on the opportunity to learn.

As noted earlier, when adolescent readers have gaps in vocabulary knowledge, direct and explicit instruction in word meanings is often the best way to help them. A common technique is for teachers to select word meanings for study from the materials that students are reading. Increasingly, however, content-area teachers are being encouraged to allow students to select the words that will be studied (Harmon, Hedrick, Wood, & Gress, 2005; Ruddell & Shearer, 2002).

With its emphasis on choice and independence, student self-selection would appear to be a powerful approach for motivating adolescents to improve their vocabularies. Two factors limit its effectiveness, however. First, students do not always select the most appropriate words to study. For example, Harmon et al. (2005) found that when eighth graders were asked to select the most important words for learning the concepts from an informational text, students' choices differed as a function of reading ability. Those reading at grade level and above were most likely to choose words based on the topic of the passage. But students reading below grade level were just as likely to choose words for more personal reasons (e.g., they already knew the meanings or the words just seemed to be important to them).

Instruction could address ways to help students make better choices.

But this leads us to the second limitation of the self-selection technique: texts do not always explicitly include the most important vocabulary words for students to know. For example, consider a textbook passage that describes the origin and effect of Jim Crow laws, but never uses the words *prejudice* or *discrimination*. A student (or teacher) who selects vocabulary words for instruction based on the words appearing in the text will end up missing out on the key concepts that struggling readers need to know.

An alternative approach that has proven successful for students like Mark is for their teachers to identify word meanings for instruction that have high utility, ones that can apply across a variety of different topics, content areas, and contexts. These include widely and frequently used academic words like *analyze, create, define,* and *identify* (Corson, 1997 & Coxhead, 2000 are excellent sources.) Once teachers have introduced the meaning, students and teachers can discuss how the word's meaning relates to what students are reading in a variety of content areas, providing additional contexts for word learning. Activities that encourage students to actively process new word meanings and provide students with opportunities to apply and use new vocabulary knowledge are key features of successful instruction (see Curtis & Longo, 2001).

While it is essential that students read texts that lend themselves to application of the vocabulary they are learning, we have found that it is not necessary that the vocabulary words appear in the actual text. Instead, the link to text is made via written questions that accompany what students are reading and that incorporate their vocabulary words. For example, with a text about the pyramids, a question we have used that incorporates the vocabulary we are teaching is the following: "Reaching a *consensus* on how the pyramids were built has been *elusive*. What's your *hypothesis?*"

Students who received the kind of vocabulary instruction I have described have made, on average, one year's growth in both vocabulary and comprehension over the course of a semester (see description of *Reading Is Fame*, in Deshler, Palincsar, Biancarosa, & Nair, 2007). As mentioned earlier, informational texts seems particularly well suited to the approach, perhaps since students recognize that a well-written informational article can enhance their general knowledge about the world, as well as their specific knowledge of vocabulary words. Table 11.3 lists some recommendations at various reading levels. Included in the list are magazines—a material source rated very highly by students when asked what they like to read (Ivey & Broaddus, 2001), along with some collections of articles that emphasize life lessons, a topic that appeals to adolescents (Moje, 2006).

TABLE 11.3. Recommended Sources of Informational Texts for Vocabulary Discussions

Second- to fourth-grade reading level

The Contemporary Reader (Jamestown Education): nonfiction selections
In the Spotlight (Jamestown Education): biographical selections
Passageways (Curriculum Associates): nonfiction selections
Reading Expeditions (National Geographic): nonfiction books

Fourth- to sixth-grade reading level

Calliope (Carus): world history magazine with nine issues per year
Cobblestone (Carus): U.S. history magazine with nine issues per year
Faces (Carus): world cultures magazine with nine issues per year
True Stories (Longman): human interest selections

Sixth- to eighth-grade reading level

Critical Reading Series (Jamestown Education): nonfiction selections
Dig (Carus): archeology magazine with nine issues per year
Everyday Heroes (Townsend Press): biographical selections about ordinary people
What a Life (Longman): biographical selections about famous figures

PROFILE 3: COMPREHENSION

To comprehend, readers must engage actively with a text, constructing an understanding that is valid and supportable (Alexander & Jetton, 2000). A number of factors can affect students' success in constructing this understanding (RAND Reading Study Group [RRSG], 2002). One factor is the students themselves—their knowledge and experiences related to the topic, their skills and strategies for working with text, and their motivation for doing so. A second factor is the text—its content (the words, concepts, and ideas it contains), as well as its structure (the way the content is organized and presented). A third factor is how understanding is defined. For instance, are students being judged on their ability to get the gist, or are they being judged on their ability to evaluate the information in a text? A fourth factor is the context in which the understanding is taking place. Is reading occurring in school or out? Success in understanding will also be affected by what we decide to call a text (Wade & Moje, 2000). Is it a textbook, a teacher- or student-generated material, an electronic text, a graphic novel, or a picture book?

Consideration of all four of the factors identified by the RRSG (2002) is beyond the scope of this chapter. Instead, I have chosen to focus on the second factor that the RRSG identified—text content and structure—since content-area literacy is at the core of adolescents' academic success (Heller & Greenleaf, 2007).

Jessica is an example of a student who struggled with content-area literacy tasks. An eleventh grader, she had no difficulties in recognizing words in context and out when she was tested. Her oral reading was fairly fluent (averaging about 140 wcpm on grade-level text), and her knowledge of the meanings of high school-level words was fairly strong. But when she was asked to read passages silently and answer multiple-choice questions, she began having difficulty with seventh-grade-level texts. With texts at even lower levels of difficulty, Jessica was not able to recall much about what she had read. When asked about textbook reading, she said she often completed the pages her teachers assigned without ever understanding anything she had read.

As Torgesen et al. (2007) conclude, consensus now exists that strategy instruction is one of the most effective ways to improve adolescents' comprehension. Strategies identified as important to teach include paraphrasing, summarizing, and question generation (Deshler, Schumaker, Harris, & Graham, 1998; Pressley & Woloshyn, 1995). The best results are found when instruction is direct and long-term, includes modeling of the strategy, provides frequent and informed practice of strategy use, and emphasizes when and where the strategy can be used.

Increasingly, however, experts are cautioning that generic strategy instruction per se may not be enough to improve the comprehension of students like Jessica. As Heller and Greenleaf (2007) note:

> To become competent in a number of academic content areas requires more than just applying the same old skills and comprehension strategies to new kinds of texts. It also requires skills and knowledge and reasoning processes that are specific to particular disciplines. (p. 10)

More research will be needed before we understand the appropriate balance between strategy and content in comprehension instruction. In addition, important questions still remain about the role that text level, quality, and type play in effective strategy instruction. Reciprocal teaching (RT)—probably the best known of the strategy interventions for adolescents—was validated using informational texts, ones that struggling readers could decode but still had difficulty in understanding (Palincsar & Brown, 1984). At present, however, students at all ability levels are being taught the approach using narrative as well as informational text, with little research support as yet for these adaptations.

Both fiction and informational text are used in concept-oriented reading instruction (CORI), an approach that has improved students' engagement with text and their comprehension (Guthrie et al., 1998; Guthrie & Davis, 2003). A key component of CORI is the use of interesting texts:

> The practice of using interesting texts refers to teaching from an ample supply of books, materials, and technology that are relevant to the learning and knowledge goals. An abundance of texts within the classroom and linkages to community resources outside of the classroom, such as libraries and the Internet, are known to directly facilitate motivation and reading achievement. (Guthrie & Davis, 2003, p. 74)

Recently, Guthrie and his colleagues (2007) looked to see whether fourth graders' motivations for reading fiction and informational texts differed, and if those motivations might be related to reading achievement. They found that students' motivation for reading fiction—associated with goals such as enjoyment—was significantly related to their reading achievement. But motivation for reading informational text—associated with goals such as knowledge acquisition—was not correlated with reading achievement. Guthrie and his colleagues speculate that a lack of emphasis on informational texts in fourth grade is why students motivated to read this kind of text did not perform better on reading tests than students who were not motivated. The result could also be related to the kinds of text used on standardized tests to measure reading achievement. Regardless, a follow-up investigation with older readers would seem worthwhile.

Aside from using texts that students are able to decode and ones that they will find interesting, another feature that can influence the success of strategy instruction for students like Jessica is how "considerate" a text is (Armbruster, 1984). Considerate text is text that (1) has a clear structure (e.g., narrative, compare–contrast, description), (2) is well organized (i.e., the connections among the parts are clear), and (3) is well written (e.g., ideas are explained sufficiently, word choice is appropriate for the audience, mechanics are correct). Students find it much easier to focus their resources on strategically reading considerate text than inconsiderate text.

In marked contrast to the qualities of texts that work best for teaching students strategies for comprehending, texts designed specifically for teaching content-area information in school have often been found to be difficult, boring, and inconsiderate (Chall, Conard, & Harris-Sharples, 1991; Ciborowski, 1992, 1995; Moje, 2006). For instance, Chall and her associates (1991) assessed students' understanding of selections from their textbooks, and interviewed them about their preferences and views about texts. They found that struggling readers were the ones served least well by their textbooks, and that students themselves were aware of this situation:

> The students who read poorly were remarkably sensitive to their needs. Most wanted books that they could read and understand. They knew

why they could not understand their textbooks. The younger ones (fourth and sixth graders) said it was the hard words that made their texts difficult. The older students (eighth and eleventh graders) said they had difficulty because of their book's organization and ideas. (p. 111)

In her study of the kinds of texts that motivated (and "de-motivated") adolescents, Moje (2006) also analyzed textbooks and interviewed students. She concluded that textbooks often confuse students—presenting information in a way that fails to support their prior knowledge, and consequently, fail in engaging them. By looking at the features of texts that students chose to read outside of school, Moje was able to offer some reasons for why these materials were more motivating for students to read than their textbooks:

> Texts youth chose to read outside of school (a) represent aspects that feel *real* to the youth in terms of age, geography, and ethnicity/race of the protagonists, (b) impart life lessons (e.g., resilience/survival, inspiration); (c) offer utility/practical knowledge, and (d) allow youth to explore relationships with friends, family, and romantic partners. Such themes are not likely to be routinely reflected in content area texts, although it seems clear that the utility value of texts has a strong impact on these young people's motivations to read in or out of school. (p. 13)

Moje's (2006) results demonstrate that motivation is best thought of as "a feature of the texts and contexts" students experience rather than "a static and singular feature" of the students themselves. To engage students in classroom textbook reading, she argues, teachers need to provide instructional scaffolding—the supports that can make texts like these more interesting for students to read.

The need for this instructional scaffolding is especially important for adolescent readers like Jessica. Skill in reading can be used to compensate for gaps in knowledge, and knowledge can be used to compensate for deficiencies in reading skill (Adams, Bell, & Perfetti, 1995). But when struggling readers like Jessica are faced with difficult texts on topics about which they have minimal knowledge, it is no wonder that they become discouraged and disengaged.

The three-phase model of reading instruction (before reading, during reading, and after reading) is often presented as a model for thinking about how and when to provide the recursive and interactive support that learners require (Ciborowski, 1992, 1995; Neufeld, 2005). Researchers have also identified specific techniques for activating prior knowledge, which helps readers to relate to new information in a text. For instance, *concept anchoring* has been shown to improve secondary students' comprehension of texts describing complex concepts (Bulgren, Deshler, Schumaker, & Lenz, 2000). In concept anchoring, students connect new information to what they already know by linking key characteristics of the new concept to similar features of the familiar one. Making a comparison between a camera and an eye before reading a physical science article on optics would be an example of concept anchoring. The *prior knowledge activation* strategy is another technique that has been found to improve adolescents' attitudes about reading and their comprehension of textbook materials (Spires & Donley, 1998). In this technique, students are taught to make explicit connections during reading between the content of the text and their prior knowledge and experiences. Compared with students using a strategy for finding main ideas, students who were taught to activate prior knowledge did better on multiple-choice and open-ended questions that required them to go beyond the information in the text.

Notwithstanding their view of textbooks as boring or confusing, adolescents often have difficulty in figuring out how to use information from other sources to enhance their content-area learning (Stahl, Hynd, Britton, McNish, & Bosquet, 1996). Perhaps this is to be expected, given that the ability to consider multiple perspectives, to weigh evidence, and to engage in reflective judgment undergo change during adolescence (Wigfield, Eccles, & Pintrich, 1996). But reading widely from a broad range of complex materials—both expository and narrative—that present a variety of viewpoints is an important part of reading development at the high school level (see Chall's Stage 4). To facilitate that development, teachers need to provide texts and tasks that enable students to learn to analyze and integrate data from multiple sources.

Shanahan (2003) discusses factors to consider in selecting materials that will engage students in learning from multiple texts. Among her suggestions are: (1) choose texts that take a stance on a controversial topic; (2) make sure that the texts are easy enough for students to read so that they are able to think critically about them; and (3) limit the number of viewpoints and genres represented. Shanahan also emphasizes that just providing students with multiple texts will usually not be enough. Teachers should plan on assisting students in how to: (1) change their purpose for reading these texts; (2) make connections across them; and (3) evaluate the texts with regard to the authors' purpose, perspective, and credibility.

While Shanahan's focus is on improving students' ability to read critically, Bean (2003) discusses how to use novels to augment the content that students learn from their textbooks. Bean recommends that teachers use a single novel in their content area each year, and he advises teachers to choose books that contain "highly lyrical, captivating language; interesting multidimensional characters; and an absence of simplistic stereotypes" (p. 22). Many of the books listed in Table 11.2 fit these criteria. For instance, *Lyddie* focuses on the experiences faced by factory workers during the mid 19th century. *Letters from Rifka* describes the Jewish immigrant experience, from the Ukraine to Ellis Island. (See also Readence, Bean, and Baldwin [2004] for lists of young adult novels by content areas.)

At the middle school level, teachers have begun to explore the effects on content-area comprehension and learning of having students read and discuss multiple novels that are related by a common theme (e.g., see Kettel & Douglas, 2003; Robb, 2002). I have found that a similar approach—using informational texts—can be successful with older readers like Jessica. In particular, students' ability to integrate perspectives and viewpoints represented in multiple texts can be helped by asking them to situate their own opinions on a topic within those expressed in texts. This requires, as Alvermann (2002) has pointed out, teaching adolescents that all texts—even their textbooks—take a stance. For example, students can be asked to discuss the points of view represented in two history texts that describe the same incident as either "a battle" or "a massacre," or two science texts that define *famine* as either "a condition" or "a crisis."

CONCLUSION

I have argued in this chapter that knowing the kinds of reading texts that will best meet the needs of adolescents requires that we understand their literacy development, along with recognizing what has failed to develop, or perhaps has developed differently, in teens who experience reading difficulty.

Selecting texts for struggling adolescent readers based on a developmental perspective has many advantages. Students can be engaged with materials that are at the appropriate level of challenge. The focus of instruction becomes the knowledge, strategies, and skills needed to move the students to the next level of development. Students come to understand why they are engaged with certain texts and what they will be able to accomplish once they are finished reading. And teachers are freed up to focus instructional time and energy on those aspects of literacy most appropriate to their students' strengths and needs.

REFERENCES

Adams, B. C., Bell, L. C., & Perfetti, C. A. (1995). A trading relationship between reading skill and domain knowledge in children's text comprehension. *Discourse Processes, 20,* 307–323.

Adams, M. J. (2006). The promise of automatic speech recognition for fostering literacy growth in children and adults. In M. McKenna, L. Labbo, R. Kieffer, & D. Reinking (Eds.), *Handbook of literacy and technology* (Vol. 2, pp. 109–128). Mahwah, NJ: Erlbaum.

Alexander, P. A., & Jetton, T. L. (2000). Learning from text: A multidimensional and developmental perspective. In M. L. Kamil, P. B. Mosenthal, P. D. Pearson, & R. Barr (Eds.), *Handbook of reading research* (Vol. 3, pp. 285–310). Mahwah, NJ: Erlbaum.

Alvermann, D. E. (2002). Effective literacy instruction for adolescents. *Journal of Literacy Research, 34,* 189–208.

Armbruster, B. B. (1984). The problem of "inconsiderate texts. " In G. G. Duffy, L. R. Roehler, & J. Mason (Eds.), *Theoretical issues in reading comprehension* (pp. 202–217). White Plains, NY: Longman.

Bean, T. W. (2003). *Using young-adult literature to enhance comprehension in the content areas.* Naperville, IL: Learning Points. Retrieved March 29, 2007, from *www.learningpt.org.*

Beck, I. L., McKeown, M. G., & Kucan, L. (2002). *Bringing words to life: Robust vocabulary instruction.* New York: Guilford Press.

Biemiller, A. (1999). *Language and reading success.* Cambridge, MA: Brookline Books.

Blachowicz, C. L. Z. (2004). *Reading fluency.* New York: McGraw-Hill.

Bristow, P. S., & Leslie, L. (1988). Indicators of reading difficulty. *Reading Research Quarterly, 23,* 200–218.

Bulgren, J. A., Deshler, D. D., Schumaker, J. B., & Lenz, B. K. (2000). The use and effectiveness of analogical instruction in diverse secondary content classrooms. *Journal of Educational Psychology, 92,* 426–441.

Chall, J. S. (1983). *Stages of reading development* (pp. 85–87). New York: McGraw-Hill,

Chall, J. S. (1983, 1996). *Stages of reading development.* New York: Harcourt Brace.

Chall, J. S., Bissex, G. L., Conard, S. S., & Harris-Sharples, S. (1996). *Qualitative assessment of text difficulty: A practical guide for teachers and writers.* Cambridge, MA: Brookline Books.

Chall, J. S., Conard, S. S., & Harris-Sharples, S. (1991). *Should textbooks challenge students? The case for easier or harder books.* New York: Teachers College Press.

Chall, J. S., Jacobs, V. A., & Baldwin, L. E. (1990). *The reading crisis: Why poor children fall behind.* Cambridge, MA: Harvard University Press.

Ciborowski, J. (1992). *Textbooks and the students who can't read them: A guide for the teaching of content.* Cambridge, MA: Brookline Books.

Ciborowski, J. (1995). Using textbooks with students who cannot read them. *Remedial and Special Education, 16,* 90–101.

Corson, D. (1997). The learning and use of academic English words. *Language Learning, 47,* 671–718.

Coxhead, A. (2000). A new academic word list. *TESOL Quarterly, 34,* 213–238.

Curtis, M. E. (1995). *Teaching troubled adolescents to read: A final report to the Jessie Ball duPont Fund.* Boys Town, NE: Father Flanagan's Boys' Home.

Curtis, M. E. (1996). Intervention for adolescents "at risk. " In L. R. Putnam (Ed.),

How to become a better reading teacher (pp. 231–239). Englewood Cliffs, NJ: Prentice-Hall.

Curtis, M. E. (1997). Teaching reading to children, adolescents, and adults: Similarities and differences. In L. R. Putnam (Ed.), *Readings on language and literacy* (pp. 75–88). Cambridge, MA: Brookline Books.

Curtis, M. E. (2004). Adolescents who struggle with word identification. In T. L. Jetton & J. A. Dole (Eds.), *Adolescent literacy research and practice* (pp. 119–134). New York: Guilford Press.

Curtis, M. E., & Longo, A. M. (1997a). *Reversing reading failure among students in Lincoln Northeast High School: A final report to the Woods Charitable Fund.* Boys Town, NE: Father Flanagan's Boys' Home.

Curtis, M. E., & Longo, A. M. (1997b). *Field test of the Boys Town curriculum in a public school environment: A final report to the Jessie Ball duPont Fund.* Boys Town, NE: Father Flanagan's Boys' Home.

Curtis, M. E., & Longo, A. M. (1999). *When adolescents can't read: Methods and materials that work.* Cambridge, MA: Brookline Books.

Curtis, M. E., & Longo, A. M. (2000). Helping teens reverse reading failure. *Currents in Literacy, 3,* 16–17.

Curtis, M. E., & Longo, A. M. (2001). Teaching vocabulary to adolescents to improve comprehension. *Reading Online, 5*(4). Retrieved March 29, 2007, from *www.readingonline.org/articles/curtis/.*

Curtis, M. E., Longo, A. M., & Chmelka, M. B. (1994). *Teaching basic reading skills at the high school level.* Unpublished manuscript.

Deshler, D. D., Palincsar, A. S., Biancarosa, G., & Nair, M. (2007). *Informed choices for struggling adolescent readers.* Newark, DE: International Reading Association.

Deshler, D., Schumaker, J., Harris, K., & Graham, S. (Eds.). (1998). *Teaching every adolescent every day: Learning in diverse high school classrooms.* Cambridge, MA: Brookline Books.

Grigg, W., Donahue, P., & Dion, G. (2007). *The nation's report card: 12th-grade reading and mathematics 2005 (NCES 2007-468).* U.S. Department of Education, National Center for Education Statistics. Washington, DC: U.S. Government Printing Office.

Guthrie, J. T., & Davis, M. H. (2003). Motivating struggling readers in middle school through an engagement model of classroom practice. *Reading and Writing Quarterly, 19,* 59–85.

Guthrie, J. T., Hoa, L. W., Wigfield, A., Tonks, S. M., Humenick, N. M., & Littles, E. (2007). Reading motivation and reading comprehension growth in the later elementary years. *Contemporary Educational Psychology, 32,* 282–313.

Guthrie, J. T., Van Meter, P., Hancock, G. R., McCann, A., Anderson, E., & Alao, S. (1998). Does concept-oriented reading instruction increase strategy-use and conceptual learning from text? *Journal of Educational Psychology, 90,* 261–278.

Harmon, J. M., Hedrick, W. B., Wood, K. D., & Gress, M. (2005). Vocabulary self-selection: A study of middle-school students' word selections from expository texts. *Reading Psychology, 26,* 313–333.

Heller, R., & Greenleaf, C. L. (2007). *Literacy instruction in the content areas: Getting to the core of middle and high school improvement*. Washington, DC: The Alliance for Excellent Education. Retrieved July 30, 2007, from *www.all4ed.org/publications/LiteracyContent/LitCon.pdf*.

Hiebert, E. H. (2007). The word zone fluency curriculum: An alternative approach. In M. R. Kuhn & P. J. Schwanenflugel (Eds.), *Fluency in the classroom* (pp. 154–170). New York: Guilford Press.

Hiebert, E. H. (2008). *AMP QReads*. Shoreview, MN: Pearson.

Hyland, T. (1998). Readers play catch up—and win. *Technos, 7*, 23–26.

Ivey, G., & Broaddus, K. (2001). "Just plain reading": A survey of what makes students want to read in middle school classrooms. *Reading Research Quarterly, 36*, 350–377.

Kamil, M. (2003). *Adolescent and literacy: Reading for the 21st century*. Washington, DC: The Alliance for Excellent Education. Retrieved March 29, 2007, from *www.all4ed.org/publications/AdolescentsAndLiteracy.pdf*.

Kettel, R. P., & Douglas, N. L. (2003). Comprehending multiple texts: A theme approach incorporating the best of children's literature. *Voices from the Middle, 11*, 43–49.

Knott, G. (1986). Secondary school contexts of reading and writing instruction. *Theory Into Practice, 25*, 77–83.

Kuhn, M. R., & Stahl, S. A. (2003). Fluency: A review of developmental and remedial practices. *Journal of Educational Psychology, 95*, 3–21.

Marchand-Martella, N., Martella, R. C., Orlob, M., & Ebey, T. (2000). Conducting action research in a rural high school setting using peers as corrective reading instructors for students with disabilities. *Rural Special Education Quarterly, 19*, 20–30.

Moje, E. B. (2006, Summer). Motivating texts, motivating contexts, motivating adolescents: An examination of the role of motivation in adolescent literacy practices and development. *Perspectives,* pp. 10–14.

National Institute of Child Health and Human Development. (2000). *Teaching children to read: An evidence-based assessment of the scientific literature on reading and its implications for reading instruction*. Washington, DC: U.S. Government Printing Office.

Neufeld, P. (2005). Comprehension instruction in content area classes. *Reading Teacher, 59*, 302–312.

Palincsar, A. M., & Brown, A. L. (1984). Reciprocal teaching of comprehension fostering and comprehension monitoring activities. *Cognition and Instruction, 1*, 117–175.

Perie, M., & Moran, R. (2005). *NAEP 2004 trends in academic progress: Three decades of student reading and mathematics* (NCES 2005-464). Washington, DC: U.S. Department of Education.

Pressley, M., & Woloshyn, V. (1995). *Cognitive strategy instruction that really improves children's academic performance*. Cambridge, MA: Brookline Books.

RAND Reading Study Group. (2002). *Reading for understanding: Toward an R&D program in reading comprehension*. Pittsburgh, PA: RAND.

Rasinski, T. V. (2003). *The fluent reader*. New York: Scholastic.

Rasinski, T. V., Padak, N. D., McKeon, C. A., Wilfong, L. G., Friedauer, J. A., &

Heim, P. (2005). Is reading fluency a key for successful high school reading? *Journal of Adolescent and Adult Literacy, 49,* 22–27.

Readence, J. E., Bean, T. W., & Baldwin, R. S. (2004). *Content area literacy: An integrated approach.* Dubuque, IA: Kendall/Hunt.

Robb, L. (2002). Multiple texts: Multiple opportunities for teaching and learning. *Voices from the Middle, 9,* 28–32.

Roswell, F. G., Chall, J. S., Curtis, M. E., & Kearns, G. (2005). *Diagnostic assessments of reading.* Itasca, IL: Riverside.

Ruddell, M. R., & Shearer, B. A. (2002). "Extraordinary," "tremendous," "exhilarating," "magnificent": Middle school at-risk students become avid word learners with Vocabulary Self-Collection Strategy (VSS). *Journal of Adolescent and Adult Literacy, 45,* 352–363.

Shanahan, C. (2003). *Using multiple texts to teach content.* Naperville, IL: Learning Point. Retrieved March 29, 2007, from *www.learningpt.org.*

Spires, H. A., & Donley, J. (1998). Prior knowledge activation: Inducing engagement with informational texts. *Journal of Educational Psychology, 90,* 249–260.

Stahl, S., Hynd, C., Britton, B., McNish, M., & Bosquet, D. (1996). What happens when students read multiple source documents in history? *Reading Research Quarterly, 31,* 430–457.

Sternberg, R. J. (1987). Most vocabulary is learned from context. In M. G. McKeown & M. E. Curtis (Eds.), *The nature of vocabulary acquisition* (pp. 89–105). Hillsdale, NJ: Erlbaum.

Therrien, W. J. (2004). Fluency and comprehension gains as a result of repeated reading. *Remedial and Special Education, 25,* 252–261.

Torgesen, J. K., Houston, D. D., Rissman, L. M., Decker, S. M., Roberts, G., Vaughn, S., et al. (2007). *Academic literacy instruction for adolescents: A guidance document from the Center on Instruction.* Portsmouth, NH: RMC Research Corporation, Center on Instruction. Retrieved March 29, 2007, from *www.centeroninstruction.org*

Valencia, S. W., & Riddle Buly, M. R. (2004). What struggling readers REALLY need. *The Reading Teacher, 57,* 520–533.

Valleley, R. J., & Shriver, M. D. (2003). An examination of the effects of repeated readings with secondary students. *Journal of Behavioral Education, 12,* 55–76.

Wade, S. E., & Moje, E. B. (2000). The role of text in classroom learning. *Handbook of reading research* (Vol. 3, pp. 609–627). Mahwah, NJ: Erlbaum.

Wigfield, A., Eccles, J. S., & Pintrich, P. R. (1996). Development between the ages of 11 and 25. In D. C. Berliner & R. C. Calfee (Eds.), *Handbook of educational research* (pp. 148–185). New York: Macmillan.

Part IV

Pulling It Together

✦ 12 ✦

Teachers Using Texts

Where We Are and What We Need

ANNE McGILL-FRANZEN

As anecdotal reports from across the country have suggested, and a recent survey of teachers' beliefs about reading and present-day practices in one state has demonstrated (Love Zeig, 2007), teachers have shifted fundamental aspects of their instruction to comply with highly constrained policy guidelines and mandates. In particular, the requirement that high-poverty schools implement with fidelity a commercial core reading program in order to be eligible for Reading First funds and the movement toward commercially produced standard treatment protocols (Mesmer & Cumming, Chapter 8, this volume) in response to intervention (RTI) initiatives have influenced both text and program selections on the part of schools and, arguably, constrained teachers' ability to optimize instruction for struggling students. The purpose of this chapter is to present additional research that confirms what the authors of chapters in this volume have been saying: (1) Core reading programs and the guidance provided to teachers in the manuals are inadequate to support the yearly progress of at least 20–35% of students; and (2) the most effective program incorporates the scaffolds for reading text that the chapter authors suggest. Studies on summer reading, also described briefly in this chapter, further support the authors' stance on matching

253

texts to readers, reading volume, choice, and the benefits of engagement with challenging topics and a community of peers.

EFFECTIVENESS OF CORE READING PROGRAMS: WHAT DO WE KNOW?

Despite decades of large-scale research demonstrating the primacy of teacher variables in improving student achievement, including the First-Grade Beginning Teachers Study (Bond & Dykstra, 1967) and the more recent Prospects Study (Rowan, Correnti, & Miller, 2002), current policy initiatives privilege commercial reading materials over the development of teachers' expertise and autonomous decision making. Given the mandates for Reading First schools and the high stakes for low-income and low-achieving children in particular, it behooves educators to evaluate the effectiveness of such programs.

Only two recent studies have examined the relationship between core reading programs and student achievement; both of these studies took place in Florida, a state that early on adopted federal education guidelines and successfully aligned teaching practices with these guidelines (Love, 2007). Similar to other states, six programs were approved by the Florida adoption committee: Harcourt, Houghton-Mifflin, Macmillan/McGraw Hill, Scott Foresman, Open Court, and Reading Mastery. According to the adoption committee, these programs were congruent with the Florida Sunshine State Standards (SSS), and by implication, with the state assessment, Florida Comprehensive Achievement Test (FCAT). The first study examined the structure and content of two core reading programs, particularly the guidance offered teachers, and correlated the use of the programs with third graders' performance on the FCAT; both programs were identified by the Florida Center for Reading Research (FCRR) as research based (McGill-Franzen, Zmach, Solic, & Love Zeig, 2006). Significant differences between programs were found in content: One program included more comprehension and interpretation segments and the other more segments preparing students for independent practice—more independent practice and more instruction in vocabulary and fluency than the first program. The latter program, with more upfront instruction in word-level strategies and more opportunities for reading practice, was significantly more successful in the pass rate for students in high-poverty schools.

Using Florida again as a case-study state, a second investigation (McGill-Franzen, Solic, Love Zeig, Zmach, & Mathson, 2005) examined school-level data for third, fourth, and fifth grades for the 2002–2003 school year to ask: What is the relation between students' performance on the FCAT and the core reading program used by the schools they attend? A census survey of every school district in Florida identified which core program was adopted by each school (number of schools that responded = 1, 743). By using third-, fourth-, and fifth-grades FCAT scores after a year of instruction in these core programs, researchers related core program to school outcomes. Only five of the six approved core programs were entered into the analysis (Harcourt, Houghton-Mifflin, Scott-Foresman, Open Court, and Reading Mastery; the sixth core program, Macmillan/McGraw-Hill, had too few cases). The 2002–2003 school year was selected because this was the initial year of implementation for the newly adopted core program and for new retention in grade policy, and it was the year preceding the tiered model of reading support. The sequence of policy mandates was important in the context of this study. As the authors noted, retention in grade may inflate test score data in the year following retention, and layered programs, in this case, the core reading program and tiered intervention programs, may make disambiguating program effects impossible. The timing of this core program study circumvented these problems.

Not surprisingly, univariate and multivariate analyses revealed an inverse relationship between poverty and FCAT scores, regardless of the core program. Upon closer inspection, however, the data revealed significant variation at the upper and lower levels of achievement as well as in subtest performance across grades. Significantly fewer students who used the core program described as more effective in the first study failed the FCAT, regardless of whether the students were third, fourth, and fifth graders. Similarly, students who used the most effective program were likely to score higher on test items that assessed word knowledge and main idea (Clusters 1 & 2 on the FCAT) across all the grades.

How did the content of the most effective core program differ from the other core programs? At least at the third-grade level, the only level analyzed for content and structure in the first study (McGill-Franzen et al., 2006), the most effective program provided word-level and repeated reading passages near the beginning of the year and more preparation before reading the texts as well as a higher frequency of opportunities for independent practice. The most effective program offered students more than twice as many words in text as the less effective program, had a higher percentage of nonfiction texts, and was slightly more difficult; text materials developed for struggling readers in the less-effective program were actually slightly more difficult on the Flesch-Kincaid readability scale than texts in the grade-level anthology. The study authors hypothesized that the content and structure of the most effective core program offered more support at the outset for low-achieving readers and more volume throughout, thereby disrupting a cycle of failure.

Nonetheless, these differences between core programs across the grades, while significant, point to a larger issue: Regardless of core program, between 20 and 35% of students failed the FCAT, leading to retention in grade (see Figure 12.1 for a distribution of third-grade mean FCAT achievement, Levels 1–5, according to the core program in use). At the end of the 2003–2004 school year, the year following implementation of the core program and retention policy, approximately one in four third graders scored at a Level 1 on the FCAT and failed. Of those who failed in 2002–2003, nearly half (41%) failed the FCAT a second time, presumably after 2 years of instruction in the core reading program. The analyses in these studies revealed that, contrary to policy goals, the core reading program mandate did not enable the lowest quintile of students to achieve grade-level standards, and may have, in fact, limited opportunity for these students by limiting teachers' decision making. Core reading programs, weighted heavily with whole-group instructional approaches, did not provide adequate support for a range of diverse learners, particularly low-achieving children.

Although the two studies summarized above dealt with the effectiveness of core reading programs as implemented in Florida, there is no reason to believe that results would vary in other contexts. Critiques of core programs have suggested that the majority offer little in the way of conceptual development to support vocabulary knowledge and comprehension of challenging texts (e.g., Hirsch, 2003; Walsh, 2003). A recent content analysis of fourth-grade core programs found that 75% of the

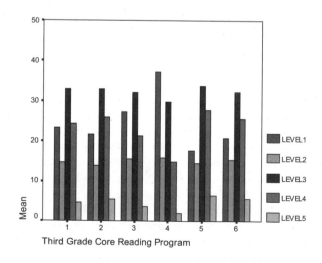

FIGURE 12.1. Achievement levels by program, grade 3.

texts do not develop a conceptual framework sufficient for understanding the overarching themes of a cluster of selections (Dewitz, Jones, & Leahy, 2006), but rather one selection may be plopped on top of the previous selection.

Hiebert and Martin (Chapter 3, this volume) have meticulously established the mismatch between the word-recognition tasks inherent in core reading program anthologies and the likely word-recognition skills of beginning or struggling readers in second grade and above. Not only are the words in current core programs more likely to be uncommon, or outside the reader's curriculum experience, than in past editions, but all words—highly frequent words as well as less commonly occurring words—are also less likely to be repeated in text. As Hiebert noted, a high percentage of words make a single appearance in text, making it highly unlikely that beginning or struggling readers would be able to remember even frequently occurring words, let alone be able to apply knowledge of letter–sound patterns to unfamiliar words or develop analogous decoding strategies.

READING BEYOND THE CORE PROGRAMS: WHAT DO WE KNOW?

The most widely known study is that of Fielding, Wilson, and Anderson (1984), in which fifth graders kept track of their out-of-school activities. Researchers found that even a few minutes of out-of-school reading translated into increased achievement on standardized tests, and their recommendations for increased emphasis on independent reading were incorporated into *Becoming a Nation of Readers: The Report of the Commission on Reading* (1985). Less well known are studies of reading achievement gains and losses over the summer months. However, studies as early as the 1970s established the connection between reading outside of school in the summer months and reading proficiency. Using fall and spring standardized test scores for elementary children in the Atlanta public schools, Heyns (1978), for example, found that "the single summer activity that is most strongly and consistently related to summer learning is reading" (p. 161). In fact, children in high-poverty communities, the focus of this volume, may lose as much as 2½ months in reading achievement each summer (Downey, von Hippel, & Broh, 2004). Cumulatively, not reading during the summer months can have devastating effects. Looking across the elementary school years in New York City, another group of researchers estimated that 80% of the reading gap at the sixth grade level between children in high-poverty schools and those from more advantaged communities could be attributed to setbacks in summer learning (Hayes & Grether, 1983).

Of course, one reason why children may not read outside of school is that they have no access to books. A recently completed experimental project that provided elementary school children in high-poverty communities with 10 to 12 free books for three consecutive summers found that such access to self-selected books does indeed significantly increase students' reading performance on high-stakes reading assessments—in this case, the FCAT (Allington, McGill-Franzen, Camilli, Williams, Graff, et al., 2007). Another study of a voluntary reading project with Baltimore sixth graders found that reading four or five books over the summer lessened the expected setback in learning (Kim, 2004).

Given the limitations of the texts in core programs, and the potential benefits of wide reading outside the core program, what do teachers do? Hiebert (Chapter 1) and others (McGill-Franzen et al., 2006) have suggested that teachers who exclusively use core program anthologies may be disadvantaging students who are already behind their peers. By comparing the results of surveys of teachers' self-reported beliefs and practices in the 1990s with those reported in the early 2000s, there may be cause for alarm.

CURRENT TEACHING PRACTICES: DO THEY ALIGN WITH READING PROGRAMS?

According to Love Zeig (2007), compared to teachers of the recent past who were surveyed by Baumann, Hoffman, Duffy-Hester, and Ro (2000), the vast majority of teachers today (71%), in at least one typical textbook adoption state (Florida), reported that they "use the basal reading program as the foundation of [the] reading program; in other words [the] reading program is structured around the basal, but [they] incorporate trade books within the basal program" (p. 125). As compared to teachers in the 1990s, teachers today spend considerably more time daily on skill or strategy lessons and less time on activities described as "applying, practicing, and extending reading," such as reading aloud and independent reading (p. 100). From a list of types of trade books, contemporary teachers report using fiction and chapter books most often; teachers also report that they teach reading through the content areas. Unlike teachers in the 1990s, who report frequent use of literature anthologies (Baumann et al., 2000), Florida teachers today report using a wider variety of commercially produced materials including commercial classroom libraries, guided reading books, and phonics and skills workbooks (Love Zeig, 2007). Although the recent survey is limited in that it does not represent a national sample of teachers, Florida policies are often harbingers of national trends, and as a state, Florida's schools are more diverse and disadvantaged than the national average (*nces.ed.gov/ programs/stateprofiles*).

Not only is the trend toward a greater variety of instructional materials evident in this country, but a recent investigation of primary instruction conducted by the University of Auckland found at least 12 different instructional programs per school and two new literacy initiatives underway each year of a 6-year longitudinal study (Auckland Uniservices Limited, 2004). Further, teachers in this study most often identified "more resources"—commercial reading programs (23%), instructional aides to implement these programs (approximately 25%), or district-developed materials (9%)—as the best way to meet the needs of diverse learners and struggling readers. The most frequent strategy for accommodating diverse or struggling readers that teachers reported using in both the recent Florida survey and the New Zealand survey was to "adapt" classroom instruction. Teachers did not specify the nature of the adaptation in the Florida survey, but they stated that struggling children were likely to receive "pull out" services or "tutoring" (Love Zeig, 2007), whereas New Zealand teachers were most likely to "vary the level of the shared book or choose an appropriate level for the individual or adapt the task" (47%) (Auckland Uniservices Limited, 2004, p. 29).

Although an abundance of instructional resources is unquestionably a good thing, teachers must be able to critically evaluate the appropriateness of particular texts for particular instructional purposes and particular children. Of course, teachers may mediate the difficulty of texts within the context of the classroom—through supportive language and the development of background knowledge and engagement—but as the Auckland researchers noted, "materials may be seen as providing second-level scaffolds in instructional activities" (p. 2). Unfortunately, teachers in the Auckland study, who were provided with several sets of new reading programs, appeared unwilling to critically evaluate these resources. In the view of these authors, teachers did not attempt to analyze which features of the new programs or texts might align with the demonstrated needs of their students, nor whether use of the new programs improved student outcomes. In fact, the researchers reported "significant lack of evidence-based decision making with respect to the use of the resources" (p. 71).

This finding resonates with those of us who teach in U.S. schools today, as well as with those who teach prospective teachers or observe contemporary teaching practices. By identifying particular core reading programs or interventions as "scientifically based" and mandating their use, policymakers inadvertently may have marginalized teachers as instructional decision makers. Mandated programs have been characterized as "shackles" for some beginning teachers (Valencia, Place, Martin, & Grossman, 2006) who cannot call upon years of teaching experiences with different iterations of instructional materials to help evaluate the legitimacy of such claims to efficacy, science, or research.

Clearly, the demand for fidelity of implementation privileges the knowledge of program authors or editors over that of the classroom teacher who is closest to the needs of students. Similarly, by layering one concurrent program with its accompanying texts upon another, as in the tiered model of interventions (Kim & Snow, Chapter 7, this volume), the administrators or teachers selecting these interventions may not be able to distinguish the outcomes of one program versus another. In other words, the core reading program may influence the achievement of struggling readers who receive one or more interventions in positive and negative ways that cannot be discerned easily, and vice versa—interventions may influence performance on and success with the core program. What is important to bear in mind is that teachers must monitor the effects of their instruction by observing the responses of the students they teach.

Another critical finding from the research data is that most experienced teachers do adapt reading programs somewhat, even highly scripted programs (Datnow & Castellano, 2000; Auckland Uniservices Unlimited, 2004), and as the authors of this volume state unequivocally, teachers must adapt reading programs if they are to reach beginning readers and struggling students at any grade level. How they may adapt matters more than the reading materials themselves—what teachers do with the texts they select, or that are selected for them, is by far the most important factor in improving students' achievement. An experimental study of the effectiveness of a trade-book intervention implemented by inner-city teachers, for example, found that the classes of teachers who received new classroom libraries of appropriate trade books but no professional development on how to use these books scored no better than control classes whose teachers received neither new books or professional development (McGill-Franzen, Allington, Yokoi, & Brooks, 1999/2000). Thus, fidelity of implementation is not the critical issue in evaluating reading programs, but rather, how teachers adapt these materials and selectively use texts for particular instructional purposes with individuals or groups of students. And, as the reanalysis of the Tennessee Class Size Study demonstrated, what teachers do matters most for children in high-poverty schools where teacher effects are the most variable and the most powerful (Nye, Konstantopoulos, & Hedges, 2004).

DEVELOPING TEACHERS' EXPERTISE:
USING AND SELECTING TEXTS

The overarching theme of this volume is that teachers must match the type of text to the reader's developmental level. Each chapter author called upon teachers to adapt, in particular ways, reading programs and the texts included within these programs. However, what emerges first from these chapters is a sense of the importance of teachers knowing specifically where the student is developmentally, no matter whether the child is a preschooler just starting kindergarten (Brown, Chapter 9, this volume) or a struggling adolescent (Curtis, Chapter 11, this volume). Chapter authors reference several different developmental frameworks (e.g., Chall, Jacobs, & Baldwin, 1990; Ehri, 1995; Riddle-Buly & Valencia, 2004) to assist them in identifying students' strengths and weaknesses and what kinds of support would move development forward. Second, chapter authors stress that teachers also need to understand the characteristics of text—informational text as well as narrative—in order to maximize the potential of text to scaffold reading development. Chapter authors specify which features might be supportive or challenging for students at different developmental stages. Also, chapter authors note that the context within which instruction takes place—the purposes of the text, the authenticity of the task, the support of peer or teacher interactions, and the background the reader brings to the text, the task, and the interaction—should contribute mightily to teachers' decision making about appropriate adaptations to reading programs and the texts included within. Finally, each and every chapter author recommends that struggling readers need to actually read and reread text— what some researchers have called "high-success reading experiences" (Allington, 2006).

The sections that follow highlight the major recommendations in this volume. Chapter authors introduce their topics with an emphasis on the reader, move to a consideration of texts and text features, and then pack a toolbox of ideas on how to select and use particular texts with particular groups of students.

• *Recognize students' developmental reading stage and monitor their progress.* Curtis (Chapter 11, this volume) proposes that recognition of the source of the adolescent's reading difficulties is the necessary first step in selecting appropriate texts. To illustrate this point, she describes the cognitive profiles of a number of adolescents, places their strengths and weaknesses within a developmental perspective, and identifies the specific support that each would need to improve their ability to read increasingly challenging text. Similarly, Mesmer and Cumming

(Chapter 8, this volume) provide case studies of a beginning struggling reader, an intermediate reader, and a small group of low-achieving students. Mesmer and Cumming demonstrate that knowledge of each student's developmental stage enables the teacher to match text with the reader and to monitor readers' responses to the intervention. Likewise, Brown (Chapter 9, this volume) proposes that teachers must first ascertain a student's developmental stage in order to scaffold new learning and prompt for appropriate strategy use. By describing the development of a young child as he traverses the path from novice to beginning reader under the expert instruction of his kindergarten and then first-grade teacher, Brown demonstrates what expert text scaffolding might look like. The recommendations by chapter authors to first determine the needs of beginning and struggling students and then to locate these within a developmental framework would go far to mitigate the most alarming of the Auckland findings—that teachers did not attempt to match reading programs with the needs of readers, nor monitor the effects of programs on students' achievement.

• *Identify text features—use text with supportive features to scaffold reading development and explicitly teach those features that challenge.* Brown (Chapter 9, this volume) explains text control in terms of the dominant patterns that are repeated in text—refrains, high-frequency words, orthographic patterns—and the characteristic development of students who might benefit from guided and independent practice with these texts. Hiebert (Chapter 1, this volume) recommends that the anthologies in core programs not be used at all for beginning readers, except as read-alouds, and instead, teachers should inspect and sequence decodable texts and leveled books for the kinds of word-level features that warrant exposure and repetition.

Because informational texts are less likely to be prominent in core programs, these texts with accompanying graphics, navigational aides, and linguistic features may be more challenging for beginning readers and struggling students. Duke and Billman (Chapter 6, this volume) suggest that informational books with repetitive formats and features—for example, an informational series on a particular content topic or theme—support beginning readers. On the other hand, generic nouns and timeless verbs, words that convey denotative versus connotative meanings, or technical vocabulary that represents key text concepts are features of informational text that challenge beginning readers and struggling students. Not all stylistic and linguistic modifications to simplify informational text actually make comprehension easier, according to Duke and Billman. Personification of animals and plants, extraneous but "seductive" details, and substitution of an everyday word for a technical term may actually promote misconceptions about content information, rendering the text more difficult to read.

Involvement with the ITUBE project in South Africa (Sailors, Hoffman, & Condon, Chapter 4, this volume) confirm the importance of text that features the content of lived experience and indigenous or mother-tongue language, both issues of accessibility in reading texts for immigrant children in the United States. Without the shifting educational mandates in South Africa as here, chapter authors were confident that the ITUBE project would be an opportunity to design text that better accommodates a developmental perspective.

• *Create supportive instructional contexts—including multiple texts and text sets—that develop conceptual knowledge and vocabulary, authentic purpose, choice, and collaboration.* In a similar vein, Billman, Hilden, and Halladay (Chapter 10, this volume) tackle the various stumbling blocks that struggling readers might face, depending on the development of the individual in decoding ability, knowledge of vocabulary, experience with text features of different genres, and engagement with the topic. They urge teachers to clarify what they mean by the "just right" book and to reflect on their purposes for selecting the book. They also urge teachers to consider how challenging particular texts might be for individual students before deciding to use these texts or develop strategies to scaffold the reading of the texts. In recognition of the context within which students read a particular text, the authors propose multitext strategies for supporting struggling readers—that is, texts graded in difficulty on a similar topic or as part of a well-developed unit or theme, with peer discussion and partner work to mediate conceptual understandings and word-level demands. Duke and Billman (Chapter 6, this volume) also emphasize purpose as a mediator in text difficulty; they make the point that the purpose for reading should be authentic—that is, based on a real-life reason for reading rather than just because the text is the next selection in the core program, a "school-only" reason for reading. In her work with struggling adolescents, Curtis (Chapter 11) identifies other attributes of texts that relate to the reader's purpose and perspective. She suggests that teachers select texts that allow students to situate their own perspective within the theme or topic of the text, or texts that are controversial. Curtis notes that engagingness is not simply an attribute of the text, nor is motivation simply a characteristic of the learner. Instead, both are embedded in context, including degree of choice and self-selection, support by teachers and peers—such as collaborative oral reading and concept anchoring—and having a real purpose for reading the texts. The recommendations by chapter authors are consistent with insights gained from a recent meta-analysis of classroom practices that are associated with motivation—emphasis on gaining knowledge, choice, interesting texts, and peer collaboration (Guthrie & Humenick, 2004).

• *Increase volume of reading.* Mesmer and Cumming (Chapter 8, this volume) caution teachers to not be carried away by unidimensional skill and strategy programs but instead to keep in mind that the goal of any intervention is to improve students' ability to read text. Therefore, they submit that increased amounts of text reading and rereading should be an integral part of the instructional plan. Like Mesmer and Cumming, Brown holds that "core programs and guided reading leveled libraries may not be sufficient with regard to text type, level of difficulty, nor sufficient titles for independent practice. To provide sufficient textual scaffolding for all of their students, educators may need to supplement with additional texts" (p. 196).

Other chapter authors echo these concerns. Even with students who fall in the bottom 10% of achievement, Hiebert (Chapter 1, this volume) recommends extensive reading for increased exposure to rare as well as high-frequency words and encourages the use of voice-recognition technology and audiotapes with appropriate texts. Recent research studies have demonstrated that extensive or wide reading develops fluency at a faster rate than repeated readings and, as an added benefit, contributes to vocabulary growth (Kuhn, Schwanenflugel, Morris, Morrow, Woo, et al., 2006). Additional support for wide reading may be found in recent studies of summer reading, especially those studies that provide children from high-poverty communities access to books (Allington et al., 2007).

FINAL THOUGHTS

Core reading programs are probably more alike than different in content and contribution to variance in achievement. Research thus far on core programs shows that current policy mandates for fidelity of implementation of these programs do not enable the lowest quintile of students to achieve grade-level standards and may actually limit their opportunities. One area of concern is that the texts of core programs do not embed or sequence word features appropriately, nor do the texts provide sufficient exposures to enable beginning and struggling readers above second grade to develop automaticity. A longstanding research program into the match between text and reader, explained in detail in this volume (Hiebert, Chapter 1; Sailors, Hoffman, & Condon, Chapter 4), presents a theoretical base for designing reading texts that would be more appropriate scaffolds for the reading development of beginning and struggling readers than those texts provided in the currently mandated core programs.

A second area of concern is that little is known about teachers' adaptations of core programs or teachers' text selection and use within core programs. Without a doubt, what teachers actually do with reading materials matters more than the program itself. Recommendations in this volume suggest a direction and provide a knowledge base for practitioners, researchers, and curriculum developers who use, study, and create text—that is, attend to students' reading development, the features of text, the context within which text is read; and enable access to books and promote wide reading. New policy initiatives should focus on developing teachers' expert text selections and adaptations, not teacher-proof programs! In all of this, there is a proactive role for knowledgeable teachers: Teachers should dig beneath the surface, take a critical eye toward marketing hype and policy pronouncements, and use text as they determine is in the best interests of the students who depend on them.

REFERENCES

Allington, R. (2006). *What really matters for struggling readers* (2nd ed.). New York: Pearson, Allyn & Bacon.

Allington, R., McGill-Franzen, A., Camilli, G., Williams, L., Graff, J., Zeig, J., et al. (2007, April 11). *Ameliorating summer reading setback among economically disadvantaged elementary students.* Paper presented at the American Educational Research Association, Chicago, IL.

Auckland Uniservices Limited of the University of Auckland (2004, February). *An evaluation of the use and integration of readymade commercial literacy packages into classroom programmes.* Retrieved from the Ministry of Education. Retrieved on September 1, 2007, from *www.minedu.govt.nz.*

Baumann, J. F., Hoffman, J. V., Duffy-Hester, A. M., & Ro, J. M. (2000). "The first R" yesterday and today: U.S. elementary reading instruction practices reported by teachers and administrators. *Reading Research Quarterly, 35*(3), 338–377.

Bond, G. L., & Dykstra, R. (1967). The cooperative research program in first-grade reading instruction. *Reading Research Quarterly, 2*(4), 5–142.

Center for the Study of Reading. (1985). *Becoming a nation of readers: The report of the commission on reading.* Champaign: University of Illinois.

Chall, J. S., Jacobs, V. A., & Baldwin, L. E. (1990). *The reading crisis: Why poor children fall behind.* Cambridge, MA: Harvard.

Datnow, A., & Castellano, M. (2000). Teachers' responses to Success for All: How beliefs, experiences, and adaptations shape implementation. *American Educational Research Journal, 37*(3), 775–799.

Dewitz, P., Jones, J., & Leahy, S. (2006, November 30). *The research base of com-*

prehension instruction in five basal reading programs. Paper presented at the National Reading Conference, Los Angeles, CA.

Downey, D. B., von Hippel, P. T., & Broh, B. A. (2004). Are schools the great equalizer?: Cognitive inequality during the summer months and the school year. *American Sociological Review, 69*(5), 613–635.

Ehri, L. C. (1995). Phases of development in learning to read words by sight. *Journal of Research in Reading, 18*(2), 116–125.

Fielding, L., Wilson, P., & Anderson, R. (1984). A new focus on free reading: The role of trade books in reading instruction. In T. Raphael (Ed.), *The contexts of school-based literacy* (pp. 149–160). New York: Random House.

Guthrie, J., & Humenick, N. M. (2004). Motivating students to read: Evidence for classroom practices that increase motivation and achievement. In P. McCardle & V. Chhabra (Eds.), *The voice of evidence in reading research* (pp. 329–354). Baltimore: Brookes.

Hayes, D. P., & Grether, J. (1983). The school year and vacations: When do students learn? *Cornell Journal of Social Relations, 17*(1), 56–71.

Heyns, B. (1978). *Summer learning and the effects of schooling.* New York: Academic Press.

Hirsch, E. D. (2003, Spring). Building knowledge, *American Educator,* pp. 1–25.

Love Zeig, J. (2007). *Reading instruction during the No Child Left Behind years: The first R revisited.* Unpublished doctoral dissertation, University of Florida, Gainesville, FL.

McGill-Franzen, A., Allington, R., Yokoi, L., & Brooks, G. (1999/2000). Putting books in the classroom seems necessary but not sufficient. *Journal of Educational Research, 93*(2), 67–79.

McGill-Franzen, A., Solic, K., Love Zeig, J., Zmach, C., & Mathson, D. (2005, November 30). *Examining the fit between core reading programs and FCAT achievement.* Paper presented at the National Reading Conference, Miami, FL.

McGill-Franzen, A., Zmach, C., Solic, K., & Love Zeig, J. L. (2006). The confluence of two policy mandates: Core programs and third grade retention in Florida. *Elementary School Journal, 107*(1), 67–92.

Nye, B., Konstantopoulos, S., & Hedges, L. V. (2004). How large are teacher effects? *Educational Evaluation and Policy Analysis, 26*(3), 237–257.

Riddle-Buly, M., & Valencia, S. (2002). Below the bar: Profiles of students who fail state reading assessments. *Educational Evaluation and Policy Analysis, 24*(3), 219–239.

Rowan, B., Correnti, R., & Miller, R. J. (2002). What large-scale, survey research tells us about teacher effects on student achievement: Insights from the Prospects study of elementary schools. *Teachers College Record, 104*(8), 1525–1567.

Valencia, S., Place, N., Martin, S., & Grossman, P. (2006). Curriculum materials for elementary reading: Shackles and scaffolds for four beginning teachers. *Elementary School Journal, 107*(1), 94–120.

Walsh, K. (2003, Spring). Basal readers: The lost opportunity to build the knowledge that propels comprehension. *American Educator,* pp. 1–25.

Index

Page numbers followed by an *f* or *t* indicate figures or tables.

267